Contents

Urban Villages and the Making of Communities

Edited by Peter Neal

Spon Press
Taylor & Francis Group

LONDON AND NEW YORK

First published 2003 by Spon Press
11 New Fetter Lane, London EC4P 4EE

Simultaneously published in the USA and Canada
by Spon Press
29 West 35th Street, New York, NY 10001

Spon Press is an imprint of the Taylor and Francis Group

Typeset in Univers and Charter by Ninety Seven Plus
Printed and bound in China by Everbest Printing Company

British Library Cataloguing in Publication Data
A catalogue record for this book is available from the British Library

Library of Congress Cataloging in Publication Data
Urban Villages and the making of communities / edited by Peter Neal.
        p. cm
      Includes bibliographical references and index.
1. City planning. 2. Community Development, Urban. I. Neal, Peter,
1963-
HT166.U7457 2003
307.1'216–dc21

ISBN 0-415-32124-7 (hb)
ISBN 0-415-26273-9 (pb)

ST. JAMES'S PALACE

Many have been inspired by the notion of the village in the city, not least by the example of London, with its numerous historic settlements, each congealing over time into a single metropolis, yet retaining a distinctive sense of locality and place. It was this characteristic – and the desire to see a revival of the principles behind it in relation to our built environment – which led me, some fifteen years ago, to start persuading people to think in terms of an *urban village*. This was an oxymoron I suppose, but a concept that nevertheless conjures a vision of neighbourhood, of conviviality and character, within an urban environment on a far broader scale than the rural village. It is a notion with a universal appeal, reflected in terms like *quartier* in France, or *neighbourhood* in the United States, suggesting a timeless and human scale to urban development, a form of urban planning that has a fresh relevance in the modern world.

The original Urban Villages Forum, a group of planning, architectural and property experts that we brought together, took this idea and examined how it may offer clues for a new generation of urban planners. In a series of visits which I initiated and sometimes led, they began to look carefully at some of the outstanding examples of historic urbanism – in places like London's Clerkenwell, Edinburgh's New Town, Charleston, South Carolina and parts of Paris. The group, under the chairmanship of Trevor Osborne, produced a book, entitled 'Urban Villages' published in 1992, that I'm afraid was greeted by many professionals as well-intentioned, but rather naïve! Yet the years since its publication have challenged some of the sceptics and, indeed, have brought the term *urban village* into common use. I am pleased to see that the concept now even enjoys favour in many official planning policies. The original Urban Villages Forum has developed into a highly regarded projects team, and a network of practitioners, that spans the United Kingdom and beyond. The Forum is now incorporated within my own charitable Prince's Foundation where it works with national, regional and local organisations to bring about examples of the *urban village* in practical projects, some of which are featured in the pages that follow.

This welcome renewal of interest in many of the features of the *urban village,* has particularly focused on the need for more mixed developments, for a more efficient use of land and on the need for the imaginative regeneration of many areas of urban dereliction and blight. On greenfield sites, too, there has also been a keen interest in using the *urban village* as a model for the sensitive and sustainable extension of

historic towns where development pressure cannot be met on brownfield sites alone. My own efforts, on land owned by the Duchy of Cornwall at Poundbury, on the edge of Dorchester, have proved that it is perfectly possible, both technically and commercially, once again to build places that can stand proudly alongside some of the finest historic settlements; places that will not become blots on either our landscapes or townscapes, and where factories and shops can be happily interspersed with homes for rent and sale, along streets that are shared by pedestrians and vehicles. And, of course, it is important to remember that one of the most crucial, underlying features of the *urban village* is that it is designed with the pedestrian, not the car, as the primary priority.

This new book brings together some of the keenest minds and most creative practitioners to explore both the theory of the *urban village* and its practical application. I am extremely pleased that it is able to include contributions not just from the United Kingdom, but also from the United States where the 'New Urbanism' is so successfully showing how the principles behind the *urban village* can help prevent sprawl and regenerate neglected cities. My thanks go to all the contributors.

I am also very grateful to Spon Press, the publishers of this collection, and to Clear Channel Communications who have generously sponsored the book. I hope that it serves to stimulate not just discussion, but also practical project work that can help to establish the wholesale revival in traditional, or sustainable, urbanism that is so desperately overdue if we are to design urban habitats fit for the future.

Notes on contributors

Peter Neal

Peter Neal is a landscape architect and urban designer specializing in urban regeneration and the public realm. Initially trained at Manchester University, he completed a Master's degree in Landscape Planning and Ecology at Harvard University's Graduate School of Design. He has worked with several design consultancies, including The ROMA Design Group in San Francisco and EDAW in London. He completed work on this book as part of a research post with The Prince's Foundation in which he looked at best practice in mixed-use urban development and regeneration. He currently manages the Enabling and Delivery Team of Cabe Space, part of the Commission for Architecture and the Built Environment.

Roberta Brandes Gratz

Roberta Brandes Gratz is an award-winning journalist and urban critic, lecturer and author of *The Living City: Thinking Small in a Big Way*, and *Cities Back from the Edge: New Life for Downtown*. She is an international lecturer on urban development issues and former award-winning reporter for the *New York Post*. In 2001, the Rockefeller Brothers Fund published her report, *A Frog, A Wooden House, A Stream and A Trail: Ten Years of Community Revitalization in Central Europe*, which she is now converting into a full-length book. She is a native and resident of New York City and her articles have appeared in numerous publications including the *Wall Street Journal*, *New York Times Magazine*, *The Nation*, *Tikkun*, *Planning Magazine*, *New York Newsday*, the *Daily News* and the *Planning Commissioners Journal*. She was a member of the New York Governor's and Mayor's Task Force on Planning Manhattan's West Side Highway and Waterfront. She founded the Eldridge Street Project to restore the first synagogue on Manhattan's Lower East Side built by East European Jews and has been appointed by Mayor Bloomberg as one of 11 commissioners on the NYC Landmarks Preservation Commission.

Peter Hall

Peter Hall is Professor of Planning at the Bartlett School of Architecture and Planning, University College London, and Director of the Institute of Community Studies. From 1991 to 1994 he was Special Adviser on Strategic Planning to the Secretary of State for the Environment. In 1998–99 he was a member of the Deputy Prime Minister's Urban Task Force. He received his Master's and Ph.D. degrees from the University of Cambridge and has taught at the London School of Economics, served as Dean of the Faculty of Urban and Regional Studies, University of Reading (1968–88) and was Professor Emeritus of City and Regional Planning at the University of California at Berkeley (1980-92). He is author or editor of more than 30 books on urban and regional planning and related topics. He has received the Founder's Medal of the Royal Geographical Society for distinction in research, is an honorary member of the Royal Town Planning Institute and was knighted in 1998 for services to the Town and Country Planning Association.

David Lock

David Lock is chairman and managing director of David Lock Associates Ltd, a practice of planners and urban designers in Milton Keynes and Melbourne, Australia. He is also chairman of DLA Architects Practice Ltd and a director of Integrated Transport Planning Ltd and of Rapid Transport International Plc. He was Chief Planning Adviser (half-time) to the Department of the Environment from 1994 to 1997, and is Visiting Professor in the Centre of Planning Studies at Reading University's School of Business. He is chairman of the Town and Country Planning Association and chair of the environmental education charity City Discovery, based in Milton Keynes. He also acts as an expert adviser on regional planning and transport strategies in Northern Ireland.

William J. Mitchell

William J. Mitchell is Professor of Architecture and Media Arts and Sciences, Head of the Media Arts and Sciences Program and Dean of the School of Architecture and Planning at MIT. He teaches courses and conducts research in design theory, computer applications in architecture and urban design, and imaging and image synthesis. A Fellow of the Royal Australian Institute of Architects, he has taught previously at Harvard's Graduate School of Design and at UCLA. His publications include *City of Bits*, *E-topia*, and the forthcoming *Me + +: The Cyborg Self and the Networked City*, all published by the MIT Press. He is a Fellow of the Royal Australian Institute of Architects and Fellow of the American Academy of Arts and Sciences.

Andrés Duany

Andrés Duany is a principal of Duany Plater-Zyberk & Co., a leading organization in the New Urbanism that seeks to end suburban sprawl and urban disinvestment. DPZ first received recognition as the designers of Seaside, Florida, and have since completed designs for over 200 new towns, regional plans and community revitalization projects. Andrés Duany received his undergraduate degree in architecture and urban planning from Princeton University and studied for a year at the Ecole des Beaux Arts in Paris before completing a Master's degree in architecture from the Yale School of Architecture. He has received honorary doctorates from Rollins College and the University of Pennsylvania, as well as the Brandeis Award for Architecture, the Thomas Jefferson Memorial Medal of Architecture from the University of Virginia and the Vincent Scully Award from the National Building Museum. He is a Fellow of the American Institute of Architects and a founder and a member of the board of directors of the Congress for the New Urbanism.

David Taylor

David Taylor is a partner of Alan Baxter & Associates. He leads project work on urban design, transport and movement, with a particular interest in advancing the creative engineering and holistic approach that the practice brings to projects. He has led the authorship of many publications on urban design, including *Places, Streets and Movement, a companion guide to Design Bulletin 32*, which was the first guide published as part of the government's integrated transport campaign. Its aim is to promote developments in which the design and layout encourage people to walk, cycle or travel by public transport rather than use the car. *Paving the Way*, published in 2002 by the Commission for Architecture in the Built Environment, highlights the impediments to achieving successful streetscapes in urban environments and sets out 12 action points for the future. David Taylor's team has also contributed the engineering aspect to *The Urban Design Compendium* and *Better Places to Live*. The principles established within this work on strategic guidance are taken through to the many projects that the practice is dealing with in the UK and Europe.

Ken Worpole

Ken Worpole is one of Britain's most influential writers on urban and social policy, and the author of many seminal books and reports. He has travelled and lectured extensively in Europe and Australia. In 1999 he was awarded an honorary doctorate by Middlesex University for his work on social policy. He has worked as an independent researcher and writer and has been principally associated with two leading research and policy think tanks in the UK, Comedia and Demos. He is particularly interested in issues associated with the quality of contemporary urban life, new forms of civil society, and the planning and design of urban landscapes and institutions that support more convivial forms of democracy. In 2001 he was appointed to the UK Government's Urban Green Spaces Task Force. His most recent books include *Here Comes the Sun: architecture and public space in 20th century European culture* (Reaktion Books, 2001) and *Last Landscapes: the architecture of the cemetery in the West* (Reaktion Books 2003).

Mike Hollingsworth

Mike Hollingsworth is planning director in the Land Development and Legal Services Division of the Welsh Development Agency (WDA), which works in partnership with the private, public and voluntary sectors, including local authorities and housing associations, and has undertaken over £1 billion in strategic investment for the economic and social regeneration of local communities throughout Wales. He has a long association with the Prince's Foundation and serves as chairman of the projects panel. He is jointly responsible for the planning and development of a series of major urban renewal and sustainable urban extension projects in Wales, most notably the Llandarcy Urban Village project near the town of Neath. This scheme is being undertaken by the WDA in partnership with BP, Neath Port Talbot County Borough Council and the Prince's Foundation.

Ben Denton

Ben Denton is a senior director of ABROS, a specialist financial advisory team focusing on Public Finance Initiatives (PFI), Public Private Partnerships (PPP) and regeneration project finance and implementation. Upon graduating from Reading University, he worked for Hillier Parker and KPMG on funding and delivering major mixed-use regeneration and property funding projects. He became a founding member of ABROS in 1996, and now leads the company's regeneration, property finance and social housing PFI work. In these sectors, he has advised on five of the eight Pathfinder social housing PFI projects in the country. His recent property and

regeneration projects include Bath Western Riverside, Newham Arc, South Telford, Canning Town and the Meden Valley Housing Special Purpose Vehicle. He has also worked on the funding and delivery for the Great Northern Warehouse and the MEN Arena in Manchester, the transfer of the former British Coal non-operational portfolio to English Partnerships and the funding, business planning and formation of the English Cities Fund. He serves on the enabling panel of the Commission for Architecture and the Built Environment, and has served as a specialist adviser on the finance panel of the Urban Task Force.

Chris Brown

Chris Brown is chief executive of Igloo Regeneration and development manager of the Igloo Regeneration Fund, which is backed by Norwich Union and managed by Morley Fund Management. Igloo invests in the development of mixed-use, environmentally sustainable, well designed, urban regeneration projects on the edge of the UK's top 20 city centres. He is a member of the government's Urban Sounding Board, a former chair of the RICS Regeneration panel, a member of the Prince's Foundation projects panel and of the Regen-Now centre of excellence steering group, and Regional Design Ambassador for the Commission for Architecture and the Built Environment.

David Lunts

David Lunts joined the Office of the Deputy Prime Minister's Urban Policy Unit as director in June 2002. He was previously chief executive of the Prince's Foundation, the Prince of Wales's urban regeneration and building charity, and before that he was director of the Urban Villages Forum, a membership and lobby group for sustainable urban development. In these posts he put together regeneration project teams that worked closely with English Partnerships, the Regional Development Agencies and local communities. Before moving to London in 1995, he worked in Manchester, running regeneration and housing projects. He chaired the City Council's Housing Committee and the board of Hulme City Challenge in the early 1990s.

Acknowledgements

This book has been a collaborative venture from the start and without initial guidance and continued encouragement from David Lunts, David Taylor and Caroline Mallinder the process would certainly have foundered at an early stage.

All the contributors deserve particular recognition, for they have given freely and generously of their knowledge, experience and time whilst being extremely busy within their own professional and academic fields. Particular appreciation is due to William Filmer-Sankey and Jaimie Ferguson from Alan Baxter & Associates, who made a significant contribution to the chapter on Connectivity and Movement. Thanks must also be expressed to Mark Gallimore of Living City Ltd for his timely assistance with the practice of neighbourhood management, and to Tom Ostler of the City of Toronto Urban Development Services, who provided invaluable help with the King-Spadina case study. I must also thank my colleagues at the Prince's Foundation, and in particular Ben Bolgar, who initiated my research post, and Dr Matthew Hardy, secretary of www.intbau.org, who has provided a continual information stream on all things urban.

Many others have assisted in providing help, facts, figures, information and illustrations that have been used throughout the book. I particularly wish to thank: Steve Alderson, Argent Group Plc; Bruce Allen, Portland Development Commission; Neil Baxter, Neil Baxter Associates; Jonathan Bewley, Sustrans Picture Library; Rebecca Bubenas, Moore Ruble Yudell Architects; Dianne Bunton, University of Strathclyde Archives; Rosa Clark, Countryside Properties Plc; Simon Conibear, The Duchy of Cornwall; John Creaser, University of California, Berkeley; Ingeborg de Roode, Stedelijk Museum, Amsterdam; Gary Dunn, Delfin Lend Lease, Australia; Mark Fiennes, Photographer; Edward Fortier, Department of City Planning, New York; Paul Frank, City of Austin, Texas; Fellene Gaylord, TriMet Creative Services, Portland; Emma Gilliam, BBC Sheffield; Dr David Gordon, Queen's University, Ontario; Robert Grahn, www.luftbildpressefoto.de; Eric Greimann, Landslides Aerial Photography; Jeff Hamilton, Ankrom Moisan Associated Architects; Prof. Lee Hardy, Calvin College, Grand Rapids; David Harrison and Claire Zapiec, John Thompson & Partners; Susan Hartung, Werner Huthmacher; David Hogg, Turner & Townsend; John Hopkins, Landscape Design Associates; Flea Keeble, Andrew Wright Associates; Peter Kermode, Mirvac Group, Australia; Christoph Kohl and Dorothea Wagner, Krier Kohl Architects; Robert Lancaster, First Garden City Heritage Museum; Sylvia Lewis, American Planning Association, Chicago; Jens Lindhe, Photographer; Róisín McCarthy, Temple Bar Properties; Mary McIntyre, Architects Alliance/Planning Alliance; Erik Møller, Technical Department, City of Aalborg, Denmark; Carlos Morales and Shannon Tracy, Duany Plater-Zyberk; Phil Mullan, Cyberia, London; Vincent Nadin, University of the West of England; Liz Neal; Sheila Noble, Edinburgh University Library; Nigel Rice, Little Germany Urban Village Company Ltd; Eva Dalman and Göran Rosberg, Malmö Stadsbyggnadskontoret; David Sucher, www.citycomforts.com, Seattle; Klas Tham, Lund University, Sweden; Ben Thompson, BBC Open Centre, Blackburn; Robert Torday, Richard Rogers Partnership; Adam Varat, Calthorpe Associates; Catherine Vibert, United Nations Division for Sustainable Development; and Volker Welter, University of California, Santa Barbara.

Illustration acknowledgements

Thanks are due to the following individuals and organizations for permission to reproduce material. Every effort has been made to contact and acknowledge copyright owners, but the editor and publishers would be pleased to have any errors or omissions brought to their attention so that corrections may be published at a later printing.

Aerofilms xiv, 5(R), 207
Ankrom Moisan Associated Architects 222(M), 223
Argent Group Plc 134, 185
Argent St George Ltd 150
City of Austin, Texas 41
Alan Baxter & Associates 102, 105(T,B), 235
Julia Bayne/Sustrans 115(TL)
BBC 74(T)
Calthorpe Associates 8(T,&B), 32, 44(B), 45, 46, 61, 68, 93(TL), 108, 112(R)
Catellus 77(T)
Bruce Cheyne 218(M)
CJB Photography 140
Congress for the New Urbanism 7(L)
Harry Connolly/Duany Plater-Zyberk 101(T)
Countryside Properties 182
Crown Street Regeneration Project 117(L), 136, 159, 200(T), 226(R), 227
Cyberia Group 75
CZWG 226(ML)
Delfin Lend Lease/Mawson Lakes 71(L), 74 (BL, BR)
Duany Plater-Zyberk 87, 88, 89(L), 90, 91, 92, 95, 96, 97, 99, 100, 110
The Duchy of Cornwall 160
du toit ALLSOPP HILLIER 219
EDAW Ltd 149, 206(L), 238(M, B), 239
Edinburgh University Library 94(R)
English Partnerships 105(L), 238(T)
Mark Fiennes/The Duchy of Cornwall 84, 101(B), 117(R), 191, 199(B), 242(TM), 243
First Garden City Heritage Museum 50(R), 52(TB), 53(R)
Free Press/Simon & Schuster 10(L)

GBD Architects 222(T)
Gemeentearchief Amsterdam 123
GLA/Mayor's Transport Strategy 113
Groth Gruppe/Archiv Allod 124(BL), 246(T)
Groth Gruppe/H G Esch 246(M)
Peter Hall 4(B), 10(R), 18, 20(T), 35, 43, 44(TL, TR), 49(L), 111, 114, 115(R), 128(T), 226(TR)
Simon Hazelgrove (020 7924 1222) 189
Hulme Regeneration Ltd/Paul Tomlin 5(L)
Werner Huthmaher 72(T), 180
Leon Krier 11(R), 86(TR), 242(BR)
Krier · Kohl 246(B)
Jens Lindhe 230(BL), 231
Little Germany Urban Village Company 156, 210(R), 211(LR)
David Lock Associates 48, 59, 62, 63(T)
London County Council 137
London Transport Museum 54
Alex S. MacLean/Landslides 6(B), 42
Malmö City Planning Office 230(R)
Mirvac Lend Lease 250(T, M, B)
Norman Mitz 25(BL, BR), 26, 28
Moore Ruble Yudell 72(B)
Moule & Polyzoides 65
Peter Neal 2, 3(L), 4(TM), 14(B), 20(B), 21(T,B), 22, 23(R), 25(TR), 29, 39, 47, 51, 53(L), 55, 63(B), 77(B), 106, 109, 116(T,B), 118, 121, 124(TL), 125(B), 126, 129(B), 130, 152, 163, 173, 184, 187, 199(T), 200(B), 210(L), 214(RT, RB), 222(B), 234(M), 250(M), 251
New York City, Department of City Planning 25(TL)
Jens V. Nielsen 58
Paul Osborne/Sustrans 115(LM)

H. Th. Oudejans Collection 124(TR)
PA Photos Ltd 6(T)
Barry Parker/Raymond Unwin 86(B)
Playa Vista 81(R)
Portland TriMet 67
The Prince's Foundation 3(R), 7(R), 11(B), 15, 20(M), 23(L), 34(TL), 36(TB), 37, 86(TL), 112(L), 120, 127(B), 139, 144, 190, 226(BL)
Ben Rahn, Architects Alliance 218(TR, BL)
Antonia Reeve 11(T)
Richard Reid/Max Lyons/ Urban Villages Forum 12–13
Roma Design Group 80–81
South East Planning Council 40
Morley von Sternberg 64
Strathclyde University Archives 93(B)
Temple Bar Properties 214(L), 215
Klas Tham 230(TL)
Percy Thomas Architects 234(T), 234(B)
John Thompson & Partners 143, 155
Tibbalds Monro 14(T)
United Nations Division for Sustainable Development 56
Urban Design Compendium 114
Urban Splash 34, 198
VROM, Dutch Ministry for Spatial Planning and Development 57
WAC Corp. 71(R)
David Warburton 89(R), 94(L)
Western Australia Planning Commission 9(B)
Simon Wilson/Berkley Homes 16, 38, 186, 196, 206(R)
Larraine Worpole 122, 125(T), 127(T), 128(B), 129(T)
Andrew Wright Associates 9(T), 145
www.luftbild-pressefoto.de 247

An urban village primer

Peter Neal

The latter half of the twentieth century was marked by a significant decline in the quality and vitality of many of our urban centres. The manufacturing and heavy industrial base, upon which many of our cities originally grew, began to rapidly contract. The commercial heart of many centres dissolved as shops and offices increasingly chose to relocate to out-of-town retail and business parks, whilst vast housing estates, built just a decade or two earlier, began an intense and painful process of social, economic and physical disintegration.

As with the garden city and new town movements of the last century we again find ourselves searching for long-term solutions that can address the immediate and often acute urban problems we now face. But unlike these previous initiatives that sought an escape for specific urban ills, the answers are now being sought within the towns and cities themselves. We are now embarking on a policy of urban renaissance which has at its heart a vision that is attempting to re-establish our neglected towns and cities as thriving and attractive urban districts. The neighbourhood has a central role in this process, for urban neighbourhoods are the primary social and physical foundation upon which our towns and cities will flourish.

The challenges are immense, but maintaining the status quo is no longer a viable option. On the one hand we are faced with the massive task of transforming dysfunctional and under-employed urban districts that are suffering blight and dereliction. On the other there is increasing pressure to sacrifice yet more of our finite countryside for new development to meet a critical shortage in housing. The solutions will not be found simply through geography and planning policy, for we face an immediate need to establish better and more effective ways to design and construct our urban neighbourhoods. Not only must the solutions be efficient in terms of land use and economics, but they also need to offer a far greater density of jobs, services, and leisure and recreation facilities – essentially, they must increasingly be socially, economically and environmentally sustainable. Above all, our challenge is to create neighbourhoods that will be popular, productive and beautiful places to live both now and for many generations to come.

Left:
The distinctive traditional urban character of Rye, East Sussex, derives from a fine-grained pattern of streets and a rich mix of uses

The village model

In the late 1980s the concept of the urban village was developed as an important and viable approach to creating successful and long-lasting neighbourhoods. It emerged as a way to alleviate the prominent failures in urban planning of our more recent past and a means to re-evaluate and re-establish many of the time-honoured principles of successful town-making that have been with us for centuries. Such places have provided some of the most popular places to live, for it is clear that people choose to gravitate towards successful, often compact, urban neighbourhoods that provide vitality and proximity to many of the amenities necessary for everyday life. But it must be remembered that these attractive and integrated urban environments do not simply happen by their own accord; they have been created by choice, by sound design and by efficient organization.

For many the term 'urban village' appeared at first perplexing, a near-perfect oxymoron that although innately familiar, projected a potentially ambiguous and even schizophrenic identity. Is it possible, yet alone sensible, to try to place the idealized charm of the village within a large and at times hostile urban environment? 'How can you have a place that feels like a village and a big city at the same time?' asks David Sucher. 'The village is small, intimate, quiet; one knows the other villagers and may even be related to them. The city is big, busy, diverse and filled with strangers. Life can be lonely in the big city.'[1]

In unravelling the complexity that lies behind the term it is perhaps worth risking the danger of oversimplifying a few of the formative principles upon which our urban centres have been built – for here lies much of the essence and purpose for making urban places. Although LeGates and Stout's expansive *City Reader*[2] provides a far more comprehensive overview than can be achieved here, one of the most succinct and long-lasting definitions can be attributed to Aristotle: 'A city should be built to give its inhabitants security and happiness.'[3] 'What is a City?' questioned Lewis Mumford in a 1930s edition of the *Architectural Record*.[4] It is 'a geographic plexus, an economic organisation, an institutional process, a theatre of social action, and a symbol of collective unity.' In the 1960s Jane Jacobs, from whom we shall learn more in the following chapter, suggested that 'the real value of cities lies in their diversity, architectural variety, teeming street life and human scale. It is only when we appreciate such fundamental realities that we can hope to create cities that are safe, interesting and economically viable, as well as places that people want to live in.'[5] Certainly such noteworthy and respected urban critics were able to clearly articulate an appreciation of the complexity and vitality that is inherent within our urban environments – but where do the characteristics of the village fit with this?

Historically, the form and purpose of the village provide important precursors to the majority of our towns and cities. Many of the innate qualities found in villages have been retained in perpetuity to provide a type of metropolitan code, or urban DNA if you like, which continues to subconsciously guide our urban development. 'Much of the City was latent, indeed visibly present, in the village,' suggested Mumford, in his urban biography *The City In History*.[6] Throughout time we have seen human life swing between two poles, from movement to settlement. From the earliest settlements, a sense of community was forged to meet the needs of nutrition and reproduction in relative safety – a new order, new regularity and new security was established in everyday life. 'From this permanent

Right:
Rye's network of attractive streets and public spaces gives priority to those on foot yet still accommodates the needs of vehicles

Left
A traditional European urban fabric of distinctive civic buildings, busy streets and popular public squares in Pollença, Majorca

Right:
The pedestrian-scaled streets of Clerkenwell in central London support a rich mix of popular social activities

association of families emerged the neighbour – he who lives near at hand, within calling distance, sharing the crises of life,' wrote Mumford. In time, the neighbour became the neighbourhood and village culture began to diversify rapidly. New individuals bought a new mix of skills and activities and larger urban centres began to form. Even if the order, stability and simplicity of the village became lost within the expansion of the city at large, the life-enhancing qualities of communal identification and neighbourliness of the village remained latent in the urban neighbourhood. And certainly some would suggest that without the initial energy and loving nurture provided by the village, the city could not have been created.

Such innate village qualities – security, sociability and economic purpose – still provide many of the essential ingredients found within our successful, and much loved, neighbourhoods. They set the benchmark upon which the success of existing places and new developments are valued and measured. It is easy to recognize and identify places where these qualities are embodied, and certainly early urban village literature aligned itself closely with the characteristics of places like Rye in Sussex, Richmond in Yorkshire and the neighbourhood of Clerkenwell in London. Yet we continually find ourselves up against the paradox that although we understand and appreciate these qualities, many of our new urban neighbourhoods fail to deliver such cherished expectations. 'Why, given that traditional urban environments worked so well in the past, do we seem incapable of building places with these same qualities today?' questioned HRH The Prince of Wales at the outset of the Urban Villages Campaign in 1990.[7]

Much of the answer lies in the fact that for over a century planners and architects have been given almost free rein to experiment at will with large parts of our towns and cities. Wave after theoretical wave has brought new and contrasting approaches to the way our urban environments have been allowed to change – occasionally for the better, but often for the worse. Many of the early attempts to create new communities came about through a reaction to the real and perceived excesses that the Industrial Revolution unleashed on our cities and citizens. Led by a number of prominent and familiar philanthropists and utopian thinkers, they sought to create immediate, idealized and enduring societies that embodied a wide variety of industrial, religious and political

Top:
Letchworth Garden City, established by Ebenezer Howard in 1903

Above:
Hampstead Garden Suburb, planned by Parker and Unwin in 1906

beliefs. Many of these planned developments, including the likes of Port Sunlight, Bournville and Saltaire, laid out in the 1800s, have clearly influenced the form and architectural vocabulary of our current urban neighbourhoods. Turn to Gillian Darley's meticulously referenced *Villages of Vision*[8] and you can see the evolution of these model communities in detail, for it is clear that they still provide latent inspiration for many of the more successfully designed neighbourhoods in Britain and abroad in recent years.

Perhaps one of the most significant influences that has been attributed to urban villages came at the turn of the twentieth century, when Ebenezer Howard spearheaded the Garden City movement. *To-morrow: A Peaceful Path to Real Reform* was published in 1898 and appeared in its second edition as the more familiar *Garden Cities of Tomorrow*.[9] It was written to address the familiar problems of Britain's decaying industrial cities and the plight of the urban poor and its impact was momentous. It stimulated numerous urban programmes in Britain and abroad that now house millions of people, and the movement directly contributed to the creation of the town and country planning profession. These garden cities, planned with the formative and perceptive architectural hand of Raymond Unwin and Barry Parker, were generally developed around the nucleus of rail stations. They were formally configured and often strengthened by powerful civic spaces that were enclosed within village-scaled neighbourhoods. The social and physical morphology of the original village had become reincarnate in a new semi-urban and suburban geography typified by the likes of Letchworth Garden City and Hampstead Garden Suburb.

Right:
Port Sunlight on the Wirral, W. H. Lever's 1880s alternative to inner-city squalor

Modernism and segregation

Probably the most fundamental influence on the development and form of our modern urban neighbourhoods came from the International Congress of Modern Architecture (CIAM), established in 1928. Dominated in the 1930s by Le Corbusier, the organization became the chief instrument for disseminating modernist ideas on architecture and town planning. CIAM's influential Charter of Athens, issued in 1933, established their principles for urban planning.[10] The primary urban functions were identified as 'residential', 'work' and 'traffic'. The diverse mixture of uses on which our neighbourhoods, towns and cities thrived was to be no more, for they were now to be segregated and zoned in a clinical, technical and compartmentalized manner.

During the post-war years and on throughout the 1950s and 1960s the modern movement held the development of our cities in an ideological vice. From Tony Garnier's *Cité Industrielle*, which isolated different uses and freed buildings from the street, Le Corbusier was able to expand his modernist vision: the segregation of use, the love of the car and the dominance of private over public space. In these new utopias the street as the community's habitable common ground disintegrated. Corbusier relentlessly continued with his creation of his 'dream city'. This so-called 'Radiant City' was composed of skyscrapers housing people at a density of more than 1,200 persons per acre in a vast wilderness of open space. For over half a century architects and town planners throughout the world have replicated numerous versions of Le Corbusier's vision, creating soulless tower block estates that have had a fundamental impact on the form, structure and social cohesion of our cities. To our further detriment the situation has been compounded by the near-wholesale adoption of the private car as the main form of transport, triggering unstoppable urban sprawl. Jane Jacobs concisely concluded:

These conceptions have merged into a sort of Radiant Garden City Beautiful. Throughout the post-war period, planners temperamentally unsympathetic to cities have been let loose on our urban environment. Inspired by the ideals

Above:
The deck-accessed housing estates of Hulme in Manchester lasted barely 20 years before demolition

Right:
Post-war neighbourhoods, including Park Hill in Sheffield, were directly influenced by modernist principles of urban planning

of the Garden City or Le Corbusier's Radiant City, they have dreamt up ambitious projects based on self-contained neighbourhoods, super-blocks, rigid 'scientific' plans and endless acres of grass. Yet they seldom stop to look at what actually works on the ground.[11]

Such urban degradation has been wrought on an international scale. As Howard Kunstler poignantly observed:

All places in America suffered terribly from the way we chose to arrange things in our post-war world. Cities, towns and the countryside were ravaged equally, as were the lesser orders of things within them – neighbourhoods, buildings, streets, farms – and there is scant refuge from the disorders that ensued ... to me, it is a landscape of scary places, the *geography of nowhere*, that has simply ceased to be a credible human habitat.[12]

The search for a new urbanism

Such flawed urban theory and practice has directly contributed to the decline of our urban neighbourhoods in the latter part of the twentieth century. This situation was further compounded in Britain with the loss of large sections of manufacturing industry to foreign competition. Vast areas of land became physically and socially blighted through contamination, dereliction, high unemployment and rising levels of poverty. Local authorities began to adopt policies for slum clearance during the 1950s, although it was not until the 1970s, suggests Ian Colquhoun,[13] that the first public recognition for the need for urban regeneration in Britain emerged, with Peter Walker, the Secretary of State for the Environment, in his 1972 Inner City Review. The 1978 Inner Urban Act switched Central Government resources from new towns to inner cities, although it was only when the inner-city riots in London, Birmingham, Manchester and Liverpool occurred that political attention finally began to focus on the urban environment. Following Margaret Thatcher's memorable visit to Teesside in 1987, the Government finally began to establish significant initiatives to tackle the problems of inner-city decline.

Throughout the 1980s and 1990s we have seen a wide variety of Government intervention within the urban environment, culminating in the more recent work of the Urban Task Force and the publication of an Urban White Paper in 2000.[14] Through the work of the Social Exclusion Unit, Central Government has now chosen to focus its funding towards the neighbourhood. Its New Commitment to Neighbourhood Renewal programme, prepared at the beginning of 2001, established a new National Strategy Action Plan to ensure that 'within 10 to 20 years, no one should be seriously disadvantaged by where they live' This new initiative attempts to balance funding between the core economic, social and physical

problems of deprived urban areas. In addition, it clearly recognizes the important role that local residents and community groups can play in turning their neighbourhoods around.

Towards an Urban Renaissance, the final report of the Urban Task Force,[15] sets out in significant detail a physical agenda for tacking urban decline and promoting urban community. Described in more detail within Peter Hall's chapter, the report illustrates the key benefits that mixed-use and integrated urban neighbourhoods can offer through proximity to work, shops and basic social, educational and leisure activities. 'Good urban design,' the report suggests, 'should encourage more people to live near to those services which they require on a regular basis.'

In parallel, American urban policy has begun to refocus on the role and value of the urban neighbourhood. Blighted by vast swathes of monotonous urban sprawl, America's cities have rapidly decentralized over the last 50 years into the surrounding countryside, leaving in their wake huge areas of urban blight and intense social deprivation. The rise of sprawl, outlined in Duany, Plater-Zyberk and Speck's book *Suburban Nation*,[16] was triggered primarily by vast post-war building programmes, an expansive interstate highway

programme and an almost unilateral adoption of the single-use zoning strategies promoted by the modernist movement.

'After 1950 the hollowing-out of the urban fabric began in earnest,' suggests Professor Michael Hebbert:

> With it, began a reappraisal of the founding axioms of urbanism, and a sequence of enquiry and experiment that was as international and as eclectic as the original movement. By way of Rossi, Alexander, Jacobs, Cooper, Panerai, Krier, and DPZ, we have arrived at a new urbanism for the close of the twentieth century; now the street which was the problem has become the solution.[17]

New Urbanism became formally recognized in the early 1990s following the First Congress for the New Urbanism that was held in 1993 at Alexandria, Virginia. At this meeting key American practitioners came together to present and debate alternative and considered solutions to current models of suburban sprawl that were seen clearly as unsustainable in terms of future urban growth patterns. 'The New Urbanism is a movement that I feel will be of great relevance to future planning efforts in this country,' suggested Peter Katz in his

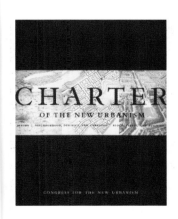

Top right:
**Proposals for a 40-acre
mixed-use, high density
redevelopment at Bay
Meadows, California**
Calthorpe Associates

Below right:
**The proposed development
plan for Bay Meadows,
California**

book, *The New Urbanism*.[18] 'It addresses many of
the ills of our current sprawl development pattern
while returning to a cherished America icon: that
of a compact, close-knit community.'

Yet New Urbanism should not be considered
just a revival of traditional or historic planning
strategies. It proposes new solutions that are being
prepared to serve the needs of our changing pattern
of society and is trying to embrace the opportunities
offered by new technology. The movement sees as
critical the promotion of land-efficient planning
methods that it believes can deliver a higher, and
more sustainable, quality of life to a majority of
America's citizens. Peter Calthorpe concludes: 'the
New Urbanism is not just about the city or the
suburb. It is about the way we conceive our
community and how we form the region – its
diversity, scale and public space in every context.'[19]

New Urbanism is concerned with both the
pieces and the whole. Its key principles are set
out within the *Charter of the New Urbanism*,[20]
which defines urbanism by its diversity, pedestrian
scale, public space and structure. Articulated
by the central elements of the 'neighbourhood',
the 'district' and the 'corridor', these urban
components provide the cornerstone of the charter
and are seen as fundamental in defining a strong
sense of community that consciously asserts the
primacy of public over private space.

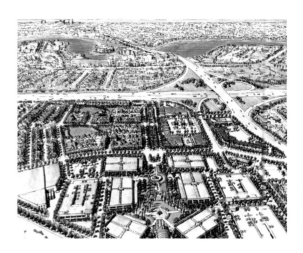

Sustainable urban neighbourhoods

It is clear that the neighbourhood is now seen as
playing a central role in both Britain's urban
renaissance and New Urbanism in the United States.
It is at the core of Rudlin and Falk's reappraisal of
the contemporary British city, *Building the 21st
Century Home: The sustainable urban neighbourhood*.[21]
Here the neighbourhood is seen as the most
important urban element that establishes the social
and economic sustainability of the area, providing
the community ties which hold it together and its
relationship to surrounding areas. By exploring a
number of complementary characteristics
represented by eco-neighbourhoods, sociable-
neighbourhoods and model-neighbourhoods,
Rudlin and Falk boldly conclude that 'the twenty-

first century will rediscover that towns and cities
are not only mankind's greatest invention and
cultural achievement, but that sustainable urban
neighbourhoods will give us back the time and
balance we have lost.'

The are a number of commonly-accepted and
now familiar characteristics that represent this
much-sought-after sustainability: adequate size;
compact form; appropriate urban density; varied
mix of uses and tenure; a range of employment,
leisure and community facilities; ready access to
public transport; and a pedestrian-friendly environment. These principles, which are central to the
philosophy of urban villages, have risen greatly in
prominence in recent years. They now form an
integral component of urban planning policy,
ordinance and guidance in many countries.

Right:
The key components of a mixed-use and integrated neighbourhood proposed by the Urban Task Force
©Andrew Wright Associates

Below:
The Western Australian Planning Commission's design code for urban neighbourhoods

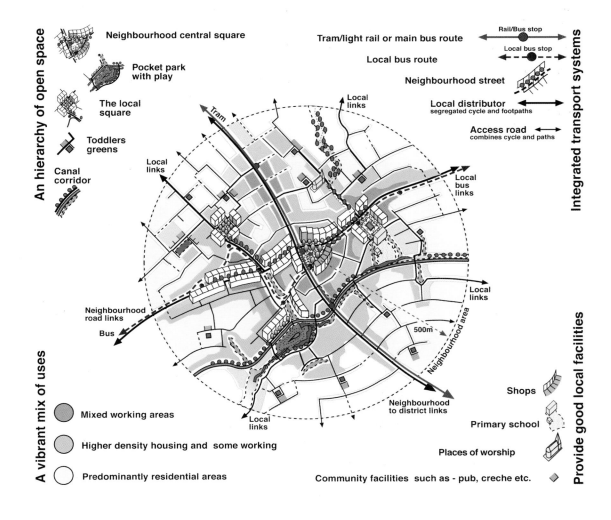

An hierarchy of open space

Neighbourhood central square

Pocket park with play

The local square

Toddlers greens

Canal corridor

A vibrant mix of uses

Mixed working areas

Higher density housing and some working

Predominantly residential areas

Integrated transport systems

Rail/Bus stop

Tram/light rail or main bus route

Local bus stop

Local bus route

Neighbourhood street

Local distributor
segregated cycle and footpaths

Access road
combines cycle and paths

Provide good local facilities

Shops

Primary school

Places of worship

Community facilities such as - pub, creche etc.

Tram

Local links

Local links

Local bus links

Local links

Neighbourhood road links

Bus

500m

Neighbourhood area

Neighbourhood to district links

Local links

Fundamentally, this now represents a significant shift away from the modernist principles of segregated use that were adopted throughout much of the twentieth century. It represents a significant change in policy, towards more traditional forms of urbanism.

The reintroduction of such time-honoured methodologies has been adopted in the United States by the planning practice of Duany Plater-Zyberk (DPZ) in an endeavour to combat sprawl. They clearly identify a need to create new regulations and a new regulatory environment to provide an alternative to existing policy of land-use zoning. In establishing a series of town-making principles that underpin the Traditional Neighbourhood Development Ordinance, DPZ have analysed the neighbourhood characteristics of many of

America's successful older cities, towns and villages and these will be discussed in more detail within Andrés Duany's chapter on the principles of neighbourhood design. This new planning code, or ordinance, has direct similarities with the initial principles of sustainable urban neighbourhoods, namely: it limits the size of the neighbourhood and defines a focused centre; it locates shops, workplaces, schools and residences for all income groups; and it sets dimensions for the street pattern so that the neighbourhood can equitably serve both the needs of the automobile and the pedestrian.

In the State of Western Australia, the Planning Commission has prepared a similar Community Design Code as part of their Liveable Neighbourhoods initiative. This sets a new approach to the creation of more sustainable suburban communities that offer a wider variety of housing types and forms of employment to support the needs of a changing population. At its heart are the now-familiar principles that lie behind the vision of Liveable Neighbourhoods: a walkable urban structure; a compatible mix of uses that can reduce car dependency; a variety of employment, retail and community facilities; and access to services and facilities for all users, including those with disabilities.

Planning Policy Guidance in Britain has adopted a similar vein. In parallel to the vision of mixed-use urban neighbourhoods proposed by the Urban Task Force, National Planning Policy Guidance (PPG), calls for the planning system to deliver high-quality, mixed-use developments characterized by compactness, varied dwelling type, a range of employment, leisure and community facilities, and ready access to public transport. PPG 1 goes further in specifically identifying urban villages as an appropriate form that these mixed-use neighbourhoods may take.[22]

The role of urban villages

Over the past decade urban villages have become widely adopted as an established component of urban planning. They have come to represent a form of shorthand to identify the regeneration of old and the creation of new urban areas embodying the principles of sustainable and tight-knit urban neighbourhoods. The origins of the term may be traced in part to the work of urban sociologist Herbert Gans. In the 1950s he undertook an in-depth appraisal of the social structure and neighbourhood of a predominately Italian-American immigrant community in Boston's West End. Describing them as 'urban villagers',[23] he published his highly descriptive findings in 1962. His in-depth analysis portrayed a vibrant, if at times down-at-heel, neighbourhood that was typified by its social mix and density of shops, houses and industrial lofts. *It was like a little piece of Italy, with narrow winding streets alive with urban social life.* Although these people lived in the great and urbane metropolis of Boston, life for the West Enders much resembled that found in the village or small town.

Urban village strategies have been adopted by many cities as a means to focus neighbourhood creation and renewal initiatives. In the early 1990s in the United States, the Mayor of Seattle, Norm Rice, proposed an ambitious new Comprehensive Plan to guide the future development of the city that included a network of urban villages – typified by dense, mixed-use developments located close to shopping and transit facilities. Similarly, in Australia, the cities of Sydney, Melbourne and Perth have all adopted strategies that identified the principle of urban villages as a means to refocus urban development at a neighbourhood scale.

In Britain, the urban village is now established within our collective planning lexicon at both a national scale, with central government planning policy, and local scale via adoption within local plans and guidance. Initial credit for the initiative must be attributed to HRH The Prince of Wales who raised the concept of urban villages in the introduction to his book *A Vision of Britain*,[24] published in 1989. His immediate concern was to define a viable framework to 'rebuild the shattered remnants of Britain's inner cities so that people once again have proper communities in which to live and which, in turn restore life and soul to such inner urban areas'. In response, the Urban Villages Group was established and charged by the Prince of Wales with the task to appraise past mistakes and learn from existing urban communities that worked. During early research the Group sought advice on urban design from a wide body of

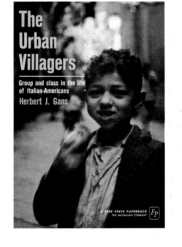

Above:
Herbert Gans's lively social analysis of Boston's West End

Right:
A Boston neighbourhood in the 1960s

theory, including the work of Leon Krier and Christopher Alexander. The Urban Villages Campaign was subsequently launched in June 1990 to promote the development of higher quality and more sustainable urban environments designed to the highest standards and with strong input from local communities.

In 1992, the Urban Villages Group published the first edition of the *Urban Villages* report, which was prepared as a discussion document, or form of manifesto, for the concept.[25] It was generously illustrated with a cross-section of urban environments, both historic and new, that promoted the urban aesthetic that was initially established in *A Vision of Britain*. The report concluded with information on urban codes and estate management and it presented the entire concept in the form of an imaginary development called Greenville that was seen to embody the key principles of the concept. These became established as the main tenets of the movement:

- a development of adequate size, or critical mass;
- a walkable and pedestrian-friendly environment;
- a good mix of uses and good opportunities for employment;
- a varied architecture and a sustainable urban form;
- mixed tenure for both housing and employment uses;
- provision of basic shopping, health and educational needs;
- a degree of self-sufficiency.

Such was the response to the report that the Urban Villages Forum, a membership organization, was established. This united many of the country's leading housebuilders, developers, funders, planners and designers to make the case for a more people-friendly approach to mixed-use development. Now integrated within the Prince's Foundation for Architecture and the Built Environment as part of the Urban Network, the work of the Forum continues to debate, promote and implement these principles of sustainable neighbourhood development throughout the country.

The original *Urban Villages* report generated

RES (ECONOMICA) PRIVATA

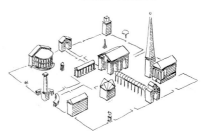

RES PUBLICA

CIVITAS

much debate and certainly received a significant amount of criticism. From a number of quarters, the concept was seen to be overly prescriptive and inflexible. The need, for example, to secure around 40 contiguous hectares of land, preferably under single ownership, was considered to be unachievable in many of our established and historic cities. By their very nature and size they would be intrusive and difficult to sell to a nation of NIMBY's (Not In My Back Yard) reluctant to support local development. A real concern was whether one could realistically expect British people to live at the kind of densities more usually found in continental Europe. It was felt that without tight control the urban village could rapidly become the suburban village.

For many, the concept was seen to be too utopian and, in the words of the Royal Society of Arts' *Journal*, easily 'dismissed by sceptics as a romantic irrelevance'.[26] Everything – from initial land acquisition, through masterplanning and

Top:
HRH The Prince of Wales initiated the Urban Villages Campaign, which drew inspiration from Leon Krier, in the late 1980s

Above:
Throughout the 1990s The Urban Villages Forum prepared a variety of guidance on planning urban villages

Right:
The domestic and the monumental, Leon Krier's familiar diagram for structuring an urban quarter

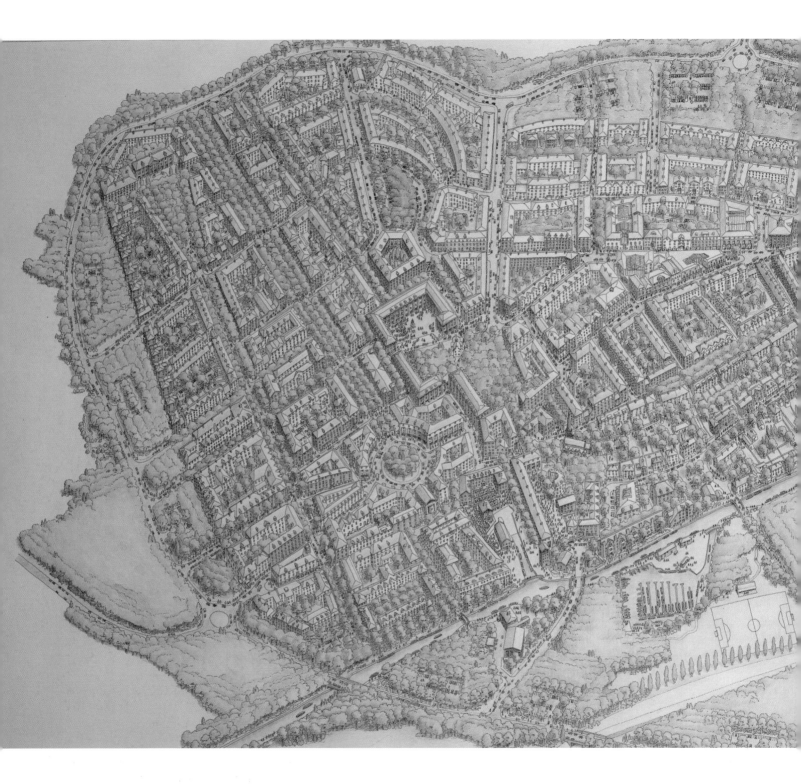

Above:

The plan of Greenville, an imaginary location, presented many of the key principles required for an urban village

on to the detailed building codes and estate management precepts – needed to be tightly controlled. This ignored much of the spontaneity and improvisation that make really liveable cities what they are today. Scant reference was given to earlier planning precedents established by the likes of Ebenezer Howard and Raymond Unwin in the early 1900s and there were real concerns as to how one could identify, yet alone involve, communities who do not exist at the time of planning. Funding

funding? Furthermore, in the long term who would be prepared to fund the unprofitable and low-income elements that would deliver a balanced community? Charles Knevitt, writing in *Building Design*, concluded that 'it might take a miracle to build something embracing more than a few of the Urban Village report's precepts.'[27]

Recent research, such as that undertaken by Cardiff University's City and Regional Planning Department,[28] continues to focus on the immense difficulties associated with the delivery of true urban villages. An analytical survey of some 55 so-called urban villages, found that the term has often been hijacked as a means to achieve planning permissions and boost final sales for developments that have generally fallen a long way short of incorporating many of the original urban village principles.

Remaking communities

This book seeks to discover what has been happening to Charles Knevitt's suggested 'miracle' over the last decade. It sets out to identify many of the now-established techniques that are being used to remake our urban communities, and identifies a series of mixed-use projects that attempt to deliver many of the early urban village aspirations.

With a desire to achieve academic depth and practical insight, key individuals with an extensive knowledge and experience of the urban environment have been invited to contribute. The book chooses to take an international perspective and focuses primarily on the making of communities in Britain and the United States, for a number of clear parallels can be drawn between our countries. Britain is seeking to establish a new urban renaissance within which urban villages can make a significant contribution. America, meanwhile, is trying to adopt models of smart growth that increasingly draw on the principles of traditional neighbourhood development.

To appreciate the broad principles of mixed-use neighbourhoods that define the model of the urban village, the book explores the concept in four distinct ways. First, it addresses the *context*. Peter Hall, Professor of Planning at the Bartlett

was considered by many to be a key concern. With investors increasingly choosing to take a shorter three- to five-year view on returns, how would it be possible to finance the initial infrastructure of the villages without significant public sector gap

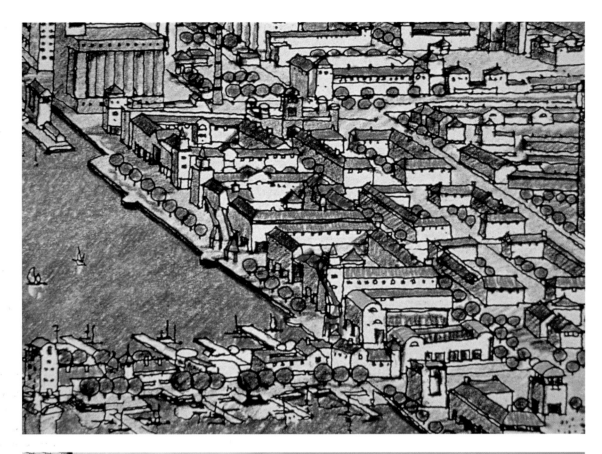

Above:
**An initial concept for
West Silvertown**
Tibbalds Monro

Below:
**New housing with a central
courtyard and ground floor
workspace, built during
the regeneration of Hulme,
Manchester**

Above:
A Planning Weekend for the West Silvertown urban village in London's Docklands, 1993

School of Architecture and Planning, reviews the primary strategies that are being adopted to reshape Britain and America's urban environments; David Lock, town planner and Chairman of David Lock Associates, establishes, from a British perspective, the current strategic planning framework within which urban villages may be placed; and William Mitchell, Professor of Architecture and Media Arts and Sciences at the Massachusetts Institute of Technology, reflects on the impact that new digital technologies will have on our changing urban neighbourhoods.

The second section takes a broad look at the *design* issues that are fundamental for the creation of liveable neighbourhoods. Andrés Duany, architect, town planner and founding principle of DPZ, writes on the physical design of neighbourhoods and focuses on neighbourhood design principles that contribute to the identity of place. Good connectivity and movement is considered to be as important as physical design and David Taylor, engineer and partner of Alan Baxter & Associates, sets out the key transport issues that contribute to the sustainability and functionality of the neighbourhood. In parallel, the social structure of the neighbourhood is considered to be equally important in the design of the place. Ken Worpole, author and national policy advisor on urban and social issues, outlines the fundamental social components and interactions that conspire to bring life and activity to the urban village.

The *implementation* of an urban village project is considered to be the most complex and challenging stage, in which a series of management and funding activities must be integrated. In reflection of its multidisciplinary nature, Mike Hollingsworth, Planning Director for the Welsh Development Agency, Ben Denton, economist and Director of ABROS, and Chris Brown, Development Manager of Igloo Regeneration Partnership, jointly draw together the key components required to initiate, implement and manage an urban village project. The section starts by introducing the key activities that are required to kick-start the inception stage of a project. It then addresses the complex issues associated with land assembly, community consultation, short and long term

funding, assessments of project viability, and the contribution of physical planning initiatives. The penultimate chapter focuses on project delivery and includes issues of project control, programming and long-term management.

In summary, David Lunts, now Director of the Government's Urban Policy Unit, draws on his long association with the urban villages movement to set out the emerging political and practical challenges that will be faced by a new generation of urban villages.

The fourth and final section of the book provides a series of case studies that represent many of the characteristics of sustainable neighbourhoods. Learning through *example* is essential if we are to appreciate the full complexity and variety of urban villages. A compendium of exemplar projects has been selected from the United Kingdom, Europe, North America and Australia. The projects have been set in a sequence that illustrates a variety of development and regeneration scenarios. These include tight urban retrofit projects, large-scale infill and brownfield renewal initiatives, and urban extension and greenfield development.

As a starting point it has been suggested that probably the most fundamental influence on both the New Urbanism movement in the United States and the aspirations for urban villages in the United Kingdom has been the observations and writings of Jane Jacobs. Almost single-handedly she took on the might of New York's Planning Department, which in turn brought into question the way we used to view our cities. In acknowledgement to Jacob's formative contribution to the way we now value, plan and develop our urban environments Roberta Brandes Gratz, New York journalist and urban critic, provides the book's keynote essay, 'Authentic urbanism and the Jane Jacobs Legacy'.

Authentic urbanism and the Jane Jacobs legacy

Roberta Brandes Gratz

Jane Jacobs changed the way the world views cities. Starting with her journalism, her pitched battles against New York planning czar Robert Moses and her first book, *The Death and Life of Great American Cities* in 1961, Jacobs articulated an accessible and potent alternative to the social science thinking of the day. In the years since, she has given us a library of books – six in all – offering insights and wisdom regarding the nature and functioning of cities and the nations that contain them. Authentic urbanism is best understood by reading Jacobs.

After World War II, viewing cities as full of problems was prevalent. This helped popularize the suburban ideal. This was the era of central planning, big highways, slum clearance, urban renewal. Expert thinking maintained that cities needed to be reconfigured. Mega-planner Robert Moses started carving up New York State under these programmes. He set a trend that spread rapidly.

Jacobs rejected all of that. Instead of looking at the city as a problem that needed fixing, she recognized the strengths of cities and sought to build upon them. She understood the challenges faced by cities. She saw cities *with* problems, not cities *as* problems. But, loudly and clearly, Jacobs said the 'experts' were studying cities in the wrong way, offering ill-considered theories and hatching half-baked, destructive policies. She accused the city planning, banking and governmental power structure of being 'anti-city' and of 'sacking' cities instead of aiding them.

Jacobs was one of the first to see cities as appealing, complex organisms while others focused on cities as full of cancers. Most importantly, Jacobs understood how cities work. She argued for common sense derived from direct observation, and related everything to peoples' daily lives. Her message was crystal-clear and totally accessible to the ordinary person. Jacobs gave voice to what many citizens were instinctively feeling. She gave encouragement to civic protestors who shared her vision, and she helped inspire the variety of citizen-based urban development and environmental movements that today are making the difference between positive and destructive urban change. The Urban Villages Forum is, perhaps, one of the most prominent campaigns in the UK to draw on her principles. Advocates of her ideas encircle the globe.

Left:
New bars and restaurants have played an important role in the revival of Shoreditch in London

Clockwise from top left:
Greenwich Village, Jane Jacob's New York neighbourhood, in the 1960s

Traditional New York apartments with ground-floor shops in the Chinese Quarter, 1960s

Inner-urban neighbourhood decline in Philadelphia, 2001

New York street life in 1965, at the heart of a lively and convenient mixed-use district

Organized complexity

She defined the city through the notion of 'organized complexity'. A city comprises what appears to be completely random activities. But, Jacobs demonstrated, these seemingly complex, ad hoc occurrences are artfully connected and interdependent in a way that comes together as a balanced whole. The micro can only be understood and studied as part of that whole, cannot be functionally separated from it and cannot be reduced to formal plans and cookie-cutter strategies. Only as part of a web can any particular strand be understood.

'Within the seeming chaos and jumble of the city, there is a remarkable degree of order', she wrote, in the form of relationships of all kinds that are absolutely fundamental to city life, more fundamental and necessary to safety, to convenience, to social action, to economic opportunity, than anything dreamed of in the image of the rebuilt city. 'Where it works at all well,' she adds, 'this network of relationships is astonishingly intricate.' It requires a staggering diversity of activities and people, variously interlocked in often-invisible ways (though often casually so) and able to make constant adjustments to needs and circumstances. The physical form of the city has to be full of variety and flexibility for people to accommodate it to their needs, not only as a family unit, but also as a living community.

Jacobs saw the city as a holistic organism at a time when prevailing movements insisted on breaking it into divisible parts. (This is still true.) Recognizing that cities have been and will always be under some kind of stress, never reaching a clear equilibrium, she illustrated that, like natural organisms, cities develop their own form of health if not inappropriately interfered with. Where her principles have been followed, her optimism has been justified.

By focusing on neighbourhoods, streets, local economies, community relationships and the like, Jacobs offered opportunities for both the average person and open-minded professional to observe and understand cities. She gave substance and encouragement, in effect, to opponents of so-called slum clearance, of neighbourhood destruction for highway construction, demolition of historic buildings and districts, of devaluation of manu-facturing areas and of the replacement of mass transit and open space by car-dependent suburbs.

'It is not easy for uncredentialed people to stand up to the credentialed, even when the so-called expertise is grounded in ignorance and folly' she wrote in the introduction to the 1993 Modern Library Edition of *The Death and Life of Great American Cities*. In this introduction, her intention was 'merely to describe the civilizing and enjoyable services that good city street life casually provides – and to deplore planning fads and architectural fashions that were expunging these necessities and charms instead of helping to strengthen them'. She quickly discovered, however, that everything she looked at was 'intimately mingled with clues and keys to other peculiarities of cities. Thus one discovery led to another, then another...'

The legacy of Jane Jacobs is as complex and innovative as the cities, the economies and the processes of nature she has written about, celebrated and defended. Sometimes elusive but always powerful, her teaching is as relevant today as it ever was, particularly in American cities where large swathes of downtowns are being cleared for mega-projects as de-urbanizing as the slum clearance and urban renewal projects she witnessed 50 years ago. And it is as relevant today in American and British residential neighbourhoods where new suburban housing is replacing the dense complexity of real urban communities. In too many places, the insights of her thinking have been stolen for promotional rhetoric but ignored in practice and application. The tendency too often seems to be to learn and unlearn lessons. Thus, the advocacy inherent in Jacob's teaching is an ongoing struggle.

The Jacobs legacy is best recognized in the places that embody her precepts: in old industrial districts showing new residential and economic life, such as New York's SoHo, the Pearl District of Portland, Oregon, London's Shoreditch, Manchester's Castlefields, Liverpool's Old Haymarket or Toronto's King-Spadina district; in traditional, mostly residential neighbourhoods, regenerated with new buildings filling empty lots on a modest scale and new uses without erasing the existing buildings and uses, such as the Greenwich Village Houses on the far west side of New York's Greenwich Village, the North Side of Pittsburgh, the Arts District in Liverpool, or the

East End of Glasgow; in a few new, dense, mixed-use neighbourhoods developed over time on already cleared land like Toronto's St Lawrence Neighbourhood and Pittsburgh's re-emerging Hill District. The good news is the large number of places embodying her legacy.

For cities of Great Britain, this is particularly relevant. The once great industrial cities, while suffering economically and dismissed as anachronistic in recent decades, retain the rich urban fabric and modest new innovations ripe for regeneration of the most enduring kind, the kind of diversified, organic rebirth about which Jacobs writes. Some, like Birmingham, suffer from large American-style urban renewal projects or, like Liverpool, from smaller ones. But recognition of these mistakes is widespread. The determination to undo them is apparent. And the impact of earlier misguided redevelopment schemes is smaller in scale than in most American cities. In effect, if the appropriate authentic urban principles are applied, British cities are poised for a remarkable resurgence.

Jacobs' neighbourhood reflects Jacobs' principles

The lesson of how to observe the particular, how to see all the connections and how to value the complexity of it all is at the heart of Jacobs' legacy. Just walking on Jacobs' Toronto block reveals a vision that, at its most complex, rests on very simple, clear principles. Her block is not unique. The lessons are universal.

Jane Jacobs lives in a medium-sized Queen Anne house built of brick on a street in a Toronto neighbourhood more typical of an American urban street than the Greenwich Village street she left behind more than 25 years ago when she, her husband and three children moved to this Canadian City. One- and two-family, detached and semi-detached houses line up close to one another, separated by driveways and with garages in some of the small back yards. Great variety of style, material and colour mark this collection of individualized houses. Small front yards, mature street trees, and a sidewalk of modest width

Top:
A leafy Toronto neighbourhood in the 1960s, incorporating houses, shops and cafés

Above:
Many of Toronto's favourite neighbourhoods are focused on popular pedestrian and transit-oriented urban streets

Right:
Street intersections, such as Five-Ways in Paddington, Sydney, can be a popular social focus for a neighbourhood

separate the houses from the street on which cars park on both sides and traffic passes slowly. The simple grid of neighbourhood streets has been modified so that cars cannot speed through the neighbourhood. Occasional directional changes, speed humps and the narrowing of intersections discourage through traffic. The streets serve well only people with local destinations. This city-implemented traffic pattern discourages intrusive car traffic, strengthens pedestrian appeal and safety and makes neighbourhoods highly liveable. Overnight street parking is limited to resident permit holders. Kerbside parking spots absorb transient parking during the day. No parking lots interrupt the continuity of houses, either between or behind houses.

Half a block from Jacobs' house is a small, tranquil park. One block in the other direction is a major neighbourhood commercial thoroughfare, Bloor Street, under which the Subway runs. An eclectic variety of businesses stands here, serving a gamut of customers from local to international. Above most of the stores are apartments or offices. This is the classic pedestrian and transit-oriented urban street with more potential for the emergence

of the new businesses that are so critical to a vibrant urban economy.

The commercial mix serves both the nearby neighbourhoods' and citywide needs. No single business overwhelms the diversity of use and scale. And when some businesses fail or move, others seem to open readily in their wake. One now-famous large department store, Honest Ed's, started as a small shop decades ago. Honest Ed's comes closest to being a single business that might overwhelm the diversity of use and scale of the street – but it is, fortunately, limited to one block. The owner is now a major popular culture producer in Toronto. Two eateries, the Country Style Restaurant and Elizabeth Deli, remain, hangovers from when the neighbourhood was the centre of the Hungarian immigrant community. The ethnic variety of live entertainment in small venues changes from year to year. Chic restaurants are scattered around, drawing from the larger city. University of Toronto students find much that is appealing on this street. A homegrown small theatre is not far from a nightclub offering live rock music. And a local store, Grass Roots, sells recycled and chemical-free products to a citywide

Above:
Pioneer Square, Seattle's reinvigorated historic quarter, is now home to a lively mix of shops, galleries, cafés and restaurants

University of Strathclyde
Dept. of Architecture and Building Science
Library

clientele. The economic ebb and flow appears reasonably in balance.

A few blocks away, perpendicular to Bloor Street, is Bathurst, another commercial thoroughfare with a streetcar line running south toward the waterfront and a longer bus route going north. Bathurst is wider and not as economically robust as Bloor but has room to grow, to house innovations, offering cheaper space where the experimental can occur. New business formations, Jacobs repeatedly points out, need cheap space in old buildings. Only established and successful businesses can occupy the more expensive space new buildings offer.

There is nothing simplistic about this combination of seemingly simple assortment of activities. The whole appears deceptively simple, if one only looks at the physical form. Many of the small changes that have occurred in recent years mirror large urban dynamics. Some of the mostly early-twentieth-century three-storey houses, for example, have been converted to two-family dwellings or contain modest apartments. Probably even more have reverted to single-family use that for many years contained apartments. But the

ability to reverse the alterations either way in the future is undisturbed, assuring small adjustments over time without destabilizing the larger neighbourhood shopping district or diminishing the intimacy of a predominantly single-family house community.

From one house to the next, one can observe the newly-planted yards, the creative new landscaping, the latest flowering tree or the newest decorative edge fencing. Jacobs is observed discussing with her neighbour, front porch to front porch, the activities of a local raccoon family. At one time, Jacobs had a rooftop garden, and while seeming to be just a garden, it reflects Jacobs' early understanding of 'appropriate technology', as green roofs are increasingly recognized. In fact, she used sawdust instead of dirt, a lighter material that would not overload the roof after a heavy rain or snowfall.

Seemingly small changes are observable along the block. Some houses have converted part of the front yard into a parking space. The reverse is also true. A variety of landscaped spaces exist where drive-in pavement once was. Near the corner is a relatively new, small apartment house on the site

Right:
The regeneration of Portland's Pearl District has made good use of a wealth of traditional railway-yard buildings

under which the Subway was built. At three corners are restaurants, two with sidewalk tables and a definite cosmopolitan air.

The overall physical appearance and neighbourly feel of the block has remained the same for years, yet the block is not frozen or museum-like. Many small initiatives over time do add up to big change without massive development overwhelming and replacing a functional place.

This block is part of the Annex, one of downtown Toronto's oldest and most desirable neighbourhoods. Annexed to the city in the late nineteenth century, this popular residential neighbourhood – like so many of today's popular urban neighbourhoods across America – was born during the era of the streetcar (tram). In Toronto, however, the streetcar survives, in sharp contrast to American cities that destroyed this most effective mode of urban transport. Toronto almost lost its streetcar system to less efficient buses in the 1970s but a citizens' coalition fought to save the system. The streetcar is key to the long-term stability of many vibrant Toronto neighbourhoods with commercial streets that would have withered if the streetcar had disappeared. (Deteriorated commercial streets in many American, English, Canadian cities – and elsewhere – once had streetcars going along them.) The Subway along Bloor is part of a system built in the 1950s and still being added to as the city grows. The streetcars, buses and subways complement each other and form an efficient transit network for the city.

Density is key

The liveability of this neighbourhood is clear to any visitor but its density – so critical to its success – is not. In formal planning terms, the Annex has at least 15–20 units per acre, a density vigorously (and wrongly) resisted in so many North American and British neighbourhoods. Yet, the range of housing choices, the vibrant commercial street and convenient mass transit options would not be viable and could not exist without the density. While the density is critical to the liveability, it is not enough. The presence of the other uses –

diversified employment, shopping, institutions, entertainment – play an equally important role. Everything is connected to everything. This cannot be reiterated often enough.

The incremental process of urban change that Jacobs celebrated is not confined to this neighbourhood. Where it spreads throughout the city, it strengthens individual neighbourhoods and the larger city at the same time. The same kind of community groups that formed in the Annex – to oppose an expressway, resist out-of-scale development, organize recycling efforts and the like – emerged in other neighbourhoods as well, setting many different priorities and defending features characteristic of their own area. But it was that process of citizen involvement and positive change that moved from block to block and neighbourhood to neighbourhood that today makes Toronto interesting and solid.

Healthy urban neighbourhoods and commercial districts anywhere must allow for the fluidity of change illustrated in the Annex. Property owners have considerable latitude to make modest alterations and express their individuality while not disturbing the overall consistency of the neighbourhood. This enables neighbourhoods to be distinguished from one another. Time, as well, Jacobs points out, 'is important in all of this. Neighbourhoods don't come into instant, finished life.' They have to be changing, growing in different ways, altering and, Jacobs asserts, 'revealing new things. A neighbourhood develops itself.'

Creative growth requires an encouraging, not constrained, environment. This cannot mean unconstrained new construction, often labelled and promoted as economic development. True economic development is about the birth, expansion, and replacement of businesses, not about new buildings. Real estate does not drive development; development drives real estate. This is the fundamental Jacobs lesson.

Downtown from Jacobs' neighbourhood, a once-thriving industrial Toronto district at the edge of the commercial core today flourishes anew, reflecting the application of more of her precepts. The old garment district, with its rich assortment of loft and early office buildings, has been

Below:
Ancoats Urban Village, close to the centre of Manchester, has worked hard to reintegrate residential and employment uses

Left:
The cultural and social focus of Birmingham's Jewellery Quarter has significantly improved in recent years

Right:
Restaurants and music clubs have diversified the Jewellery Quarter's economy and identity

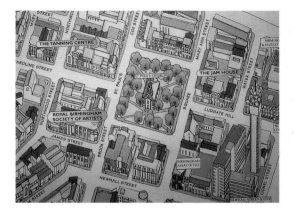

reinvented organically with new businesses and residences of all kinds attracting a broad range of people. With Jacobs' total involvement in a public planning process, the long-standing planning and zoning regulations that kept this a fully industrial district were removed. New guidelines, rather than rigid zoning policies or grandiose plans, were put in place. Now this area, known as King-Spadina, of which a vibrant Entertainment District is an unanticipated part, has evolved also into the desirable residential district that was anticipated. The same planning principles apply to a companion district to King-Spadina on the other side of downtown called King/Parliament. Together 'the Kings', as they are known, cover some 160 hectares (400 acres) and as mixed development heats up in the first, activity spreads to the second.

Former zoning and density limits were eliminated. Instead, design guidelines limit height, preserve the street wall, provide setbacks and protect sunlight. Building depth is limited, guaranteeing useful alley separations and the absence of super-blocks. All non-noxious uses are permitted, as long as they are in an urban form and meet the building code. Parking is strictly regulated with no open lots permitted. The market is the basic rule-setter but the city stands ready to step in with corrections as needed. New mixed-use buildings with high-end condos are filling vacant lots. Sports stores, recording studios, retail stores, graphic artists and conventional corporations are compatible neighbours.

A framework with limitations, not a planning and zoning code: radical? Contrary to convention? To be sure, by today's planning practice. But this

has long been the essence of Jacobs' prescriptions. They cannot be reduced to formal plans or zoning regulations. For more than 35 years, she has criticized the planning profession and focused on the ills of zoning. Toronto heard the message, absorbed lessons from her books and learned from her participation in public forums. In 1995, Chief Planner Paul Bedford, with Mayor Barbara Hall and urban designer Ken Greenberg, set out to change the declining Kings Districts. They were guided by new ideas proposed at public forums by developers and a wide range of other interest groups and citizens, including businesses and labour unions in the area – a process of listening, responding and shaping accordingly.

When asked why he followed her lead, Bedford said he viewed Jacobs' approach as perfectly logical. 'She's simply right,' he says. 'That's the obvious thing. There are so many pressures put on a planning department that it is easy to be pulled in different directions to the point that the logic of things gets lost. I absolutely told myself I would not let that happen and that I would go the full measure to change things. The reality is that a planner is trained to do the opposite. So we said, "Let's experiment, let's trust the common sense of developers." People are not going to do stupid things. Everything is always full of "what ifs?" The system bogs down. The result is paralysis when you try to anticipate everything. That's what planners usually try to do. The public goal is positive change and we are getting those results incredibly fast. It is all perfectly logical. The proof is in the pudding.'

Such common sense is refreshing.

Starting with New York's SoHo

The transformation of the King-Spadina district occurred in the hands of public officials, in itself a testament to the Jacobs legacy. This Toronto experiment brings full circle the lessons of the transformation of New York's SoHo, which started in the 1960s with a successful battle led by Jane Jacobs against a major highway and urban renewal project promoted by planning czar Robert Moses that would have wiped out what we know today as SoHo, Little Italy, Chinatown and much of Greenwich Village. With the highway – known as the Lower Manhattan Expressway – defeated, SoHo, this onetime industrial district, was transformed with little loss of the nineteenth-century buildings, without any suburbanizing adjustments, without any diminution of its authentic urbanism, and without large public funding. A more up-to-date, modern district cannot be found: in recent decades SoHo has been the birthplace of many new businesses, providing great creativity and residential opportunities for artists and artisans, single and married, young and old, immigrant and native.

In the 1960s, Jacobs, with the enormous help of hundreds of neighbourhood activists, opposed urban renewal and highway projects that would erase whole neighbourhoods in the name of progress. Jacobs argued that the dense unplanned mix of uses is what constitutes a healthy urban district and sustains a viable urban economy. She looked at the big development projects and showed them to be failures while pointing to the success of the modest new economic, social or physical initiatives that emerge, often unpredictably, but that fit in, knit into the web of an existing places.

As a basic notion, Jacobs has shown that a city by its very nature is so full of variations and differences that a universal solution is both impossible and undesirable. To even begin to solve problems in any place, you have to know what is missing to know what improvements are appropriate, and that differs from place to place. A vibrant place has to include an undergrowth, not readily apparent, of new things happening because that is where new problems are being solved. This is why the small things are so important. Their possibilities are unlimited. Growth depends on the small things. The large ones reach limits.

Such sensible and observable reality was then heresy. Today, to some planners and urban designers, like Toronto's Paul Bedford and Ken Greenberg, some public officials and millions of average citizens, this is common sense. That adds up to quite a legacy, one taking root in urban districts across American and in the rejuvenating industrial cities across Great Britain which have not experienced the massive clearance and demolition history crippling so many American downtowns today.

The value of authentic urbanism, which Jane Jacobs first wrote about so eloquently, is not sufficiently recognized. Many people don't even understand what it is or know how to recognize it. Urbanists are primarily found among those who live and work in city districts. That is why their voices are so critical to any revitalization process. They can contribute new ideas and creative solutions based on direct experience if given a genuine opportunity during a public process. The absolute key to regeneration is building on the remaining strength of authentic urbanism, where it exists. This must include human assets, in other words, people in place. Where urbanism is not fully understood, recognized and valued, the future is grim.

In too many US cities, we have mistaken for regeneration the recently-built, big, dazzling mega-projects that attract tourists but do nothing for the cities they are in. We built big, flashy projects. We replaced messy, hodgepodge genuine urbanism with pretty, neat *faux* urbanism, selectively picking and choosing appealing urban elements that don't add up to urbanism. We've transformed too much of the public realm into private enclaves. We've suburbanized so many neighbourhoods, thinned them out, and then wondered why they can't support local businesses or transit and have minimal street life. We've erased our productive districts, the ones with small and large businesses that include producers of 'things' not just 'paper', the innovators large and small that may be tomorrow's Microsoft or Cuisinart. We've replaced factory, warehouse and low-income mixed districts

Clockwise from top left:
Much of New York's identity and character can be attributed to its structure of neighbourhoods
©2002 New York City Department of City Planning, All rights reserved

Greenwich Village, New York's archetypical urban village

The streets throughout SoHo are very pedestrian-friendly

New York's SoHo is home to many businesses and is recognized for the creativity of its artists and artisans

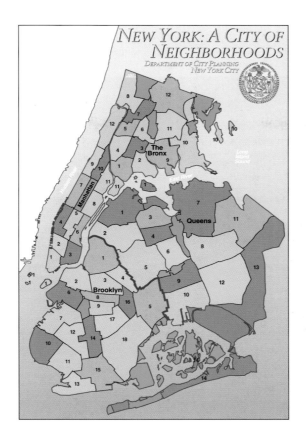

with stadiums, shopping malls, convention centres, cultural centres, aquariums and lots of parking lots. All too often we've turned city centres into assemblages of projects, killing or crippling the real city in the process. This is not regeneration. An inventory of projects is not how to measure the health of a city. They don't add up to a city. They are not about urbanism.

A big difference exists between a place rebuilt and a place reborn. Rebuilt is replacement; reborn is the regeneration of the existing fabric developed over time. Inevitably, the big, expensive projects

fail the cities they promised to improve, even if boosterism and slick public relations camouflage the failure. We've mistakenly staked our cities' future on the visits of suburbanites and tourists instead of understanding that the true strength of a place depends on its local people, places and economic innovations, a lesson Jacobs has promoted since the 1960s. Sadly, also, we have not recognized that without a viable public school system, any regeneration effort is crippled. Nothing big happens at one time in urban districts reflecting the birth process Jacobs describes.

Lots of modest things happen over time with no singular big project overwhelming the district. The result? Big – in fact, enormous – change but gradual, incremental, enduring and not as vulnerable to national downturns as are the tourist-dependent, single dominant industry and mall store areas. The result: genuine urban districts, always adapting, always changing, always receptive to innovation, continuously spawning new businesses, some of which will grow and spread their impact. Some will fail; but small failures do not endanger the diverse assortment of activities around them.

No one big project overwhelms the district or makes the area dependent on it. And as the district grows successful, parts of it may get too successful and too expensive for the new small innovation. Room must exist elsewhere in the urban fabric for that energy to move into. The process works best where the urban fabric – even with some destructive intrusions – is still dense enough, still filled with the great mix of old and new buildings inviting to new people and new businesses. Great Britain's historic industrial cities reflect this potential. The potential is more limited in American cities so 'over-renewed' by big projects that only remnants of genuine urbanism remain.

If the surviving urban fabric is valued and not eviscerated and the human assets recognized and nurtured, then whatever remains of authentic urbanism can be the foundation for regeneration, once again serving as centres of innovation, strength and enduring character. With luck, that regeneration process can spread and extend the web that once existed in most American cities.

Jacobs' principles – beyond authentic urbanism

Jacobs is best known for these urban development ideas but in time, her economic and environmental concepts may and should gain equal attention. They already are a significant part of her legacy and when understood, enable more creative thinking about urban challenges.

Environmentalists seek to conserve and enhance what has evolved over time, to preserve natural resources rather than exploit them and to learn from and fit into nature instead of controlling and overcoming it. Jacobs cites the work of Eco-Trust, an innovative environmental organization working on conserving the rainforest of the Pacific Northwest USA and Canada by finding alternative or supplementary activities that are economically friendly. 'Conservation-based development' or 'development-based conservation', Eco-Trust calls it. Either way, the depleting of a natural resource, such as an ancient forest, is replaced with a combination of diminished logging and creative use of wood for new products, adding more human capital than logging jobs alone require. Employing farmers living next to the rainforest to grow coffee beans in the shade or extract nuts from an undisturbed forest are further examples of the 'conservation-based development' that Eco-Trust advocates.

The creative employment of 'human capital' (not just the exploitation of 'natural capital') and pursuing endeavours that use the yield from the natural capital rather than the capital itself, are key to interconnected thinking about economics and nature. If one understands the natural processes, Jacobs illustrated in her latest book *The Nature of Economies*, then one at least has a road map to the economic process. Professional economists, Jacobs argues, fail to understand the parallels between the processes of nature and economies. The real trick, the pragmatic notion, is to learn from and draw from those processes of nature. 'A system can be making itself up as it goes along,' Jacobs says. 'The weather is like that. Evolution is like that. Economies, if they aren't inert and stagnant, are like that. Since they make themselves up as they proceed, they are not predestined. Not being predestined, they are not predictable.'

In her second book, *The Economy of Cities*, Jacobs had illustrated how the economy of a city works, how interdependent all of the often invisible components are and how economies reflect a process that can't be created but can easily be undermined. In this book she also illustrated how cities are the economic engines of whole regions, the net generators of the national wealth, and how they spawn other places, like suburbs and regions. She focused on what urban economies do well, not what they don't do well. She continued

Left:
SoHo has been transformed with little loss of its nineteenth-century buildings

Above:
New buildings have filled empty lots on the far west side of New York's Greenwich Village

this idea in subsequent books, expanding her conviction that economies need to be self-sustaining, self-renewing and reliant on local initiatives instead of centralized bureaucracies.

Jacobs illustrates how the value of many modest investments is more significant than the singular mega-investment. Micro-lenders put into practice the value of small but significant economic steps, by risking small loans for the new idea, the new business that adds something to the economy instead of moving an existing business around. Micro-lenders also make capital available in deteriorated neighbourhoods where talented and energetic human capital is in place but is ignored or not valued by conventional investors. Jacobs often cites the success of the South Shore Bank of Chicago. With $600 million in assets – small as banks go – South Shore Bank's investments rescued 16,000 housing units on Chicago's South Side, stimulating a reinvestment momentum that led to the stabilization and upgrade of thousands more.

'You may think they are too small,' she says of the bank, but, in fact, they are 'making the biggest difference because they are doing something no one else is doing'. One also must calculate what would have been lost to continued decay, in order to fully value what has been gained. Economic developers who understand Jacobs' ground-breaking ideas about 'import replacement' find creative ways to encourage new small businesses, breakthrough innovations and any other ways that value human capital and strengthen local economies.

Principles, not ideology

'Ideology,' Jacobs says, 'is the hunger for certainty of some kind, the comfort of certainty'. People with an ideology, she adds, see themselves as 'keepers of the true faith'. Strict adherence to their 'version of the truth' interferes, she says, with 'dealing practically with how the world works and what each of us is trying to do'.

Jacobs' teachings are, by definition, non-ideological. No one 'movement' or 'ism' can claim to follow Jacobs' path. But many civic activists and farsighted professionals have adopted elements of her thinking. Transit advocates, sprawlbusters,

community-based redevelopers, historic preservationists, new urbanists, park restorers and public space advocates all draw from Jacobs' ideas to advance their own piece of a larger agenda. Some, however, don't embrace the full picture, don't grasp the complexity and don't provide for the full diversity of activity required for the vibrant, healthy city.

Observes urban designer Ken Greenberg: 'One of the weaknesses of certain doctrinaire elements of the New Urbanist movement has been to oversimplify and caricature the kinds of urban places Jacobs describes, to focus on a frozen "look" at a certain point in time, but fail to allow the play of forces over time that will achieve the real thing. In part, this stems from an exaggerated preoccupation with aesthetic control and an idyllic and circumscribed image of community life that eschews the inherent "messiness", incompleteness and open-endedness of true urbanity.' The great subtlety and intricacy of the mechanism Jacobs has observed cannot be designed or planned into existence. The creative unlocking of opportunities for the private sector goes beyond control, regulation and planning. This conflicts with those planners and architects wedded to a total vision. 'Some planners and architects need to shake the notion that they are making something complete instead of building a foundation for change,' Jacobs says.

Slowly but assuredly, recognition of the validity and strength of the authentic urbanism Jacobs advocates has taken hold, overcoming the formidable and entrenched view that only suburbs are the future. 'Suburbs are not where new things are happening or new problems are being solved,' she says. Diversified activities and opportunities are found in cities. Surely, the growing popularity of living in cities again, especially in 'messy' former industrial neighbourhoods, attests to this revaluation of cities. Yet the extraordinary potential inherent in fully understanding and promoting the authentic urbanism that Jacobs helps us understand is far from being reached.

The hardest lesson of the Jacobs legacy is that new cities cannot be developed from a preconceived plan. They have to evolve as innovations and new economic configurations emerge, as communities grow up with and around these innovations. Density and transit must be

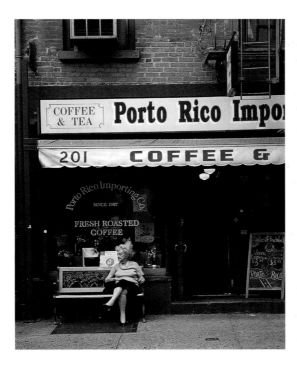

Left:
Good shops and interesting streets must be at the heart of any popular neighbourhood

Right:
Neighbourhoods should be encouraged to evolve in an organic manner to create their own unique identity

integral. The providing of flexible spaces of varying scale in which the unpredictable can happen is key to encouraging the unplanned emergence of new innovative economic and social uses. True public spaces must exist to make possible the endless unprogrammed encounters that bind people together as citizens and neighbours. Realistically, cities can be rejuvenated, added onto, or extended, assuming that variety and interconnectedness also extends and the web that defines urbanism is strengthened.

A formidable obstacle to the broader application of Jacobs' legacy is that Jacobs' ideas conflict with the misguided priority of planners and elected officials to accommodate the car. 'We can hide it, squeeze it in tight spaces and do all sorts of things to deal with it,' observes Bedford, 'but it is still about a driver, with no genuine alternative to the car'. Bedford's goal, central to all his planning efforts in Toronto, is to make it possible over time to 'lead a full life from birth to death without a car and not feel deprived as a result'. That doesn't mean eliminating the car. It means having a choice. But the option for that non-car-dependent life, he says, must be 'the core value'. Only in a few places, he notes, is that now possible. A genuine urban web, a real city, embraces that core value. Car dependency has no

place in authentic urbanism.

The forces against this and other core urban values, in America and around the globe, are powerful beyond measure. In fact, the belief that cities are bad places remains strong. The problem is not that Jacobs' ideas are not understandable, pragmatic and appropriate. 'I don't think it is hard for ordinary people to accept,' says Jacobs. 'I think it's hard for professionals and experts who've been taught differently and have a vested interest analyzing these things.' And, of course, whole industries and international institutions have a vested interest in maintaining business as usual. Overcoming established patterns of thought and action is a formidable task.

Jacobs' legacy is a guidebook to understanding authentic urbanism – what it is, how to recognize where it is weak or strong and how to add to it appropriately and solve problems over time. This legacy is a potent force, making inroads in many unpredictable places and having an enormous impact as urban districts learn to reinvent themselves without losing the fundamentals of their strength.

The book is still open everywhere on the future of cities and if you like open books, Jane Jacobs is your best librarian.

Part One

The context for urban villages

During the 1990s neighbourhood renewal became central to urban policy in both Britain and the United States, and there is now a stated preference to regenerate and extend our existing urban centres before creating more new towns and cities. The desire to create and maintain compact and mixed-use districts, typified by urban villages and championed by Jane Jacobs, can be seen as one important part of this strategy. This section presents the strategic planning context for this initiative and defines the role that the urban village can play in promoting and maintaining the vitality of our urban environments.

Through the work of the Urban Task Force in Britain three primary drivers guiding urban development have been clearly identified: changing social patterns, the importance of sustainable development, and the impact of the information age. The following three chapters explore these specific trends in detail and reflect on the ways they influence the character of the built environment.

Smart growth on two continents looks at recent urban planning initiatives in Britain and the United States. These are now beginning to address the impact of changes in our demographic structure and the effect this will have on the density, sustainability and connectivity of our urban neighbourhoods. In Britain a new urban renaissance is trying to resolve the conflict between greenfield and brownfield development as well as respond to the impact that new patterns of employment are having on our cities. In America 'smart growth' initiatives in many states are attempting to reduce car-based development and dependency by establishing more traditional neighbourhood patterns that embody a stronger communal identity and purpose.

Planning for sustainable communities sets out the main planning principles that currently guide our urban development. With growing pressure on our finite environmental resources the need to adopt a more sustainable approach to urban planning is certainly appreciated, even if it is yet to be fully understood. International agreements on sustainability forged at the Rio Earth Summit are beginning to be recognized at a local and neighbourhood level through the preparation of Agenda 21 strategies and Community Plans. In parallel, the European Union is beginning to promote regional spatial design strategies that are increasingly influencing both planning policy and guidance for our urban environments.

Emerging digital neighbourhoods reflects on the growing impact that the technical revolution will have on our urban communities. Innovations in information technology are now beginning to reinforce the role of smaller-scale, finer-grained, more humane and equitable urban environments. New and regenerating neighbourhoods that are based in part around new digital technologies are starting to support alternative ways to create, maintain and economically sustain our urban districts. It is clearly anticipated that this growth in technology will directly influence the way we choose to interact socially, conduct our business and re-establish our urban communities.

Chapter 1

Smart growth on two continents

Peter Hall

Urban planning at the end of the twentieth century has been marked by an urgent need to find solutions to the key problems facing our towns and cities – the control of sprawl, sustainable growth, more integrated transport and better-quality urban environments. In both the UK and the USA, there are parallel debates about proposals for new – and sometimes not so new – patterns of smarter and more efficient growth. They provide an essential context for the role of mixed-use urban villages and new approaches to traditional urbanism.

In Britain, the Urban Task Force has published its manifesto for an urban renaissance,[1] addressing issues of density, sustainability, integrated transportation, shifting patterns of employment, and greenfield and brownfield development. In the USA planned 'smart growth' has been adopted by numerous states as they attempt to refocus and constrain their urban growth towards more traditional forms of public transit-oriented development.

Above:
An Urban Task Force visit to the Zaan Island district of Amsterdam

Britain's urban renaissance

The Urban Task Force, convened at the behest of the Government and chaired by Richard Rogers, included a multidisciplinary coterie of urban practitioners, policy makers and practitioners. It was commissioned to identify causes of urban decline in England and recommend practical solutions to bring people back into our cities, towns and urban neighbourhoods. At the heart of the final report, published in June 1999, were two critical issues triggered by the projected shortage of housing; the first could be called the southern England agenda, whilst the second focused on the revival of our northern cities.

Around London, almost all planners agree, much recent development has contravened basic principles of urban sustainability because it has been built at densities that are too low, with virtually no access to local services or to transit. But there is a political element too: powerful local

NIMBY (not in my back yard) movements are resisting further developments on greenfield land, and some of the biggest controversies are in areas that have narrow political majorities. This highly contentious issue of brownfield versus greenfield development was the political starting point for the Task Force's appointment back in spring 1998, and has been further highlighted with the publication of the much-publicized Crow report on the public examination of the regional guidance for the south-east. As that suggests, this is mainly a southern England issue in political terms.

In parallel, in the northern cities like Manchester and Newcastle upon Tyne, there's a quite different situation and a different agenda: work by Task Force member Professor Anne Power has recently revealed a pattern of downtown renewal – including new loft-style apartment building for singles – almost next door to widespread abandonment and flight in the mid-city rings. Here, the mounting physical decay, and the

Left:
Concert Square, a new public space in Liverpool, completed in 1995
Urban Splash

Right:
Manchester's Smithfield Buildings: a vacant department store converted into popular new loft apartments
Urban Splash

associated flight from the city of many households, especially those with children, seems to be following an ominous North American pattern. This problem has been compounded by neighbouring suburban jurisdictions that have effectively welcomed developers with open arms, so that attractive new housing is available at prices that southerners can remember only from history books.[2] The agendas are linked, especially in the north, but it's best to start by treating them separately and understanding the underlying issues of sustainability, urban design and shifting patterns of employment.

Promoting sustainable urbanism

The Task Force has suggested a design prescription based on fashionable sustainability concepts reflecting much of the principles that underlay the original urban village initiatives – mixed use 'New Urban' physical structures at medium-high densities, within walkable distance of public transport. The big question is whether this prescription will encourage middle-class homeowners back into the cities. That depends a lot on the household projections, which showed an additional 4.4 million households from 1991 to 2016, later updated to 3.8 million between 1996 and 2021. But four in five of them are one-person households, a product of complex socio-demographic changes: more young people leaving home early for college, more divorces and separations, more older folk surviving their partners for longer, and above all a major shift towards more single people who have never married, a product in part of dual-career relationships. It may be that we can repopulate the northern cities by such new households, using imaginative high-density apartments like the ones Urban Splash have done so successfully in Manchester. This is now happening in other cities too, though the concern is that the families won't come back unless we give them the more conventional suburban patterns that attracted them out of the cities in the first place. But we could perhaps compromise, by replicating the patterns that are popular in older traditional suburbs like Ealing, Richmond, Wimbledon, Edgbaston or Jesmond.

Focusing on the physical environment

Many of the Task Force's proposals were criticized for being too physical. True, you can search the Task Force report from end to end and find virtually no mention of the geography of jobs, or of the relevance of employment creation to urban renaissance. Yet it should be remembered that John Prescott gave the Task Force a very definite remit, in fact a mission statement: 'The Urban Task Force will identify causes of urban decline in England and recommend practical solutions to bring people back into our cities, towns and urban neighbourhoods. It will establish a new vision for urban regeneration founded on the principles of design excellence, social well-being and environmental responsibility within a viable economic and legislative framework.' Although the final report did address the basic economics of regeneration[3] and did specifically note the pressures that were taking employment out of urban areas, it did not go into further detail because the basic problem was well analysed in many previous accounts.

One of the basic presumptions was that 'an attractive, well-designed environment can help create a framework for promoting economic identity and growth'.[4] In other words, much activity nowadays is footloose, and will flow to places that look good, feel good and have high-income people in them. I think that was the basic gut feeling that led Michael Heseltine, 20 years ago, to assume that you could turn around derelict urban areas by a strong injection of public money to promote accessibility and improve the environment, leaving it to private capital to do the rest, thus attracting the dynamic economic sectors that were seeking new locations. I think that approach, so much criticized and even vilified at the time, can now be seen to have been successful. It is essentially the same prescription as the Task Force was making, although the suggested mechanisms are slightly different from the ones Heseltine chose to use.

The Task Force concentrated very much on two aspects: First, what kind of urban environment would be attractive both to the people and to the businesses that have been fleeing the cities?

Above:
Many of London's older suburbs, including Park Hill in Ealing, continue to be much-sought-after places to live

Above:
London's Coin Street provides a good mix of offices, shops, flats and houses centred on a public park

Right:
Brownfield redevelopment in Nordhorn, Germany, has created a successful new mixed-use neighbourhood

Second, what mechanisms would be needed to create such environments? Under those headings, it produced a very detailed analysis and a host of specific recommendations. Part Four of the report (Chapters 12–13), makes a large number of proposals – new public-private investment funds for area regeneration, a package of tax measures, regional generation investment companies, and new powers for the Regional Development Agencies (RDAs). All these would specifically address employment as well as housing, although we could have been more specific about the kinds of activities that should have been targeted.

Supporting the service sector

Regeneration authorities at both local and regional level need to try to promote schemes that intelligently address known needs and likely new developments. It is essential that we have a basic understanding of what is happening to the economies of the UK, and any other developed country at the end of the millennium. It is now commonly agreed, though for a long time many people refused to accept it, that the industrial era is over and that the future lies with the service sector, above all with the services that generate and exchange and utilize information – an issue that will be explored further in William Mitchell's chapter on digital communities. Michael Breheny's report, which appeared at the end of 1999, shows just how fundamental has been this shift in the economies of British cities. Some of the most telling analysis in the Breheny study concerns the location of business services, which he finds are growing not in the cities, except in London, but in smaller towns in the western crescent of south-east England. One of the most important conclusions of the study is that traditional agglomeration economies, the kind that we always believed tied vast masses of activity together in the hearts of great cities, are at last dissolving – but they're reforming, in different kinds of place.

Well, to misquote Mark Twain, reports of the city's death may be exaggerated. British cities, above all London, still do remain our biggest single concentrations of service employment although the key issue is that in general the cities and their centres are not holding onto them. Although it is true that both London and the major cities have recorded growth in service jobs, this growth is relatively smaller than in the country as a whole. A more detailed analysis suggests that even within the cities there may be outward movement. Much has been made of the fact that Leeds seems to be the only city that has gained employment overall in the last decade, but it now emerges that much of the growth was in call centre complexes on the city's outskirts. It's those logistical economics again: the workers come by car, and these locations give the shortest commutes, hence it's easier to find the right kind of staff here.

This issue neatly illustrates one of the major dilemmas now facing planners in the UK or any other developed country today. Overwhelmingly, with the conspicuous exception of central London, people depend on the car for commuting. The more urban congestion increases, and the more policy tries to take care of that by congestion charging, the more it may increase the incentive for businesses to move out. That way, they're as close as possible to the workers who represent their sole raw material – or at least their sole material having any bulk; the remainder is information, and this is delivered by wire.

Above:
Brindleyplace in Birmingham is one of the more successful inner-city mixed-use developments of the 1990s

Repopulating cities

If we accept this rather drastic conclusion of the Task Force's study, where does that leave the final recommendations? Were we wasting our time and missing the real point? Not at all. For the entire point was to try to repopulate the cities, especially the great northern cities where, as Anne Power's recent work has shown, there is such alarming evidence of panic flight. Basically we come back to that huge and fundamental difference between London and these northern cities: in London people still are flooding in, housing markets are almost everywhere buoyant, and last year two of

Right:
**Reuse of redundant
brownfield sites, such as
Llandarcy in South Wales,
is at the heart of the
Urban Task Force's agenda**

the fastest rises in house prices were in Tower Hamlets and Hackney, two of the most depressed boroughs. As a result the problem in London is how and where to accommodate the new households, and planners there have now produced the astonishing statistic that we can house 579,000, or over 90 per cent of the projected increase – a result that confounds not only my confident predictions, but also those the Task Force got from the National Land Use Change Statistics. But in the north, the critical question is whether we can build the kinds of developments that will attract the middle class back in their tens of thousands to repopulate hundreds of square kilometres of dereliction.

If we can, then all these people will constitute the new labour force and they, in their turn, will represent a key logistical factor for new service industries as well as supporting a whole raft of employment in local services that will minister to them and in particular help them spend their salaries. But if we can't, the prospects for further regeneration are dire. I do not want to belittle what has been achieved so far, and it is certainly remarkable that parts of all these cities are being reclaimed. Brindleyplace in Birmingham, the Lace Market in Nottingham, Castlefield in Manchester, Crown Street and Glasgow Green in Glasgow, are real achievements. But they are a mere beginning; the task ahead is huge and, insofar as people continue to leave, it is growing.

Recycling northern brownfields

As stated, the Task Force started with a highly political, you could say politicized, agenda: how to deliver the target of 60 per cent of new housing development on recycled brownfield land, which the Government hastily adopted in the wake of the huge countryside revolt of March 1998. The closing pages of the final report (Chapter 14) illustrate how this might be done. There is no prescription here: it is up to Government, and local authorities, to make the choice.

The basic arithmetic, which underlies this, is set out in painstaking detail in Chapter 7. It shows that in 1996, only 47 per cent of all land changing

to residential use was brownfield. But this actually includes about 7 per cent which was rural brownfield in the form of airfields, old quarries and the like, so that only 40 per cent of new housing – and only 32 per cent of the land taken for housing – was on true urban brownfield. The figures are disturbing, because they go on to confirm what many people had been arguing: that so much of the new housing – including especially the greenfield – was being built at the very low densities of only 8–10 units per acre. This is well below Raymond Unwin's historic norm of 12, which the Town and Country Planning Association (TCPA) have faithfully followed, or Frederic Osborn's maximum allowable density of 15. So we could all agree with the proposition that these low densities represented a problem.

However, Chapter 7 underlines another difficulty: the brownfield quotient varies hugely between one region and another. In 1994, it was 81 per cent in London but only 37 per cent in the east Midlands and 34 per cent in the south-west. The Task Force's own calculations, based on the National Land Use Database (NLUD), show the London percentage for 1996–2021 falling sharply to 61 per cent. This really means, as the TCPA have always argued, that London cannot accommodate the projected figure within its boundaries. Chapter 7 shows the south-west quotient rising to a creditable 49 per cent and the East Midlands to an even more creditable 65 per cent. But in the most pressured area of all, the south-east, it shows a fall to only 39 per cent.

Refocusing southern development

So, especially in the south-east, all the key players – the government, the regional planners, the local planners, the developers – have been left with that old Ebenezer Howard question, *The People – Where Will They Go?* For the past six years the TCPA have produced a consistent set of answers: develop through clusters of urban development – extensions of both larger and smaller towns, growth of selected villages into small country towns, some new settlements where appropriate – along strong public transport corridors. Michael Breheny and Ralph Rookwood spelt this solution out diagrammatically in the TCPA's book on sustainable development[5] in 1993; Colin Ward and I worked the solution up for some real-life areas in our book *Sociable Cities*,[6] to launch the TCPA's Centenary Year, 1998. Now, to our gratification, we find it winning acceptance as Government policy. The DETR's own guide, *Planning for Sustainable Development: Towards Better Practice*,[7] devoted a chapter to it that appeared almost simultaneously with the Task Force report and now, predictably, it is becoming a topic for debate.

Our proposed corridor clusters – the City of Mercia linking Rugby, Northampton, Wellingborough and Corby, the City of Anglia linking Letchworth, Cambridge, Huntingdon and Peterborough, and the City of Kent linking the East Kent coastal resorts and ports around a core at Ashford – were all deliberately and carefully chosen, first for their distance from London, which makes them as self-contained as possible, and second for the existence of rail links together with old rights of way that could be reopened. Significantly, though we had failed to notice it when we were writing, Northamptonshire had embraced the concept almost precisely in their own corridor strategy, which is illustrated in the DETR good practice guide.[8]

My argument is that we should start discussing how we can best secure sustainable development, on urban brownfield and rural greenfield alike. For here in the south-east, at any rate, it's a certainty that we're going to need both – a lot of both.

Promoting smart growth in America

Smart growth has surely been the great planning mantra of the late 1990s for the USA and is becoming a primary ambition for planning the new millennium. In January 2000 the American Planning Association's *Planning* magazine gave it the honour of a special issue and even more recently, two of America's most distinguished architectural planning practices – Andrés Duany and Elizabeth Plater-Zyberk (DPZ) on the east coast, and Peter Calthorpe on the west coast – have published major books on the topic.[9] So if there's one thing we don't lack, it's recognition of the topic; in fact we're almost drowning in it.

In that special issue of *Planning* in January 2000, Patricia Salkin[10] showed just how huge has been the move towards smart growth, in state after state, during the last two decades. It started in a small way even in the 1970s, with state-wide planning and growth management programmes. But in the 1980s it went further: Florida, Georgia, Hawaii, Maine, New Jersey, Oregon, Rhode Island

Right:
The South East Planning Council's 1967 Strategy proposed a clustering of new developments along main transport corridors
South East Planning Council

Opposite:
A Smart Growth Map for Austin, Texas, discourages development on the environmentally sensitive western sector of the city
City of Austin, Texas

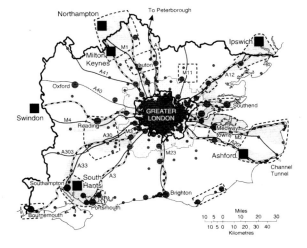

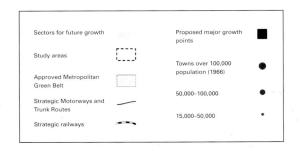

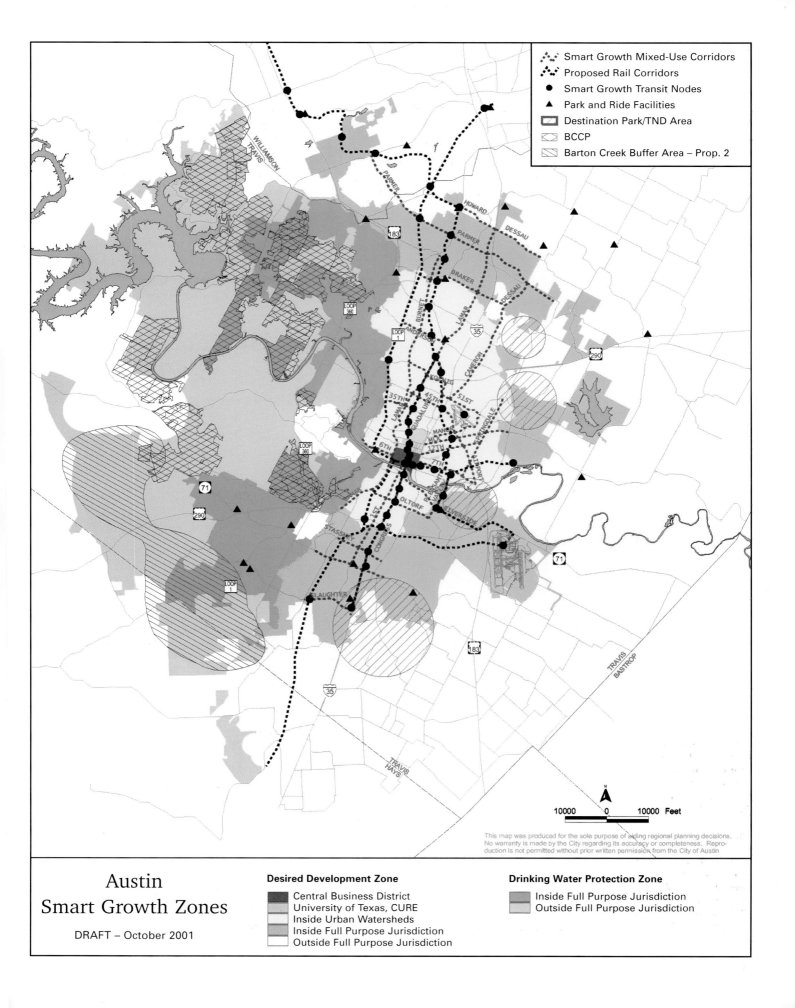

Legend:
- Smart Growth Mixed-Use Corridors
- Proposed Rail Corridors
- Smart Growth Transit Nodes
- Park and Ride Facilities
- Destination Park/TND Area
- BCCP
- Barton Creek Buffer Area – Prop. 2

Austin
Smart Growth Zones

DRAFT – October 2001

Desired Development Zone
- Central Business District
- University of Texas, CURE
- Inside Urban Watersheds
- Inside Full Purpose Jurisdiction
- Outside Full Purpose Jurisdiction

Drinking Water Protection Zone
- Inside Full Purpose Jurisdiction
- Outside Full Purpose Jurisdiction

This map was produced for the sole purpose of aiding regional planning decisions. No warranty is made by the City regarding its accuracy or completeness. Reproduction is not permitted without prior written permission from the City of Austin.

10000   0   10000 Feet

and Washington all established frameworks for state-wide comprehensive planning. Then, in the early 1990s, a host of states – California, Connecticut, New Jersey, New York, Massachusetts, Maryland, Pennsylvania, North Carolina and Virginia – all began to look seriously at options for reforming their state land-use laws, particularly those relating to comprehensive plans, coordination and cooperation among municipalities, and appropriate divisions of responsibility between state, region and locality. No fewer than 100 smart growth laws in all have been introduced across the country in 27 states, affecting more than half the land in the Union.[11]

But the key question amongst all this legislation is the one that Amalia Lorentz and Kirsten Shaw put in their article, 'Are you Ready to Bet on Smart Growth?' in that same issue. 'More than ever before, US communities are talking the talk. Do they have the political will to walk the walk?'[12] Basically, of course, most do not – or

they've only begun to take the most hesitant and tentative steps towards doing so. America has built 27.3 million new homes since 1981; in 1998 starts were higher than ever before: of the 1.6 million homes built during the year, 1,271,000 were single-family homes.[13] The gainers have been the Sunbelt and the west, the losers the Midwest, Plains and north-east. In the 39 largest metro areas, 80–85 per cent of this construction has been suburban, though recently there has been much more interest in older cities. So the question has to be: what's been happening out there in the 'burbs?

Tackling urban sprawl

Let Duany and Plater-Zyberk give you the answer. It's not smart growth; in fact it's very unsmart growth. As they argue in *Suburban Nation: The Rise of Sprawl and the Decline of the American Dream*, Americans have almost always lived in suburbs;

Below:
Commercial strip development in Orange, Connecticut: car-oriented, pedestrian-unfriendly and extremely inefficient in its use of land

America could almost be said to have invented the concept. But there's a critical difference between the kinds of suburbs America used to build, and the kind that are built now. Pre-sprawl, Americans lived in neighbourhoods that had some degree of segregation by house type but with consistent streetscapes and a shared public realm. The problem is that in the new suburbs, you can only move by car.[14] Or, as Peter Calthorpe puts it in his book, *The Regional City: Planning for the End of Sprawl*, these outer suburbs 'literally have no center or history'.[15] Too often their 'centre' is a mall, connected to the residential areas only by broad four- or six-lane roads, with totally homogeneous land uses and no possibility of making transit viable. Many such communities are frightened of the idea of mixed-use centres with multi-family housing, which they see as inviting crime and undesirable elements into their neighbourhoods; they prefer to limit growth and build bigger roads.

Calthorpe concludes that 'the relentless development at the edge around the car is unsustainable, and most of us know it. A new regional order is emerging.'[16] This new order is quite different from Howard's Garden Cities, or greenbelt new towns, or edge city sprawl[17] and perhaps more akin to a number of the principles that underlie Urban Villages. The basic design principles are 'to create places that are walkable and human scaled, that are diverse in population and varied in uses, and that are shaped around public spaces that are meaningful and memorable'.[18]

Traditional neighbourhood development

So there is a huge challenge in the USA, but it does appear that some places are walking the walk, pretty smartly. Basically, you can identify two groups of tools they've been using. One group is to do with urban design: essentially, it consists of ordinances to reintroduce traditional kinds of neighbourhoods – in other words, that major 1990s theme, New Urbanism, which could quite easily have been called old urbanism. Communities are adopting a Traditional Neighbourhood Development Ordinance (TND) which is an

alternative zoning code based on the evident advantages of America's older cities, towns and villages. Variants include Sacramento County's Transit-Orientated Development Ordinance and Pasadena's City of Gardens Code. Municipalities using TNDs include Miami-Dade County, Orlando, Columbus, Santa Fe and Austin. New Jersey law establishes a clear ideal for a full range of models, from rural conservation to urban redevelopment. Florida's growth management laws have a strong compliance review process, but lack New Jersey's vision.[19] 'Over time, the success or failure of these pioneer states in fighting sprawl will show other states which model is worth emulating.'[20]

But traditional urban designs are not enough in themselves; because of course they say nothing about the regional relationships of the new neo-traditional developments to the entire metropolitan area. New Urbanism is all about a return to traditional urban forms, with high-density housing including houses, flats and apartments along traditional residential streets with sidewalks and a liberal mix of shops and services within easy walking access. New Urbanism philosophy also stresses good access by transit, and the west coast version builds that in to the plan by grouping all development around a combined commercial-transit core: what Calthorpe calls TODs (Transit-Oriented Developments) and what Michael Bernick and Robert Cervero have called transit villages: developments that are deliberately designed at densities higher than conventional automobile-oriented suburbia, that have shopping and other essential daily services within easy walking distance, and that are above all grouped around good-quality transit.[21]

The evidence so far

With a few exceptions, such as Peter Calthorpe's work in San Jose, it is disappointing that most actual examples of New Urbanism are either new suburbs on greenfield land such as Laguna West in California and Kentlands in Maryland, or resort/retirement communities typified by Seaside, Florida. Kentlands, which is a pure piece of auto-oriented suburbia some five miles beyond the Shady Grove terminus of DC Metrorail's Red Line, can hardly qualify as smart growth and nor, unhappily, does Peter Calthorpe's own ambitious essay in the genre, Laguna West south of Sacramento. Calthorpe himself regards Laguna West as a failure, and advised me not to go and see it; I ignored his advice, and was glad I did, because the failure teaches important lessons.

The first failure, which is obvious within minutes of arrival, is that something went wrong with the design. The houses that follow Calthorpe's original concept, grouped tightly around the Town

Top left:
Laguna West's main boulevard reflects dependency on the car rather than public transit

Top right:
Suburban housing at Laguna West fails to deliver the density aspired to in the original masterplan

Right:
The initial 800-acre masterplan for Laguna West in Sacramento, California
Calthorpe Associates

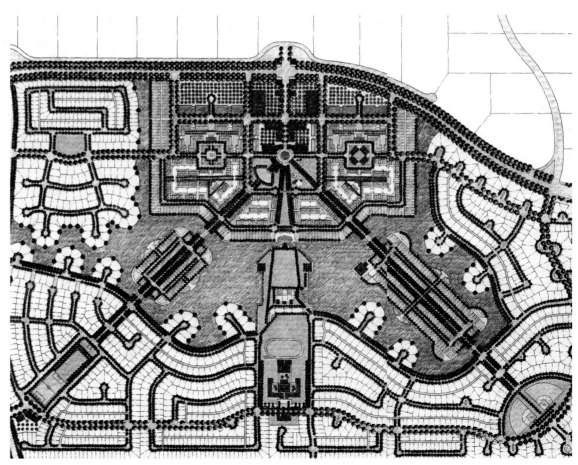

Hall and lake, are few in number; all around them are streets of banal tract-home development. What intervened was the failure of the original developer in the great Californian economic meltdown of the early 1990s and his replacement by a different developer who had none of his idealism or imagination.

But there is another, deeper failure, which is that in hardly any sense can this be called a transit-oriented development. The visitor or resident approaches at 70 miles an hour via Interstate 5, exiting on to Laguna Boulevard, a monster six-lane arterial. The southern line of the Sacramento light rail system, around which the entire development is based, is at last under construction, but the first and even the planned second stage will get nowhere near Laguna West – indeed, they are heading in the wrong direction.

This, interestingly, underlines a central feature of Calthorpe's design. He has done much smaller TODs elsewhere, for example at Aggie Village in the campus town of Davis, close to Sacramento, which is bus- and bike-based, or around a new train station at Mountain View in Silicon Valley. Here he has been compelled by physical and fiscal necessity to build closely and densely around transit and retail. At Laguna West he was free to indulge in a grand vision and what he did, in clear tribute to Ebenezer Howard, was to recreate the original 1898 diagram of the ideal garden city.

To be specific, in order to accommodate the transit station he had to chop Howard's circular central space in half. But otherwise it is all there just as Howard saw it: a vast formal central space, with radiating processional ways leading out over the lake and through parks and school playing-fields, and with key public buildings like a town hall, a day centre for children, and a school and then beyond to the residential districts. It is all the more astonishing, because neither Letchworth nor Welwyn turned out like that in practice; it is just like seeing *Garden Cities of Tomorrow* in a dream.

It could have been brilliant, and it still may be. The few original houses, designed in a fresh idiom that evokes subtle but conscious echoes of century-old Californian streetcar suburbs, show the urban qualities that could have been achieved. When the transit arrives, Calthorpe's own realization could still be brilliant.

Establishing growth boundaries

So, with an analysis of the failures so far, we need more than just urban design. We need a coordination of transit planning and land use planning which, as Sacramento has shown, is not always easy. Eighty miles south in the Bay Area of San Francisco they have been trying to encourage higher-density development around the Bay Area Rapid Transit stations. It's been a slow progress, with only one or two successes, and partial ones at that. At the Del Norte station, on a difficult site with low-density single-family housing to the east and big box development across a six-lane arterial to the west, 'citizen concerns about traffic and the developer's failure to secure financing for retail as well as housing made for a less than perfect TOD'.[22]

So, say the advocates of smart growth, you're never going to get the pressure to develop density around transit unless you put in negative growth controls as well. And this is where we come to what could be called the regional part, as distinct from the design part, of the smart growth agenda. The best-known, and most widely used, of these devices is the Urban Growth Boundary, most famously been used in Portland, Oregon, represented by a line that defines the edge of the metropolis, based on land capacity to house a growing population. But it seems that after 20 years, the jury is still out,

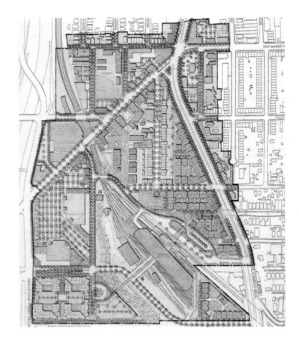

and the key proponents of New Urbanism have yet to agree on the verdict. Duany and Plater-Zyberk condemn it because, originally drawn many miles out, 'anticipating and effectively sanctioning 20 years of bad growth … the growth boundary contains *within* it thousands of acres of the most mundane sprawl'.[23]

A rather different approach is the Countryside Preserve, which sets aside multiple parcels of conservation land independent of their relationship to the Centre City. It is based on objective, not arbitrary, criteria; if possible it should form continuous green belts.[24] Perhaps the classic case is the regional park system in the San Francisco Bay Area, which follows the crest line of the coastal ranges on both the ocean and the land sides of the Bay, and which was brought under public ownership mainly on the grounds that it was vital watershed land. Another long-established example is Boulder in Colorado, which in 1967 became the first community in the nation to levy a 1-cent tax on itself to encourage infill and preserve open space, buying land and easements that now cover an area twice that of the city itself to form a continuous green belt of 28,906 acres plus 55,000 preserved by the county. The downside of this strategy is that the city's success has created a housing shortage, which means people have been forced out to nearby communities, increasing traffic in and out of a city that is job-rich and housing-poor.[25]

A key fact is that these schemes depend on a whole raft of individuals to do the right thing and *Planning* magazine's review concluded that the weakest link to smart growth will be willingness of individuals to embrace the change in their own community. Furthermore, developers are reluctant to invest in alternative kinds of development unless they see market support, thus ending up in a chicken-and-egg dilemma.[26] A subsequent review by Harold Henderson of Timothy Beatley's *Green Urbanism: Learning from European Cities*, in *Planning* a few months later, suggested that 'Most green-city initiatives seem to require stronger central planning, higher taxes, and denser development patterns than Americans have been willing to impose on themselves. The author alludes to, but does not squarely confront, one

fundamental reason for this difference: Europe has a dense population and a shortage of land, and North America does not … Advocates of green urbanism have a hill to climb because they want Americans to *choose* to behave as their European cousins *must*'.[27]

Transatlantic comparisons

So, are Britain's campaign for an urban renaissance and America's search for smart growth and New Urbanism two sides of the same transatlantic coin? Many observers, looking at the key design chapters of the Urban Task Force report, would conclude they are – urban growth limits need to improve the efficient use of both brownfield and greenfield land and car dependency must be reduced through orienting development towards efficient public transport networks.

For Britain, the Urban Task Force report started with the aim of encouraging maximum reuse of brownfield land within city limits. For London, it will not be difficult, indeed it is already happening: inner-city housing markets are buoyant, even frenetic, with prices rising as much as 25 per cent a year, and old blue-collar boroughs being discovered and gentrified. Yet more recent experience close to the city at Greenwich's Millennium Village and

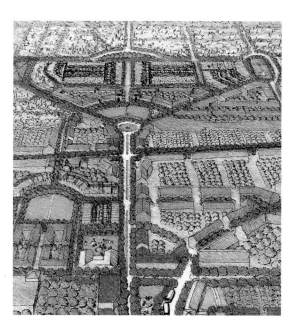

Right:
Transit-oriented mixed-use development, as proposed for Orenco Station, near Portland in Oregon
Calthorpe Associates

Left:
The light rail stop will provide an increasingly important focus for the development of Orenco Station

Right:
A mix of shops, offices and homes is beginning to provide a neighbourhood structure for Orenco Station

West Silvertown in the Docklands has yet to deliver good public transport.

In the great ex-industrial cities of the north, it is going to be harder to stimulate growth. There is a long tradition here, going back a century and more, that if you are successful you take your family out of the city. Here, urban renaissance will need to depend on new and growing demographic segments – above all the young and the young-middle-aged unmarried professionals, living alone – who may reject the suburban ideal. It is starting to happen, as we've seen. But they may not be enough to fill the growing voids, so the answer for these cities may be to build a new generation of sustainable in-town suburbs, recalling the villa suburbs of a century ago.

The Urban Task Force report concludes that with an effort, the UK could achieve more than 60 per cent of all new urban development on recycled brownfield land. This still leaves a substantial share of development on greenfield land. The important point is that the same principles of sustainable development, or smart growth, should apply. New greenfield development needs to be concentrated at moderately high densities, close to shops and other local services and transit. The TCPA have shown how this can be done: small, medium-density developments in the form of country towns, clustered along transit routes.[28] There is an astonishing degree of similarity – given

that they were developed quite independently – between their prescriptions and those of Peter Calthorpe. It now seems more than likely that, at least in certain areas, these principles will actually shape new development. In that event, the American New Urbanism will truly find its expression in the English countryside. History could thus repeat itself, as when, half a century ago, Lewis Mumford ruefully reflected to Frederic Osborn that the principles of the Regional Planning Association of America had been realized not in their homeland, but in the English new towns.

What is yet unclear, either in the USA or in England, is whether planners can achieve what their Swedish counterparts achieved around Stockholm half a century ago: new greenfield developments structured around high-quality transit and with retail and other key services right outside the transit stations, within easy walking access for all. We know how to do it; we did it in those classic railway suburbs a century ago, which people love so much that they are prepared to pay a lot of money to live there. The Swedes did it, and New Urbanists, like Peter Calthorpe, have shown that it can be done in America. Now, if only we can coordinate transit planning with new residential development and find developers with the courage and the vision to implement these integrated schemes, then the future prospects for our urban neighbourhoods look encouraging.

SWANSCOMBE
PENINSULA

WEST

EAST

GREENHITHE
WATERFRONT

NORTHFLEET
EMBANKMENT

STONE
CASTLE

EBBSFLEET

Bluewater

EASTERN
QUARRY

SPRINGHEAD

A2

Chapter 2

Planning for sustainable communities

David Lock

In the previous chapter we saw how North America and Britain are both 'talking the talk' of a more sustainable urbanism that plans to bring people closer together in stimulating and attractive, transit-orientated places surrounded by beautiful, diverse and vital countryside. In the preceding chapter, Peter Hall has shown that while people on both sides of the Atlantic may be 'walking the walk' at different speeds – not least because Britain has less space – we share an immediate need for smarter forms of growth.

In this chapter we look further at the strategic planning that is needed to take us where we need to be. The achievement of sustainable urbanism requires conscious design and management of growth at local, regional, state and perhaps even national scales, to provide the framework within which local communities can make successful and durable places. We find ourselves able to draw in part upon the timeless way in which humankind has made towns and cities.

Unlike most previous generations, however, we are better informed to appreciate the global context of our urbanism, and the duty of care we owe to our planet. This understanding introduces obligations against which our approach to place-making must be tested. In short, to be able to apply the ideas of the urban village at the local level successfully – the formative building block of sustainable urbanism – we also need to consider the bigger picture and the longer view.

Left:
A strategic planning framework for the development of the Kent Thames-side
David Lock Associates/Land Securities/Kent Thames-Side Association

Historic planning strategies in Britain

Britain was the first part of the world to experience full industrialization. Streets of densely-packed and cheaply-built houses were hastily laid out to accommodate migrants from the countryside. The industrial machine took precedence: the priority was to process raw materials and distribute products. The wealthier families moved upwind and on to higher ground, where the air was cleaner and where their neighbours were like themselves.

Thus suburbanization followed hot on the heels of industrial urbanization.

Rapid industrial expansion created appallingly unhealthy conditions for most of the people, inducing the drive for clean drinking water, drainage, and for reduced risk of fire. Standards were evolved for the layout of streets, for the design of replacement housing, and to ensure a degree of privacy, daylight and fresh air.

Humanitarian movements to provide education for all introduced local schools, which –

Above:
New Lanark, Robert Owen's famous model industrial community, was founded by David Dale in 1785

Right:
The Social City, Ebenezer Howard's diagram for a network of garden cities connected by railways and canals

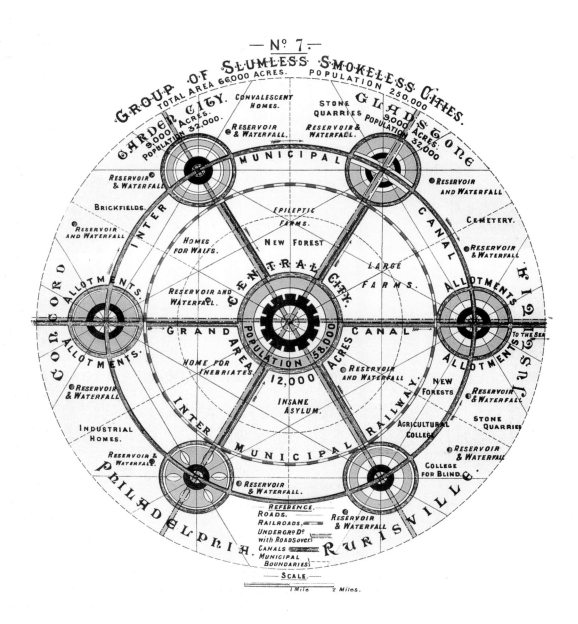

Right:
**Civic buildings make a
significant contribution to
the urban structure of
Letchworth Garden City**

together with local hospitals, workhouses and other community facilities – started to give physical form to what might later be called neighbourhoods, nascent urban villages. The wealthy increasingly accepted a civic responsibility, acting as benefactors for theatres, museums and other institutions. Local government systems were established. The process of industrialization was now yielding not only a new urbanism, but a new urban culture.

From Robert Owen at New Lanark as early as the eighteenth century, there had been a small minority of industrialists who believed that their mills and factories could form the foundation for a carefully designed and caring community rather than a vulgar work camp. Titus Salt at Saltaire and Lever at Port Sunlight stand in this line, as do the Quaker families of the Rowntrees at York and Cadburys at Bourneville.

By their example of making civilized places and harmonious communities the foundations were laid for conscious city planning: here were models both for efficient industry, and for healthy and cultured living for ordinary families. Here also were living examples of the benefits of single ownership of land and of masterplanning, which highlighted the merits of having a vision for a place, of single-minded implementation, and of self-governance and long-term management.

The garden cities movement was the first serious attempt to weave these threads into a comprehensively-planned approach to the design of whole towns and even for management of urban growth on a large scale. The movement was formed around Ebenezer Howard's manifesto *Tomorrow* (1898), which explained how philanthropic landowners and investors might develop complete mixed-use industrial towns ultimately owned and managed by their residents, whose efforts would be rewarded by the increasing yield from their commonly-held estate, which would not only provide the civic necessities of life but might eventually provide pensions.

The need for people to be able to walk and cycle around their town, and have ready access to a surrounding country belt that would also provide the town's food, provided a theoretical urban footprint which, with housing developed at

medium densities in the range 35–55 dwellings per hectare (as currently targeted in the UK), would accommodate around 30,000 people. Clustered together and connected by transit, a collection of such towns might support a high order central city, the whole 'social city' cluster accommodating perhaps 250,000 people.

Here was an approach to regional planning that married town and country into a viable ecology, rooted in proven neighbourhood planning yet capable of supporting metropolitan culture, and drawing together the lessons to be learned about land ownership and the capture of land value by the community that creates it. Practical demonstrations of the idea were attempted at Letchworth Garden City (1909) and Welwyn Garden City (1919), though industry in those days was still a 'bad neighbour' and the mix of uses is not as fine-grained as we would seek today. The idea was interpreted in various ways all over the world, and was immediately adapted as a means of handling the peripheral expansion of towns, notably at Hampstead Garden Suburb on the edge of London.

Patrick Geddes, a contemporary and supporter of Howard and his colleagues, provided a deeper

The Broadway, Letchworth.

Above:
The centre of Welwyn has a semi-formal arrangement of open space, shops and houses

Right:
Louis de Soissons's masterplan for Welwyn Garden City – an early twentieth-century version of transit-oriented development

DIAGRAM OF GENERAL TOWN-PLAN

Top left:
The formal alignment of The Broadway was one of the first elements constructed during the early development of Letchworth

Below left:
Central to the concept for Letchworth was the location of industrial and manufacturing activities on the edge of the Garden City

intellectual foundation for the planning of regions. Both Howard and Geddes were certain of the need for town and country to be locally connected and mutually dependant, but Geddes was equipped by his background in botany, biology, sociology and economics to go further in expounding what we would recognize today as the ecology of human settlement. He was also inclined to go further than Howard in developing practical techniques for regional survey, analysis and planning, and had the opportunity in India to pilot regeneration of old cities through what he called 'conservative surgery'.

Right:
**Rapid 'Metroland'
development of London
was triggered by the
expansion of the tube and
train network**

After the First World War the massive unplanned sprawl of Britain's cities was under way, even while Letchworth and Welwyn were being developed, and the young Town Planning Institute was encouraging the British government to require town-planning schemes from local government. 'The key in London and Birmingham, as in New York or Chicago, was of course transport … the growth of speculative housing in London – which roughly trebled the capital's area in twenty years – depended on rail transit.'[1] New suburbs were laid out around stations on new railway lines reaching out from the cities, and houses with gardens were made available at affordable prices by speculative developers. This 'Metroland' was attractive to those whose parents had toiled from insanitary workers' homes outside the gates of smoky factories. Ribbons of new homes lined either side of the main roads out into the countryside. Parliament passed legislation to try to control the worst of these excesses, but the scene was set for the establishment of a national planning system as soon as possible after the Second World War.

Town and country planning and new towns

The Town and Country Planning Act 1947 nationalized the right to develop land, and for the first time planning from the strategic to the local scale was possible. Every local authority was required to produce a comprehensive town planning scheme, and although the rules and requirements have changed over the years, this remains the situation today. With the exception of certain types of relatively small-scale development specified by government from time to time, all land use change in Britain requires permission from the local planning authority.

Howard's demonstrations were not overlooked. Where cities were overflowing, regional plans were devised and provision was made for the government to create complete new towns. The New Towns Act 1946 was to lead eventually to the creation of 32 new towns in Britain, home today to around two million people. Most were successful in providing fine homes and good jobs to people who otherwise would have

Top:
Milton Keynes sought to provide sustainable models for housing using renewable energy and maximizing solar gain

Above:
The local centre of Shenley in Milton Keynes provides a limited range of basic neighbourhood facilities

Right:
High-density housing at Albion Dock in Surrey Quays, created by the London Docklands Development Corporation

had little chance to improve their lot. All experimented, with varying degrees of success, with the current fashions in architecture and urban design. Many, such as Warrington, Washington and Milton Keynes, remain spectacularly successful and manage to constantly reinvent and refresh themselves. Others, such as Cumbernauld, Corby, and Skelmersdale have fared badly, with fragile local economies, dilapidated town centres, and public housing estates in need of wholesale renewal or replacement.[2]

Refocusing on older cities

Despite the establishment of a planning system throughout Britain, and associated initiatives in managing urban growth, by the 1970s it was clear that local planning authorities were unable to prevent the physical concentration of poverty and social deprivation in or near the core of the older cities. As in North America, manufacturing industry has moved out to large industrial estates where there was room for expansion, good road access, and easier access to the skilled labour that had already moved out to the suburbs. The poor – apart from the minority given the chance to move to a new town – were unable to escape. Immigrants, who typically accepted the worst-paid jobs in the cities to get themselves started, formed part of these inner city communities.

In 1977, Peter Walker, the Secretary of State for the Environment, published a report on inner-city deprivation, which stated that the plight of the inner cities 'was no longer a matter of individuals or households falling below the poverty line; rather it had become a matter of the failure of entire urban economies'.[3] Riots in various inner-city areas induced government action faster than might otherwise have been the case, and the 1978 Inner Urban Areas Act created an Urban Programme that applied public monies and tax breaks to try to kick-start regeneration.

The people and their neighbourhoods needed urgent attention, but unlike their counterparts in North America, the inner-city areas were not at this time threatened with abandonment by their residents: there was nowhere else for the people to go.

By 1980 the government had decided that local authorities were not able to manage the recovery of the inner cities themselves, and that small-area initiatives were not having enough effect. Urban Development Corporations (UDCs) were brought into being. These took control of all publicly-owned land in large tranches of selected inner-city areas and, using public money and conferring tax breaks on special zones, cleared the dereliction and contamination and carried out large-scale environmental improvements. This in turn attracted private investment in office developments, small factories, retail and leisure attractions, and housing for sale.

There is some controversy over the extent to which the poor directly benefited from the work of the UDCs in their midst, but there is no dispute that the UDC areas have been physically uplifted. Some have been economically transformed, an effect seen most dramatically in London's Canary Wharf, and others, such as Quayside in Newcastle and Cardiff Bay, now host vibrant urban communities.

Looking back at Britain over the period from the 1960s to the 1980s, it is possible to see that

there was some amnesia in all that activity. The government's own new town programme had shown the merit of comprehensive land assembly at 'no new town' values, followed by investment in masterplanning, environmental improvement and social development by a single-purpose body that was also a planning authority in its own right. This had involved, in turn, disposal of serviced land to developers and occupiers on a competitive basis, with as much concern given to the quality of proposed development as to land value. These good experiences were overlooked: UDCs were not given plan-making powers, they had a limited brief and a shorter life, and they were controlled project-by-project by a remote central government.

Neither was the lesson learned that experimentation in architecture and urban design caused us to wander away from traditional urbanism. In mass public housing projects the eventual occupiers were never consulted, and speed of construction and the search for ever-lower costs became the primary – and, at times, the only – concern. Those much-trumpeted innovative housing schemes created a legacy of relatively modern neighbourhoods that soon needed radical upgrade or total redevelopment.

The need to balance housing growth with the development of a strong and broadly-based local economy was often forgotten, so today we see the geography of jobs barely fitting the geography of the homes of the people that want them.

Planning sustainably

Awakening environmental consciousness world-wide meanwhile led to the international commitment to sustainable development secured at the Earth Summit in Rio de Janeiro in 1992. This followed the initial United Nations World Commission on Environment and Development (Brundtland) report in 1987. The UK and the USA, along with the majority of democratic nations, made commitments that have immediate implications for our generation and for those that will follow.

The Rio agreements reflected a consensus that our planet has been abused and, if that trend were to continue, the planet would be destroyed. Hence the commitment to clean air, clean oceans and rivers, restoration and respect for our ecological biodiversity, the use of naturally renewable sources of materials, and the construction of participative and cooperative methods of governance for living in harmony with our neighbours and with the Earth.

The 500-page *Agenda 21* established at Rio is radical. Its practical and political implications are only just dawning on us all, and are currently proving painful to implement. It throws into sharp relief the unfinished business of the Rio summit; demonstrators at meetings of the World Trade Organization shout that 'business as usual' is not an option; agitation at the institutions of global capitalism and the activities of multinational corporations make the same point. Since Rio, everything we do must be reviewed and reoriented to the pursuit of sustainable development if our planet is to survive and continue to support humankind.

The words 'sustainable development' can present some difficulty. Sustainable development is not a masterplan or blueprint for an end-state arrangement for the planet – it is not an object, but a dynamic process. Fundamentally, it is a way of thinking about how we must proceed in a way that enables us to meet 'the needs of the present without compromising the ability of future generations to meet their own needs'.[4] In addition, it carries other behavioural and social obligations, such as a requirement for development and change to be participative processes, and for us to give thought to matters of inter-generational equity.

The high-level commitment to sustainable development bites hard in town and country planning at the strategic level. Accepting the fact that 'the future will be predominantly urban, and the most immediate environmental concerns of most people will be urban ones',[5] we are taken quickly to the point that the achievement of sustainable urbanism is a major part of the task that faces us.

There is coincidence of view about the characteristics of sustainable urbanism. Approached from an ecological modal of development, as described in the *Gaia Atlas of Cities*,[6] this defines the need for close proximity of

Below:
The United Nation's *Agenda 21* provides a localized programme of action for sustainable development
United Nations Division for Sustainable Development
©2001 United Nations Division for Sustainable Development

A VISION FOR NORTH WEST EUROPE
An agenda for a sustainable and balanced development

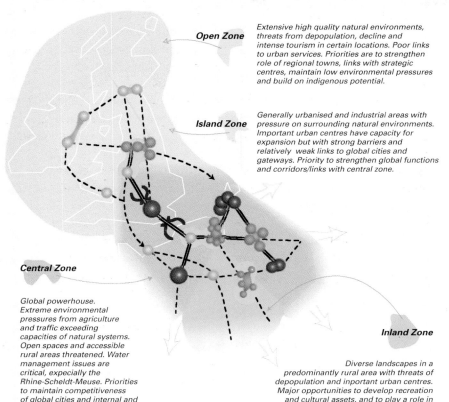

Open Zone
Extensive high quality natural environments, threats from depopulation, decline and intense tourism in certain locations. Poor links to urban services. Priorities are to strengthen role of regional towns, links with strategic centres, maintain low environmental pressures and build on indigenous potential.

Island Zone
Generally urbanised and industrial areas with pressure on surrounding natural environments. Important urban centres have capacity for expansion but with strong barriers and relatively weak links to global cities and gateways. Priority to strengthen global functions and corridors/links with central zone.

Central Zone
Global powerhouse. Extreme environmental pressures from agriculture and traffic exceeding capacities of natural systems. Open spaces and accessible rural areas threatened. Water management issues are critical, expecially the Rhine-Scheldt-Meuse. Priorities to maintain competitiveness of global cities and internal and external accessibility, whilst containing physical growth and relieving pressure on environment.

Inland Zone
Diverse landscapes in a predominantly rural area with threats of depopulation and inportant urban centres. Major opportunities to develop recreation and cultural assets, and to play a role in improved connections to the east and south.

Cooperation zones

Inland Zone   **Central Zone**   **Open Zone**   **Island Zone**

Global cities and gateways · cities of major economic importance for north-west Europe/rest of the world with high level of access to and from them

Strategic polycentric areas · cluster of cities, high level of economic activity, key role in inward investment to north-west Europe

Strategic centres · monocentric, high level economic activity, key national/regional role and focus for inward investment

Eurocorridors

Corridors/transport axes to be strengthened

Communication bottlenecks

Enhanced external connections

Counterweight global gateways and economic centres

Above:

The European Spatial Development Perspective identifies strategic urban centres and strengthens public transport corridors

home and work, integrated public transport systems, energy conservation and efficiency, renewable energy technology, longevity of built structures, and 'circular metabolism', in which staple foods are supplied from local sources and waste is recycled to support that process.

The *European Spatial Development Perspective* (EDSP)[7] confronts the pressures for further urbanization with insistence upon urban renaissance rather than the wanton consumption of the countryside, connections made by public transport rather than by cars, social inclusion, and respect for local building traditions.

We must be cautious about imprecise language. This especially applies to the literature on the density of sustainable urban development, about which there is a terrible tangle between net and gross densities, town densities and site densities, and measures that variously use people, floor space or even bed spaces per hectare. We also need to be cautious about the assumptions we make about the energy consumed by different intensities of urban form. Nevertheless, almost all commentators view the following three objectives, familiar to the philosophy of urban villages, as necessary for moving towards sustainable urbanization:

– the achievement of mixed-use neighbourhoods, integrating work, service and living functions as far as possible;
– the achievement of densities sufficient to ensure the viability of public transport and other services (30 people per hectare appears to be the minimum, approximately); and,
– the achievement of 'decentralized concentration', by which everyone is within walking or cycling distance of a connection to high-quality public transport, from where higher-level service functions, such as higher education, specialized healthcare and entertainment can be accessed.

These have been clearly expressed in the Aalborg Charter of 1995. Following this, strategic agreements between a network of European cities have led to the establishment of the European Sustainable Cities and Towns Campaign.[8]

Right:
The Blue House – part of
Aalborg's Urban Ecology
Project, which contributes
to the European
Sustainable Cities and
Towns Campaign

Current planning policy and guidance

The UK Government's overarching policy on
sustainable development is set out in *A Better
Quality of Life*.[9] This provides a framework within
which more specific guidance on urbanization has
been developed within the series of Planning
Policy Guidance notes (PPGs), each of which seeks
to apply the principles of sustainable development
to town and country planning.

By way of context, it is government policy that
'each household has the right to a decent home'[10]
and demographic projections indicate that at least
5 million new households will require accommodation in England over the period 1991–2016 or
thereabouts. This, not surprisingly, has caused
great consternation in parts of England that have
already been heavily urbanized in recent decades.

The greatest growth in households is projected
in the country towns to which many families
migrated from the former industrial cities. Much of
this expansion is led by an increasing demand for
one-person households, greater divorce rates and

people living for significantly longer. Paradoxically,
it is now these residents of the country towns and
outlying villages who, although the cause of much
of the growth in new households and the need for
new homes, are the ones most disturbed by the
possibility of further development in their locality.
'Not in my back yard!' they shout, apparently
unaware that it is the needs of their children, their
parents, and their former partners, that they address.

The Government's PPGs seek to steer
household growth to the idle, vacant and under-
used land and buildings within older cities.
Specifically, PPG guidance is now beginning to
promote the creation, and reinvention, of dense,
mixed-use neighbourhoods, typified by the urban
village model. The fact that so much of the
household growth appears likely to be in one-
person or small households is felt to be very
helpful. Such households, comprised primarily of
the young and the elderly and with no children,
will benefit from the proximity to new work
opportunities and the attractions and
neighbourliness of mixed-use neighbourhoods in
the revitalized urban districts.

Thus *PPG 1: General Policy and Principles*
outlines the national objective of achieving at least
60 per cent of new homes on previously-developed
land. This PPG specifically commends the urban
village approach to the revitalization of the older
industrial towns and cities, and states in paragraph
12 that, 'The planning system can be used to
deliver high-quality, mixed-use developments, such
as "urban villages". Built on large sites, usually
within urban areas. They are characterized by:

- compactness;
- a mixture of uses and dwelling types,
  including affordable housing;
- a range of employment, leisure and
  community facilities;
- appropriate infrastructure and services;
  high standards of urban design;
- access to public open space and green spaces;
  and
- ready access to public transport.'

PPG 3: Housing outlines a 'sequential approach' to
the identification of land for new development, in
which the first priority is to use previously-

Right:
**Ebbsfleet is set to become
a new urban centre on the
Channel Tunnel Rail Link**
David Lock Associates

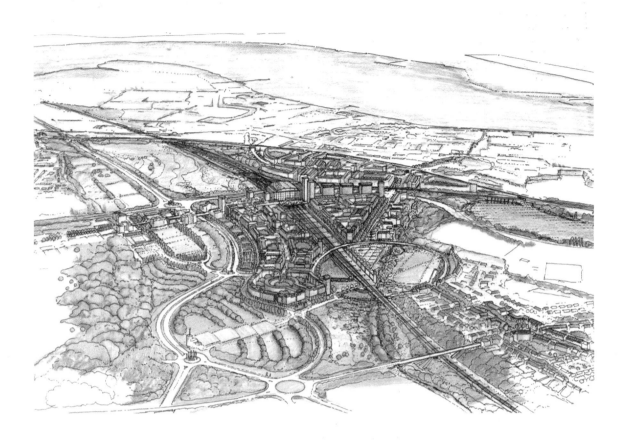

developed land inside existing towns and cities. Second, if necessary, 'sustainable urban extensions' along public transport corridors at the edges of the built-up area are to be encouraged and, as a third step, the creation of properly-planned new towns (euphemistically called 'new settlements') some distance away in public transport corridors. PPG 3 also introduces the idea of phasing the release of land for development in order to hold back green fields until previously-developed land inside towns and cities has been brought into use.

PPG 6: Town Centres and Retail Development gives its priority to the vitality and viability of town centres, and is designed to bring an end to the rash of edge-city retail sheds and superstores that have grown at the expense of the High Street. A sequential approach has to be taken, whereby the need for new retailing needs to be demonstrated, and it must be proved that it cannot be accommodated in an existing town centre, or on the edge

of a town centre, before the possibility of an out-of-town location can even be considered. This policy has had the effect of almost halting out-of-town retail development, and of stimulating the comprehensive redevelopment of existing town centres.

PPG 13: Transport, which was the first PPG to be rewritten after Rio, sets out the requirement for new development to reduce the need to travel, especially by car. In its latest revision (2001), provision for the car generally is to be constrained by the setting of maximum rather than minimum car-parking standards. All forms of development must now promote walking and cycling, and give support to good-quality integrated public transport.

While the government's PPG series has been revised to apply the priority for sustainable development and to stem the dispersal of people and jobs from the older cities, fresh impetus for urban regeneration comes from the work of the Urban Task Force.

The Urban Task Force, convened in 1998, described the issues facing our urban centres as 'Drivers of Change'. 'In the post-industrial age powerful drivers are already transforming our towns and cities beyond recognition.' The Task Force's Final Report[11] summarized the main factors that have emerged as central to this process of change:

- the technical revolution: centred on information technology and the establishment of new networks connecting people from the local to the global level;
- the ecological threat: greater understanding of the global implication of mankind's consumption of natural resources and the importance of sustainable development; and,
- the social transformation; changing life patterns reflecting increasing life expectancy and the development of new lifestyle choices.

The report of the Urban Task Force sets out numerous detailed recommendations for action by the Government if the desired urban renaissance is to be brought about. These include fiscal changes that would encourage urban development and discourage greenfield urbanization; the creation of special agencies and development trusts for rolling programmes of urban renewal; the use of masterplanning teams to promote the conscious design and enhancement of urban areas; the raising of average densities and the encouragement of mixed-use and mixed tenure development; and the higher priority to be given to public transport systems. The challenge facing the nation, as discussed in the preceding chapter, is to accommodate all the homes we need through the urban renaissance; to retain and attract people to existing cities; to tackle the poor quality of life and lack of opportunity in some urban areas; to strengthen the factors that enhance the economic success of urban areas; and to make sustainable urban living practical, affordable and attractive.

The Government's response has been the Urban White Paper *Our Towns and Cities: The Future*.[12] This accepted many of the recommendations of the Urban Task Force, though progress appears to be slow and the Task Force has found it necessary agitate for more action.

Strategic planning for sustainable urbanization

While in England the Government encourages the sequential approach to development at the regional and sub-regional scale, it is anticipated that in due course a more balanced approach will be established. Instead of a 'one size fits all' policy, strategic planning might consider what the Town and Country Planning Association calls a 'portfolio' approach. This would entail a blend of urban infilling and town extensions, country town expansion and new towns, crafted to suit the particular needs and circumstances of the region. Some of these are represented by the urban retrofit, infill and extension projects illustrated later in this book.

A more open-minded and locally-derived approach to making arrangements for the future has clear parallels with the United States and is well expressed by Peter Calthorpe in *The Next American Metropolis*.[13] In this we can see the variety of responses that need to be considered, but none pre-judged from above as to their priority. Calthorpe's diagram of a hypothetical city region, reflected in his Regional Plan for Sacramento County, illustrates the point that the renaissance of the centre is not the only requirement. New urban villages on major brownfield tracts at transport nodes, urban extensions at the edge of the city, and even a new town some distance away, will also be needed.

Beyond the edges of existing towns and cities, should further growth have to be accommodated, this strategic planning logic might lead to a pattern of development illustrated for parts of Britain by Hall and Ward in their *Sociable Cities*.[14] All towns and cities must have a stop line or growth boundary somewhere, in order for people to have contact with the countryside and in deference to environmental constraints, or simply because the feel and size of the place seems just right as it is. Some places today may sit comfortably short of their stop line and could safely be grown larger. Some new places might be made. All places within the cluster, linked by excellent public transport like beads on a string, can be moulded to satisfy the principles of sustainable urbanization and the harmonious social, economic and environmental conditions that implies.

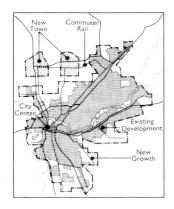

Above:
Urban development should focus on infill and adjacent new growth areas ahead of new towns
Calthorpe Associates

Right:
The adoption of Transit-Oriented Development Design Guidelines for San Diego in California
Calthorpe Associates

Planning for sustainable communities

In mending and remaking existing towns and cities, and in the design of new communities should they be needed, the core of the vision is now understood: compact neighbourhoods of housing, parks and schools placed within walking distance of shops, civic services, jobs and transit – the modern application of traditional town-building principles. In North America it has found its most succinct and powerful expression in the New Urbanism. This vision lies at the heart of the urban villages movement, and draws upon international commitment to sustainable development that has been embedded in government policy, best practice and in the popular imagination in Britain. This has been the movement's greatest achievement to date.

The transformation of 'what we have inherited' into 'what we must have in order to survive' occurs at a time of particularly significant change. As Peter Hall noted in the previous chapter, the greatest growth in new households is among single people and those without children. Many of these households, whether rich or poor, can be expected to find the characteristics of urban villages particularly suited to their needs and lifestyles. New businesses, and particularly those that depend on information technology, which will be discussed in the following chapter, tend to be small and to prefer a location that is joined into the life of town rather than a bleak edge-city business park. Successful cities are creative cities, and creativity stems from people meeting and interacting in the urban village and the metropolitan network it can support, not from lonely lives in low-density suburbs.

Experience has shown that land assembly is needed to enable the making of sustainable neighbourhoods. The Urban Villages Group has been explicit on the subject from the start,[15] and in their later report on the economics of urban villages the importance of the point is emphasized.[16] Sufficient land must be assembled not only to achieve the desired physical form and mix of uses, but also to enable a proportion of land values created to be used to cross-subsidize the ingredients that the market cannot provide. These

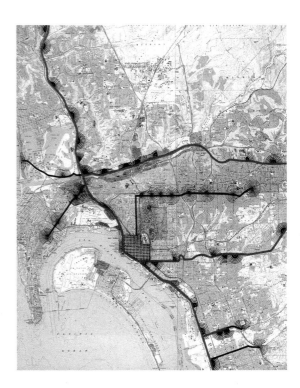

ingredients include housing for people on lower incomes, and community facilities. The money might also run to subsidizing transit, social and cultural programmes, and aspects of healthcare. It should certainly provide for the capital costs of the sustainable drainage and energy systems that are required, and for long-term management and maintenance costs of the public realm.

Where the land is held by a single landowner with a philanthropic attitude and a highly developed sense of civic responsibility, or by development companies committed to town building rather than fast profit, acquisition by a public agency – either for development led by itself, or for handing on to a credible town-building company – will not be necessary. There would be no point.

But where land carries a heavy burden of cost of clearance and removal of contamination, for example, even the most willing landowner may need to be relieved of his ownership. Where the land is in multiple ownership, or in the hands of obstructive landowners or speculative developers interested only in swift profit, assembly of the necessary land will be essential.

Cherry-picking old neighbourhoods and dismal suburbs, for small sites and characterful buildings

Right:
**The Brierley Hill masterplan
proposes a new urban
district for the former
Merry Hill Shopping Centre**
David Lock Associates

of value, is not a sound basis for the development
of successful urban villages. There should be little
attraction for the wealthy to sit behind their
security gates in even the densest streets. Sustainable
neighbourhoods must accommodate and integrate
as diverse a range of people and activity as
possible, and that requires not only careful
masterplanning, but also a degree of cross-subsidy.

In the design of sustainable neighbourhoods,
the principles outlined in the Charter of the New
Urbanism have been developed into best practice
guidance in North America.[17] The advice of the
urban planning consultancy Duany Plater-Zyberk,
which is based within the scalar system of planning
defined by the Region, the Neighbourhood and the
Block, can be summarized to show the essential
neighbourhood elements:

–   a discernible centre – often a square or green
    and sometimes a busy or memorable street
    corner – where the transit stop would be
    located;
–   most dwellings within a five-minute walk of
    the centre;
–   shops and offices of sufficiently varied types to
    supply the weekly needs of a household;

–   a small ancillary building within the back yard
    of each house that might be used as a rental
    unit or place of work;
–   an elementary school within walking distance
    of homes;
–   small playgrounds convenient to every
    dwelling;
–   connected networks of streets, providing a
    variety of routes for walking and for vehicles;
–   streets that are relatively narrow and tree-
    shaded, slowing the traffic in favour of
    walking and cycling;
–   buildings around the neighbourhood centre
    are placed close to streets, creating a well-
    defined public space;
–   parking spaces and garage doors rarely face
    the street – they are relegated to the rear of
    buildings, usually accessed by alleys;
–   prominent sites are reserved for civic
    buildings, accommodating community,
    education, religious or cultural activities; and,
–   the neighbourhood is organized for self-
    governance, with community responsibility
    for matters of maintenance, security and
    physical change.

In Britain the design specifications for
masterplanning are very similar, and are being
finely honed and widely disseminated within the
more recent design guidance that has been
provided by several organizations, including the
Commission for the Built Environment (CABE), the
government itself, the Urban Design Group and the
Urban Design Alliance.[18]

While the masterplan provides the framework
for development, and the town-builder will ensure
the delivery of the public realm and cross-subsidy
of non-commercial ingredients, most of the physical
fabric will be delivered by property developers or
occupiers for their own use, on individual parcels
of land. To provide a brief for their designers, and
to provide a basis for quality control by the town-
builder and the community at large, design codes
and development briefs will be needed.

In structuring and ordering this detailed
development guidance, there is great assistance to
be gained from the ongoing work of DPZ in the
Transect that will be discussed further in Andrés
Duany's chapter. In practical terms it helps us

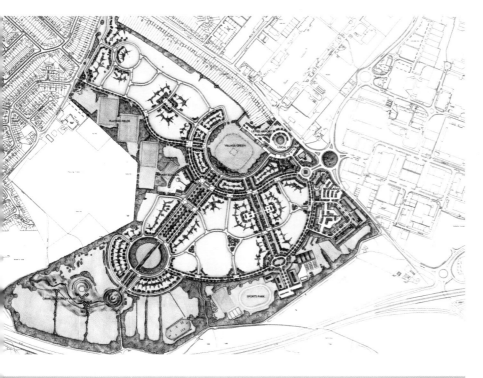

Above:
The framework masterplan for Ipswich's former airfield is structured around a series of new neighbourhoods
David Lock Associates

Below:
New medium-density housing and a network of public open space is leading the redevelopment of Ipswich's former airfield

understand that there is an appropriate place for all features of sustainable urbanism, and that most conflicts over design and urban planning arise because people are trying to do the right thing but in the wrong place. Useful American guidance on design codes and conventions that can be used to manage the quality of development is presented in detail by John Dutton in his work on reforming American suburbs.[19]

Planning for change

This chapter has explored the necessity to plan strategically for growth at national, regional and local scales to ensure that our whole environment can evolve in the most sustainable manner possible. The hard work really begins as one attempts to implement such strategies, for the ballot box cruelly demonstrates that society can be extremely resistant to change and very reluctant to plan ahead and disturb the status quo. This reluctance to change is beginning to ease as people become more aware that without such an approach there can be no urban renaissance, and no 'smart' growth.

Perhaps the strongest resistance to change is a justified disgust at the quality of the new development that finally appears on the ground. The urban village philosophy continues to play an important role in changing the culture of the development industry, and in brokering collaborations between the suppliers of development and its occupiers. New development, whether in the regeneration of older towns and cities, or in town expansion schemes or new towns, is a collective task. In conclusion, it must be:

- participative in the way it is planned and implemented;
- subsidized in part from the unearned increment in land value that comes with a planning permission;
- inclusive in whom it accommodates;
- traditionally urban and expressive of its locality in structure;
- with a connected, high-quality public realm;
- mixed in use and character;
- focused on non-car modes of travel;
- joined to neighbouring towns and cities by excellent public transport; and
- managed in perpetuity by its citizens.

By persistent application of these principles the resistance to change will begin to evaporate and the strategic planning debate can then develop along more open and intelligent lines. We shall then begin to travel faster on the path to more sustainable development and thus secure a future for the planet and its burden of humanity.

Chapter 3

Emerging digital neighbourhoods

William J. Mitchell

Our dwellings, neighbourhoods and cities perform the fundamental task of bringing us together to interact socially, conduct our transactions, construct and reproduce our cultures, and form our communities. At the same time – and this is the fundamental paradox of architecture – they separate us by providing differentiated, specialized spaces for our various activities. A very simple dwelling, for example, consists of a single enclosure, but a more complex one is divided into living room, bedrooms, kitchen, bathroom, and so on.

Different strategies for resolving this paradox – albeit imperfectly and incompletely – lie at the root of basic differences in architectural and urban form. Historically, new technologies of interconnection have enabled new strategies, and have allowed new architectural and urban forms to emerge. Today, in particular, innovations in computer networking and information technology are opening up the possibility of smaller-scale, finer-grained, more humane and equitable urban environments. We are seeing the gradual emergence of *digital neighbourhoods* as attractive alternatives to the characteristic urban and suburban patterns of the recent past.

Left:
**The City Learning Centre
in Camden, London, includes
an information technology
teaching bar**
Gollifer Langston Architects

Adjacency, proximity, and circulation networks

Architects often attempt to resolve the contradiction between the need to come together and the need to separate by first dividing a building into separate enclosures for various specialized activities, then forming adjacencies between activities that interact. Thus the kitchen of a dwelling, for food preparation, normally ends up adjacent to the dining room, for food consumption. The problem, however, is that adjacency is a very scarce resource. If you have two, three, or four distinct enclosures you can make them all adjacent to one another, but, if you have more than four spaces, it is impossible to achieve universal adjacency. In general, in the layout of buildings, architects find that there are more desirable adjacencies than they can provide.

The next best thing is to substitute proximity, via some sort of circulation space, for direct adjacency. In warm climates, this logic has often produced the form of the courtyard building. Using this pattern, you can conveniently connect every room to every other via the central circulation space. In cooler climates, you can get the same effect with an internal corridor. And you can also get it by scattering pavilions within a compound. At a larger scale, circulation spaces begin to evolve into elaborate circulation *networks* – linked structures of corridors, streets and roads.

Where the time spent circulating through a network is significant, and the cost is high, it may be worthwhile to reduce circulation costs by investing in more efficient network infrastructure. For example, if there is a dirt track connecting two sites, then travel between them will be relatively slow and expensive, but if there is a good paved road, then transportation will become more efficient and the costs of interaction will diminish – or, at least, they will do so when you have amortized the cost of the road. In general, efficient networks attempt to overcome the tyranny of distance. And they become increasingly crucial as settlements grow to the scale where simple adjacencies no longer suffice to hold them together, and as settlements are integrated into larger regional, national, and global systems.

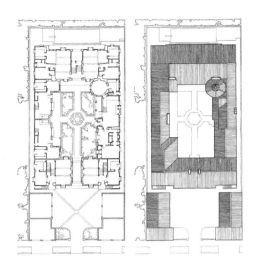

Many, varied things need to be transported between sites, so buildings and cities have evolved multiple, specialized network infrastructures. Today, there are track networks for goods and people, pipe and duct networks for water supply, waste disposal and air and gas supply, wire networks for electrical energy distribution, and both wired and wireless networks for transfer of information. By increasing the efficiency and decreasing the cost of certain types of transfers, each such specialized network selectively loosens spatial linkages among activities.

If you rely upon a village well, for example, you have to transport water in a bucket or in a jar on your head. There is a high cost per unit distance for transporting water from the point of collection and accumulation to the point of consumption, so dwellings tend to cluster tightly around the well. But if you introduce a specialized, efficient water transfer network, such as a high-volume aqueduct, you loosen the relationship between the point of collection and accumulation (a spring and reservoir in the mountains, say), and the point of consumption – perhaps the city of Rome. And if you add to the system piped water supply to residences, you allow these residences to spread out along the supply lines instead of centralizing at the well or fountain. But notice that the effect is not general, but a highly selective one; activities that are linked by intensive transfers of people, energy, or other things that don't flow through the pipes still need to be close together.

Fragmentation and recombination

As new transfer technologies emerge, and as new types of network infrastructures are overlaid on cities, the resulting selective loosening of spatial linkages allows latent adjacency and proximity demands to manifest themselves. This produces fragmentation and recombination of established room arrangements, building types, and urban and regional land-use patterns.[1] Activities that were clustered at a single location may be redistributed over multiple locations, and conversely, activities that were dispersed through a region may

condense to form new combinations and clusters.

Consider, for example, a simple dwelling that gets its heat and light from a single fireplace. Under this condition, the family clusters around the hearth in the evening. But if you introduce a heat distribution network – furnace, hot water pipes and radiators, for example – you can warm different rooms, and you eliminate the need to cluster for warmth. If you add an electric supply network and lights you also eliminate the necessity to group around the central source of light. So latent demands for separation of incompatible activities, and for varied and specialized facilities

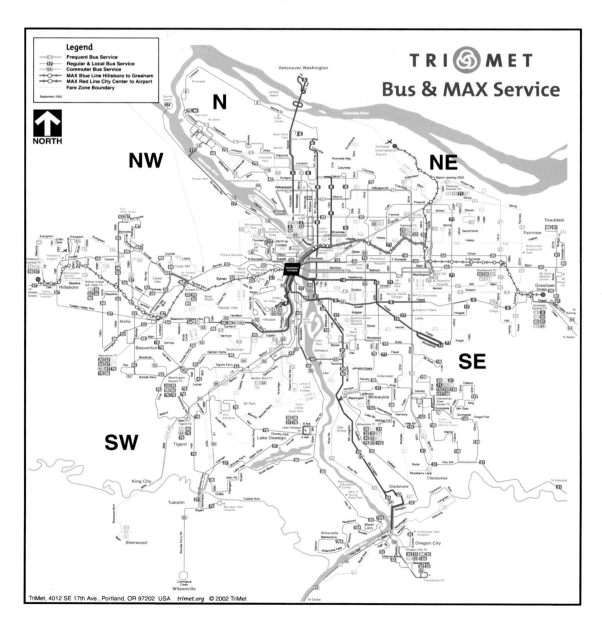

Right:
TriMet, Portland's integrated transport system, provides a network infrastructure that connects the city together
©2002 TriMet

Right:

**Portland's 2040
Framework relates
transport networks to
a strategy of neighbour-
hood development**
Calthorpe Associates

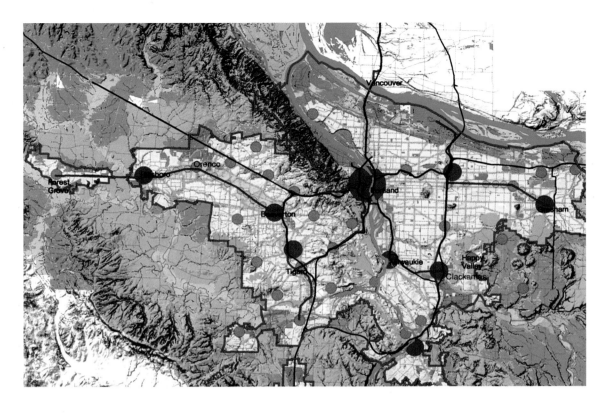

to support different activities, take over. Thus the kids disperse to their bedrooms to do their homework in quiet and privacy, and with everyone able to retreat to their own spaces, there need be no conflict between different choices of music, or lively conversation versus quiet reading. But there is a cost, of course: fragmentation and dispersal reduces internal interaction and cohesiveness of the social unit.

Or think of a traditional village well, and its role in defining settlement patterns. It is a point of water supply for drinking and cooking, so as we have noted, sites of domestic consumption need to be nearby. It is also a supply point for bathing, so in many cultures, a central, public bathing place (maybe elaborated into a bath house) is located at the well. Furthermore, because inhabitants of the village need to come regularly to the well to collect water and bathe, it serves as a social focus; the surrounding public space is a place to be seen and to represent yourself as a member of the community, to exchange news and gossip, to conduct face-to-face transactions and to strengthen social ties. When a piped water supply system replaces the well, the houses aren't just dispersed; they are also transformed both functionally and spatially. The public access point for drinking and cooking fragments and recombines with domestic space; there are now, more conveniently, taps and sinks in domestic kitchens. Similarly, the bathing space fragments, decentralizes, and privatizes; each house gets its own, private bathroom. The well can no longer serve as a magnet for social interaction; this function shifts to domestic living rooms (perhaps emphasizing the family rather than the village as the social unit), and to public spaces such as cafés, which depend upon different sorts of attractions.

Sometimes relative cost plays an important role in these processes. Spartan hotels and dormitories economize on space, plumbing costs, and cleaning costs by relying upon communal bathrooms – maybe one per floor. But more luxurious ones pay the additional price of distributing and replicating the function, and provide private bathrooms for each unit. This move becomes more likely as costs go down, or as the affluence of customers goes up.

The crucial lesson, here, is that new networks do not simply interconnect rooms and buildings within existing settlement patterns. They create strong *transformative* pressures that frequently produce new building types and neighbourhood, urban, and regional patterns, with profound economic, social, and cultural consequences. The transformation of traditional, pre-industrial settlement patterns into those of the modern city depended upon the introduction of efficient transportation networks, water supply and sewer systems, electric power distribution systems, and early telecommunication networks – particularly the telegraph and telephone systems. Today, I shall argue, the ongoing deployment of new, digital telecommunications infrastructure is opening up the possibility of creating some attractive, sustainable new urban patterns.

The effects of digital telecommunication networks

Essentially, digital telecommunications links (following in the footsteps of the telegraph and telephone) loosen the linkages between activities that had previously required face-to-face interaction. Digital storage facilities (electronic versions of files and libraries) loosen requirements for synchronization and coordination among activities. And combinations of the two (as in the Internet and the World Wide Web) are particularly powerful.[2]

The communications 'glue' that now holds organizations and communities together takes a multiple form, including face-to-face meetings, video conferencing, email and the internet. This is summarized in the Synchronous/ Asynchronous table below.

These different forms of communication have different associated costs, and provide very different combinations of advantages and disadvantages, so they do not simply substitute

Below right:
The communications 'glue' that holds communities together now has multiple forms

	Synchronous	Asynchronous
Local	Face-to-face Agora Village green Conference room	Notice board Inscriptions Non-circulating library
Remote	Telephone Videoconfrencing Instant text messaging Online virtual worlds	Email Voicemail World Wide Web

for one another. Instead, we make choices among the available possibilities within an increasingly complex 'economy of presence'.[3] Face-to-face communication is, for example, richly multimodal, emotionally intense, and often very satisfying, but can also be difficult to arrange and expensive, both in direct cost (travel to meetings, and so on) and in opportunity cost. By contrast, email is far less intense and satisfying, but its asynchronous character makes it very convenient, it can effortlessly keep us in touch globally, and its cost is extremely low. And there are important complementarities; we often use convenient, inexpensive, asynchronous email to arrange scarce, expensive, but very valuable face-to-face interaction. Conversely, face-to-face meetings often generate extensive email follow-up.

It used to be the case that all the action took place in the top-left (local/synchronous) quadrant, supported by urban and architectural arrangements such as the ancient Greek agora, the conference room, the classroom and the lecture hall, the live theatre, and the nine-to-five workplace. But the effect of new, digital telecommunications networks has been to produce a massive shift down the diagonal to the remote/asynchronous quadrant, which is supported by fibre-optics and high-speed copper wiring, personal computers, servers, routers, telecommunications protocols, and email and Web software. The dot-com bubble of the late 1990s was an over-enthusiastic short-term response to this shift, but the long-term effects are likely to be even more profound than the dot-com enthusiasts could imagine.

The loosening of spatial and temporal linkages that results from this shift has multiple, and sometimes seemingly contradictory consequences. Some activity components take advantage of new spatial and temporal freedoms to decentralize – to reach wider markets, to get closer to customers, to reduce vulnerability to attacks and outages, and so on. Others want to centralize – to achieve scale economies, knowledge spillover effects, and other classic benefits of aggregation. Others will exploit newly feasible locational possibilities; if you can now telecommute, for example, you might take the opportunity to shift your residence to a distant but highly desirable scenic site. And yet others will mobilize to respond more effectively to dynamic conditions – as when telephone call centres, which can now operate from pretty much anywhere, move around in response to geographic differences in labour costs.

Consider book retailing, for example. The traditional urban bookstore combines the activities of advertising through its sign out front and its display windows, book storage, browsing among the shelves to select books for purchase, point-of-sale activities at the cash register, and accounting and management activities in a back office. The whole system is tied together into a compact architectural package by an internal pedestrian circulation network, provisions for face-to-face interactions between customers and sales staff, and enclosure by a security and weather protection envelope. But what happens to book selling space in an online retailer, such as Amazon.com? First, the advertising function is virtualized; visibility in cyberspace, rather than in public urban space, is now what matters. Second, the space for browsing fragments, disperses, and recombines with points of Web access in homes and offices; customers now browse through an online catalogue rather than physical bookshelves. It is the same with the point of sale: an online form replaces the counter and cash register. But the book storage function condenses rather than disperses; instead of keeping inventory at multiple urban locations, online retailers seek scale economies by shifting it to highly automated, big-box warehouse and distribution centres at national and international air transportation nodes. (Incidentally, this also allows them to keep much larger lists of titles in stock.) At the same time, electronic commerce technology allows the back office to float freely to wherever appropriately skilled labour is available at an attractive price; it no longer needs to be near the books, nor near the customers.

You can take almost any traditional building type and perform a similar analysis. Digital telecommunication does not simply substitute for physical transportation and face-to-face contact (as one might initially imagine), but produces a complex restructuring of activities in which some things that had been clustered begin to disperse, other things that had been dispersed begin to cluster at new locations, and yet other things simply become less attached to particular locations.

Wireless networks

Emerging wireless networks are further destabilizing traditional patterns. Where wired digital networks primarily affect *place-to-place* relationships, newer wireless networks, combined with miniaturized, portable electronic devices, loosen the binding of *people* to places.

The telephone provides the most vivid example of this sort of transformation. Early telephones were bulky devices attached to walls; you literally 'placed' calls to these devices, and you were never quite sure who might be there to answer. In public spaces there were specialized architectural arrangements – telephone booths and boxes – for speaking on the telephone. Eventually, desktop telephones, extension cords, and modular jacks began to mobilize the act of phoning and to recombine it with different settings; you could call from your desk, your armchair, your bed, or even from the kitchen while cooking. Now, of course, tiny, wireless phones fit in your pocket. The ambiguity of calling is reversed; you generally know who will answer, but you don't know where they will be. And the act of calling is no longer associated with particular places; you can call from your home, the street, the train or bus, your car, the supermarket, or your workplace. In some contexts, such as restaurants and theatres, the incompatibility of telephone rings and calls with other ongoing activities has become a problem.

In general, miniaturization reduces the demand for specialized spaces built around fixed equipment; telephone boxes, typewriter rooms, computer rooms, and so on are fast becoming quaint anachronisms. And providing miniaturized, portable devices with wireless connectivity has the additional effect of reducing demand for spaces built around accumulations of information; when your files are online and wirelessly deliverable to wherever you happen to be, you do not need to work in a cubicle with file cabinets close at hand. At the same time, miniaturization and wireless

Above:
Wireless networks, like those available at Adelaide's Mawson Lakes, support a greater variety of activities in public open spaces

connectivity increase demand for general purpose, flexibly assignable spaces that can be used for different purposes as the need arises.

This new-found freedom can be put to different uses in different contexts, and to serve different goals. For socializing teenagers, mobile phones provide the capacity to use the city more flexibly – to arrange get-togethers on the spur of the moment, rather than meet at established hangouts at prearranged times. For managers of office space, portable equipment and online resources provide the opportunity to get rid of conventional office cubicles and move to 'hotel-style' space in which workstations are assigned temporarily, for short periods, as needed. For business executives, travel time can be put to better use; airport lounges and hotel rooms serve their needs as effectively as office desks. In pleasant climates, there may be a drift to the outdoors, as gardens, park benches, and sidewalk cafés become productive workplaces.

Reinventing neighbourhoods for the digital electronic era

One way to think of buildings and cities in the digital electronic era is to assume that they will retain essentially their current forms, but will be equipped with wired and wireless infrastructure for electronic delivery of a growing array of news and entertainment, retail, education, health care, government, and other services to homes and businesses. In other words, people might live and work in much the same sorts of places, but their consumption of goods and services – from ordering pet food on line to scanning their mutual fund balances and obtaining their drivers' licenses – would be facilitated by the Web. This was the approach taken by many of the dot-com enterprises that boomed in the late 1990s; it attracted an extraordinary amount of enthusiasm and investment for a short while, but it quickly showed itself to be very limited. It ignored the logic of fragmentation and recombination.

Alternatively, you can, more radically, conceive of information technology as an opportunity to pursue an anti-urban agenda; you can take it as a means of escape from the crowds and dangers of the big city, and a vehicle for pursuing the agrarian dream. You can imagine a world of semi-autonomous electronic cottages scattered through the woods and nestled in the mountains. These would be sites of electronically supported telework and home schooling. No doubt there is a niche in the real estate marketplace for wired writers' retreats and vacation homes, but this pattern does not scale. A wholesale shift to rural electronic cottages would obviously be environmentally destructive and absurdly unsustainable.

A far more interesting and attractive strategy than either of these is to employ information technology as a means of reinventing the small-scale, pedestrian-oriented neighbourhood for the twenty-first century. Digital telecommunications infrastructure provides an attractive opportunity to rethink the trade-offs between centralization versus decentralization, public space versus private territory, and specialized facilities versus flexibility and adaptability. The essence of the idea is to take advantage of telecommuting and electronic commerce to reduce trips *out* of the neighbourhood, while simultaneously deploying local attractions and circulation networks to encourage interactions *within* the neighbourhood.

It is far too early to provide a complete, fully exemplified theory of the digital neighbourhood, but some basic principles are already clearly identifiable. These are summarized in the following subsections.

Right:
San Francisco's popular South Park neighbourhood provided a focus for the city's dot-com enterprises in the late 1990s
©www.waccorp.com

Provide high-speed telecommunications infrastructure

A necessary – though clearly not sufficient – condition for benefiting from digital technology is to put the necessary infrastructure in place. Eliminating the digital divide does not reduce to providing connectivity, but you are certainly on the wrong side of the divide if you do *not* have connectivity.[4] In developing or rehabilitating neighbourhoods for the twenty-first century, therefore, capable digital telecommunications infrastructure should be thought of as an essential component of the utility system, along with roads, electricity supply, and water supply and sewers.

Left:
**Malmö's Bo01 housing
Expo included a digital
communications network
accessible to all homes**
Moore Ruble Yudell

Below left:
**A digital 'smart wall' runs
throughout the Tango
housing at the Malmö Expo**
Moore Ruble Yudell

One component of this infrastructure task is to provide the 'last kilometre' of high-speed connectivity from the nearest switching node on a long-distance backbone to the neighbourhood's homes and businesses. There are many technological options (among them cable modem systems, DSL, microwave links, and fibre optics to the front door), and the balance of their respective advantages and disadvantages changes with particular contexts and over time, so there would be little value in going into technical details here. The important thing is to evaluate the available options carefully, make a well-informed choice, and make sure that *some* effective system is put in place.

It is worth keeping in mind that cables are relatively inexpensive, but that ditches and culverts to accommodate them can be very costly. So it makes good sense to take an integrated approach to utility networking, and to take the opportunity to put data conduits and switching facilities in place whenever utility projects are carried out. Even if the telecommunications capacity is not immediately required, this is usually a sensible provision for the future.

A second component of the task is to provide data cabling, closets, and outlets within buildings. It is far easier, less expensive, and more graceful architecturally to do this up front than to come back, at some point after construction is completed, to retrofit telecommunications wiring. And one should not make the mistake of underestimating future need. The best strategy is to make comprehensive telecommunications infrastructure an integral part of the architectural concept from the beginning.

The effect of providing this infrastructure is to make the neighbourhood an active node in the global, electronically mediated economy. And, since access to the global digital networks matters far more than relative location within those networks, it has an equalizing effect; access creates much the same sorts of opportunities for a neighbourhood in London as it does for one in Bombay or in Sydney. Competitive success depends upon more than just network access, of course, but such access opens the door.

Add wireless capability

Wireless telecommunications infrastructure is sometimes thought of as a substitute or replacement for wired systems, and in some contexts it is, but it is better to think of wired and wireless as having complementary roles.[5] Wired provides high capacity and high levels of reliability, but it is often more difficult and expensive to put in place, and it does not provide mobile access. Wireless provides mobility and convenience, and it can quickly be put in place where terrain or urban conditions make wired systems difficult to implement, but there are some fundamental capacity and reliability limitations. By intelligently combining wired and wireless, it is often possible to get the best of both.

Wireless technology is developing rapidly and somewhat unpredictably, so the most important design issue is to make flexible provision, at both architectural and urban scales, for installation of wireless transmission and reception points. Wireless systems normally employ low-powered devices, so these installation points are required at frequent intervals, and they need electrical supply and (where they connect to wired systems) data cabling. Furthermore, they are subject to interference from topographic and architectural features, so they must be located carefully with respect to these.

Wireless connectivity has the particularly important effect of enhancing the functionality of gardens, outdoor public space, and indoor public spaces such as waiting areas and cafés – thus making these spaces even more valuable as neighbourhood assets. Such connectivity makes it possible to log in with a portable wireless device and work or conduct other transactions at these locations; you do not have to retreat to private space to get the access you need.

Create public access points

Network connectivity is useless, of course, if you don't have the necessary access facilities. These facilities consist not only of computer and telecommunications hardware, but also appropriate software (Web browsers, email

Above:
A fleet of BBC Buses has been equipped with workstations, tutors and digital studios to support the needs of local communities

software, and so on), access to subscription services, maintenance, upgrade and repair service, and perhaps advice and technical consulting. Just as connectivity to the water supply may be provided by means of a public well or private plumbing, so these access facilities may be located in public space or private – with very different social consequences.

In most contexts today, access will be provided by some mix of fixed, wired equipment and portable, wireless equipment. The balance is shifting towards portable wireless access, but fixed access points are likely to retain a role (if a diminishing one) for a considerable time to come.

Where the cost of access facilities is high relative to the general income level in a community (or some significant segment of the community), public access points are particularly attractive. These may take the form of for-profit cybercafés, non-profit community technology centres and computer clubhouses, computer centres attached to public libraries and recreation centres, installations in railway station waiting

rooms, and, in the case of the BBC, a travelling bus. Like the village well of old, they can serve as social attractors, and sites for social interaction (sometimes cross-generational) and peer-to-peer learning.

As the ratio of access cost to income drops, public access facilities tend to become less viable. For example, cybercafés remain popular in developing countries, and often play important roles in communities, but they have faded in more developed countries as personal computers providing private Internet access have become progressively more affordable. However, specialized equipment (such as large-format printers) remains expensive, and the technical expertise that can be provided by centre staff is a scarce and valuable commodity, so scale economies can still work to the advantage of public access points.

On grounds of social equity, it is important in a networked neighbourhood to provide not only private wiring for those who can afford personal equipment, but also public access points for those who cannot. These public access points can widen their appeal if they not only provide basic access,

Above:
Mawson Lakes homes are fully wired with an extensive digital communications infrastructure

Right:
The Home Management System in Mawson Lakes, Adelaide, allows owners to monitor and manage their houses remotely

Home Management System

Design. For better living

At Mawson Lakes, it all makes sense.

Mawson Lakes residents will benefit from the installation of a Home Management System that offers a number of lifestyle advantages as well as long term cost savings. Come into the Mawson Lakes Sales and Information Centre to experience our hands on display.

At Mawson Lakes all homes will be fitted with a minimum base system to which extra features can be added as desired.

Call into the Mawson Lakes Sales & Information Centre for a list of Home Management System providers and their contact details. These suggested providers can assist you with designing a system that meets your specific needs.

3 **13** **Turn on irrigation system**
Your home irrigation system can be turned on and off by telephoning the system and entering the appropriate code number.

7 **13** **Turn on air-conditioner**
Home appliances such as your home air-conditioner can be turned on and off by telephoning the system and entering the appropriate code number.

6 **9** **Intruder?**
A master switch can be installed next to the bed for control of the house lights and the security system. If you hear a noise outside press a button and the outside lights will come on.

2 **13** **Intruder?**
If the system detects an intruder in your home, lights will flash and sirens will sound. The system can be set to phone the police and the owner on a selection of preset telephone numbers.

10 **11** **Goodbye**
A goodbye switch when pressed on departure can be used to turn off every light in the house, arm the security system and open the garage door.

14 **Holiday mode**
If you are going away for a length of time the holiday switch can be used to turn on and off the television, radio and lights to emulate household patterns and give the appearance that there is someone home.

5 **Secure downstairs**
If you are home alone at night, the security system can be set to arm particular sections of the house.

Monitor consumption
The Home Management System can monitor the consumption of water, gas and electricity and help residents save money by operating appliances in off peak periods.

1 **4** **13** **Fire at home**
In the event of a fire at home, the system can be set to phone the fire brigade and the owner on a selection of preset telephone numbers.

5 **13** **Pet's locked in**
The security system can be set to detect a pet locked inside the home and can phone the owner on a selection of preset telephone numbers.

8 **12** **13** **Turn on spa bath**
A great lifestyle feature of the system is the ability to phone home in advance of your arrival and turn on the spa bath.

10 **Welcome home**
A master switch panel at the front door can be used to control many functions of the Home Management System. When you arrive home, press the welcome switch to turn on preset lights and appliances.

Please note: some of the features shown on the above diagram are not required as part of the minimum base system.

At Home   At Work   On Holiday

but also high-end equipment, advice, training, and technical consultation. They should be located and designed not only to play their direct technical roles, but also to take advantage of their 'village well' capabilities and to serve as foci of social interaction.

Public access points also have the potential to play specialized cultural roles – particularly when combined with more traditional cultural institutions. A local library, for example, might provide not only networked computers but also access to online databases and subscription services that are beyond the reach of individuals, together with librarians to provide assistance, and a congenial atmosphere for interaction and discussion. A local music centre might provide specialized digital synthesis, recording and playback capabilities, together with access to online recorded music sources, to become a focus of musical culture. A craft centre might provide access to laser cutters and other CAD/CAM equipment, a teenage hangout might be focused upon video game culture, and so on.

Establish community networks

It has often been observed that there is a choice between surfing the Web at home and going to the pub or café to hang out with your friends and neighbours. From this it is easy to jump to the conclusion that there is an inherent conflict between the development of online, geographically distributed 'virtual communities' and the vitality of local neighbourhood life.[6] In fact, electronic and face-to-face interactions do not directly substitute for one another. There are, as I have noted, different cost structures and benefits, and there are complementarity effects as well as substitution effects. And there is growing empirical evidence that electronic interaction can work to *reconnect* the disaffiliated.[7] So, instead of positing an irreconcilable opposition, it is better to seek the mix of electronic and face-to-face interactions that most effectively strengthens local community interactions and provides most effective access to local community assets.[8]

Consider, for example, the case of a customer

Above and Right:
The Cyberia Café was London's first neighbourhood-based internet café

who wants to purchase some product and runs a Web search to find a retailer who offers it. If nearby retailers do *not* have a Web presence, then the customer will take his or her business out of the community – to a more distant store that *does* have a Web presence, or to an online retailer. But, if local retailers show up in the search, there is a good chance that their greater convenience will win them the business – especially if the customer's browser sorts responses by geographic proximity. And limitations on acceptable delivery time (as, for example, with hot pizza) reinforce this effect.

One way to gain the benefits of neighbourhood networking is to create a comprehensive community portal, that is, a Web site with links to local businesses and institutions, directories and search capabilities, notice boards of events, jobs listings, news, and chat rooms. This requires a substantial investment in development and upkeep from a project developer, volunteer community group, or commercial enterprise that hopes (directly or indirectly) to make money out of the service. Another way is to provide incentives and support for local organizations to develop their own, individual capabilities in more piecemeal fashion. In any case, though, network infra-structure will do little to support the *local* community unless the software is there to take effective advantage of it for this purpose. And networking *without* such software simply directs attention out of the community, while providing nothing to counterbalance this.

There are lessons to be learned, here, from the experience of large organizations – corporations, universities, and government departments – with the Internet and the World Wide Web. These organizations swiftly learned that connectivity serves two distinct purposes – to enhance *internal* intercommunication and cohesiveness, and to maintain *external* linkages. Intranets emerged to provide the former function, and Extranets to provide the latter.

Enhance access to local resources

For local institutions, such as schools, religious centres and community groups, a neighbourhood Intranet provides an effective way to reach their constituencies, and to make their resources available to those constituencies. For individuals, email lists of neighbours, community issue chat rooms, and the like provide efficient ways to disseminate information, to advertise events, to provide danger warnings and support neighbourhood watch functions, and to organize for various local purposes. And for local government, online town meetings and committee deliberations can provide effective new ways to engage citizens.

In general, the techniques that have been developed to tie together geographically distributed, online, 'virtual' communities[9] and to accumulate social capital within those communities, also work very effectively at a neighbourhood scale.[10] If local businesses and institutions are effectively represented online, they can compete for attention and patronage with more distant ones, and their proximity will often give them an edge. Online community message centres can perform more effectively than notice boards on the village green, bells, minarets and sirens to summon the community, or old-fashioned town criers. Social interaction depends upon more than geographic proximity; a key strategy is to use networking and software to make introductions and connections that lead *to* face-to-face encounters.

There are also some potential scale economies. Universities, for example, centrally negotiate access to expensive online databases, then make these services available (with security controls) to registered members of their communities; this is generally far less expensive than obtaining multiple individual subscriptions. The same might be done by local schools and community organizations.

Create a live/work neighbourhood

Information work now constitutes a large and growing proportion of economic activity in developed parts of the world, and it is (as we have seen) mobile and reconfigurable. It can often be performed by individuals operating from modestly-scaled workplaces, and it does not necessarily demand massive concentrations of workers, tall towers, or large building footprints. Unlike industrial and earlier forms of office work, it is not incompatible with residential land uses and domestic buildings, and it can be integrated seamlessly into residential neighbourhoods. In other words, we now have the possibility of reinventing a vigorous pre-industrial urban pattern – the live/work neighbourhood – for the post-industrial era.

There is little evidence, it must be emphasized, that large communities of full-time telecommuters are likely to develop. There are still good reasons for going to the office, and for visiting collaborators and clients. But electronics and networking have certainly encouraged more flexibility in choices of workplaces and working hours. For growing numbers of information workers, shifting part of their work to the home provides opportunities to eliminate unnecessary commutes, to avoid distractions, to continue working when immobilized by injury or illness, and to combine work with child care or elderly care responsibilities.[11]

One necessary condition for successful exploitation of this trend, and development of lively live/work neighbourhoods is provision of a fast, reliable, inexpensive telecommunications infrastructure. This may not be much of a differentiator in urban areas that are generally well served by such infrastructure. But it can provide a significant competitive advantage to developments in more isolated scenic areas, and it can boost the attractiveness of rehabilitated historic neighbourhoods.

A second necessary condition is construction of housing that incorporates sufficient, appropriately configured space for working. You might occasionally work at the kitchen table, or boot up your laptop on the living room couch, but

Right:
The new mixed-use neighbourhood for San Francisco's Mission Bay includes an extensive information technology infrastructure

Below:
A new tramway along the Embarcadero will efficiently connect Mission Bay to the rest of San Francisco

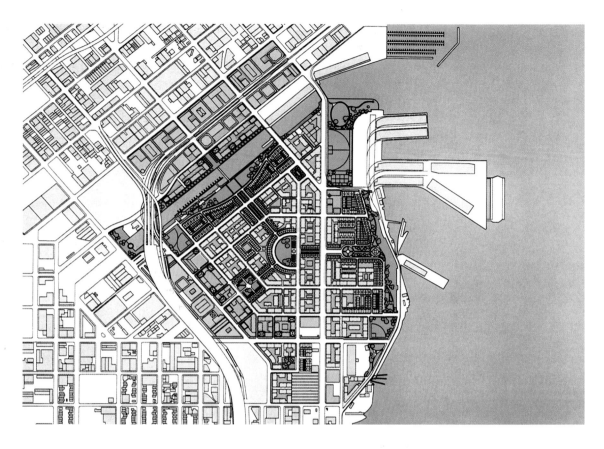

the shift of substantial quantities of daily work to the home creates a demand for quieter, more private workspace that is sufficiently differentiated from other domestic activities. There are many interesting historic prototypes for such live/work zoning, including shop-houses with workspace below on the street and family living space above, the narrow *machiya* townhouses of Kyoto with workspace on the street frontage and increasingly private living space extending back into the block, the lofts of New York artists, and farmhouses with their outbuildings.

A third necessary condition is zoning that allows and encourages these mixed uses. Traditional zoning practices often enforce a rigorous separation of workspace from residential, and this obviously inhibits the emergence of live/work neighbourhoods.

Finally, the neighbourhood should provide competitive levels of workplace amenity. If your neighbourhood is boring and lacking in services, it will not be an attractive place to work long hours; it may be far more stimulating to commute to a central workplace. But if there are scenic attractions, if it provides opportunities to take a break for exercise or recreation, and if it has places to go for a cup of coffee, or to socialize at lunch, then it will exert a stronger hold. In other words, as accessibility becomes less of a competitive advantage for a neighbourhood, local environmental, cultural, and recreational opportunities become correspondingly more crucial.

Reorganize delivery

If you order your groceries online you save a trip to the supermarket, and you can do it whenever you like, not just in opening hours. On the downside, though, you generate a trip to your door by a delivery van, and you have to be home during delivery hours to accept delivery. Nothing much is gained here. For electronic neighbourhoods to work well, we must find ways to gain the potential benefits of electronic commerce while minimizing the downsides.

One potential solution to the delivery problem is to install special delivery receptacles at individual dwellings – an elaboration of the idea of the mailbox at the front door. These receptacles might be sufficiently capacious to accept groceries and the like, they might be provided with electronic security systems to prevent tampering and theft, and they might have refrigerated compartments to handle perishable items. They eliminate the need to wait for the delivery van, but they still generate door-to-door van trips.

A more radical solution (which might be combined with front-door delivery receptacles) is to develop the neighbourhood convenience store into a delivery drop-off, temporary storage, and pick-up point. This builds upon the old idea of a local post office with a bank of mail delivery boxes for individual addressees. From the viewpoint of suppliers it is very efficient, since all the deliveries to a neighbourhood can be combined and dropped off at a central point. From a resident's viewpoint it works if the local circulation system is sufficiently pleasant and efficient. (You might either drop in to pick up your deliveries or rely upon a secondary, less intrusive, local delivery system to get your deliveries to your door.) And, if it generates sufficient drop-in traffic, it produces a 'village well' effect and strengthens local community.

Support a local centre

One of the advantages of pre-industrial, mixed-use neighbourhoods was their 24-hour population, which enabled them to support local services. By contrast, bedroom suburbs are often sparsely populated during the day when commuting workers are gone, and downtown business districts are similarly dead at night when the commuters go home. But networked live/work neighbourhoods are much less affected by this ebb and flow of population. Effectively, their population densities are higher, and they are thus better able to support local cafés and restaurants, business centres, health and recreation clubs, playgrounds, and daycare and elderly care centres.[12]

This provides the opportunity to create a viable local community centre. In addition to the standard sorts of commercial, recreational and community facilities, such a centre might also contain community technology centres and pick-up/drop-off points, as discussed above.

To make this pattern work, the centre must have convenient access to regional transportation networks, and the local circulation system must weave live/work residential areas closely around the centre. The traditional configuration of a High Street surrounded by residential blocks can elegantly satisfy these requirements. The crucial strategies are (1) to adhere to the time-honoured principle of clearly articulating the difference between small-scale, slow-paced local movement networks and long-distance, high-speed, regional networks, (2) to avoid mixing the two, and (3) to use the neighbourhood centre as the interface point.

Some examples

Since the digital telecommunications boom began in the early 1990s, these strategies have increasingly begun to appear, in various combinations, in neighbourhood developments. It has become commonplace, for example, for developers to offer high-speed network access, together with internal data wiring in businesses and dwellings, as selling points. There have also been grassroots initiatives to provide neighbourhood wireless access based upon the IEEE 802.11 standard[13] and inexpensive wireless base stations and communication cards.

The idea of community networks predates the Web era, and goes back to such pioneering efforts as the Berkeley Community Memory network, the Santa Monica Public Electronic Network (PEN), the Blacksburg Electronic Village, and the Cleveland Free-Net. An appendix to Douglas Schuler's 1996 survey *New Community Networks*[14] provides an extensive listing, and typing the name of any community into a Web search engine now stands a good chance of turning up an example.

Among the early attempts to design villages and neighbourhoods around the new capabilities of digital telecommunications were ParcBIT[15] (Balearic Park of Innovative Technology) in Majorca, the Malmö Bo01 'City of Tomorrow', and the Mawson Lakes[16] development on the outskirts of Adelaide, South Australia. Mawson Lakes –

though flawed in some ways – does provide a particularly interesting combination of digital tele-communications infrastructure, live/work space, a local town centre enlivened by educational institutions, and a landscape strategy that emphasizes water features and pedestrian and bicycle ways.

Perhaps the most ambitious and sophisticated example to appear by the opening years of the twenty-first century has been Playa Vista, adjacent to the Pacific Ocean on the Westside of Los Angeles.[17] The 1,087 acre site, comprising former industrial and airport land in the heart of the (mostly) affluent and densely populated Westside, has development plans for 5,800 housing units. The first phase, scheduled to be completed between 2005 and 2006, consists of approximately 3,200 residential units, 26,000 sq ft of retail and 5–6 million sq ft of office space. Advanced digital infrastructure and a community Intranet (PlayaLink) are planned, and the development targets information workers – particularly in the areas of software and digital content, entertainment, biotechnology, and professional services. There is a business centre designed by a team of architects including Frank Gehry, there is a strong emphasis upon recreational and open space, and the on-site circulation system emphasizes pedestrian and bicycle ways, combined with an electric tramway system. The development vigorously seeks to capitalize on the climatic and recreational advantages of the Southern California coastland, and the promotional Web site offers a digital video entitled 'Walk to Work'.

Conclusion: combine the advantages of local and global

The strategies that I have outlined, taken together, provide a way to resolve a fundamental contradiction. It is not hard to make the case that fine-grained, mixed-use, traditionally-structured villages and neighbourhoods have many attractive qualities. Jane Jacobs did so with passion and eloquence.[18] More recently, the American New Urbanists have developed the arguments in detail.[19] And many of the examples presented in this volume are immediately compelling. But there

is always a nagging question: What do you actually *do* in these sorts of places? How do you escape from the traditional problem of small-scale settlements – that local economic, social, and cultural opportunities are very limited? How do you avoid having to choose between the *Gemeinschaft* of the village and the *Gesellschaft* of the big city? How do you dodge those little-town blues that sent Frank Sinatra running for New York, New York?

On close inspection, it turns out that some of the recent developments that follow neo-traditional urban design principles are recreational or retirement communities, or mixtures of the two. Some are collections of vacation homes at scenic locations. Others are counter-culture eco-communes, supporting themselves through small-scale agricultural or craft production. Yet others are proffered as alternatives to standard bedroom suburb developments within large metropolitan

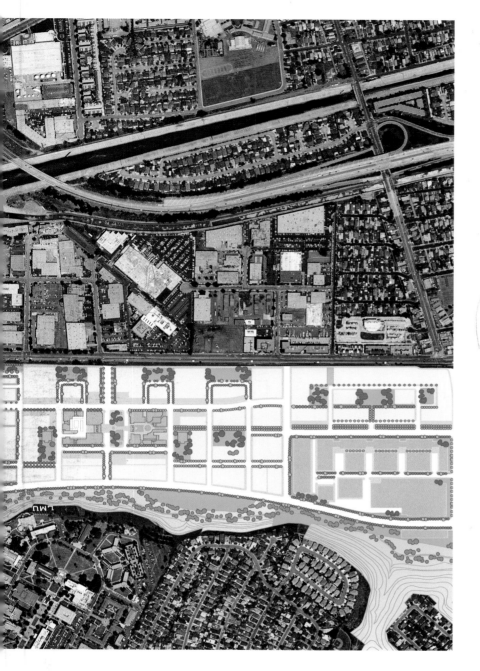

local character you want, what do you do?

As we have now seen, the combination of digital telecommunications infrastructure with live/work development can provide a community with a vital, twenty-first century economic base. By reducing the emphasis upon daily commuting to distant workplaces and service sites, this creates the conditions for local, face-to-face interaction, for supporting local service businesses, and for accumulating social capital. Urban designers and developers can take advantage of the resulting opportunity to create viable local centres, and local pedestrian and bicycle circulation systems. Simultaneously, the telecommunications infrastructure can keep residents closely in touch with a wider world, and the economic, social, and cultural opportunities that this wider world affords. Digital technology provides a new way to resolve the ancient conflict between our need to come together to form communities and our need to separate out our activities and distribute them across distinct, specialized spaces.

regions, and depend upon the assumption that inhabitants will commute to workplaces elsewhere in those regions and travel extensively to find services and recreational opportunities. This is all perfectly fine, as far as it goes. But what seems to be missing, in general, is a compelling vision of local vitality within a post-industrial, globalizing world. If pre-industrial patterns of local enterprise and employment are no longer viable, and if industrial development is incompatible with the

Part Two

Design principles for urban villages

This section establishes the key design principles needed for the creation of urban villages and mixed-use neighbourhoods. It demonstrates that the making of community is far more complex than a purely architectural activity – for the physical creation of place is but part of the challenge. Successful communities are not just built, but are developed and nurtured through a synthesis of activities that include the creation of a good urban form, clear social structure, economic purpose and supported by integrated modes of transport. The following chapters focus on the design, connectivity and social facilities that, when combined, create vibrant and sustainable urban districts.

Neighbourhood Design in Practice explores the key urban design and architectural foundations for establishing good neighbourhoods. Essentially this is about creating a legible and defined urban form

of appropriate density to provide a framework for detailed development and future change. Within this structure a clear hierarchy of streets, buildings, and public and private spaces must be established. Beyond the functional requirements of pedestrians and vehicles, the urban environment needs to be able to support and encourage spontaneous and organized social activity. In order to to fulfil the initial aspirations of the masterplan and to safeguard the aesthetic of the project, the architectural form and the building process should ideally be managed by established and accepted design codes and guidance.

Connectivity and movement describes the key principles required to establish and maintain well-connected neighbourhoods. At the outset urban village design should put people first and the well-being of the pedestrian should be considered of paramount importance. Good networks for pedestrians and cyclists and efficient public transport will make a significant contribution to environmental quality and sustainability. In reversing the traditional bias towards private transport, vehicles need to be accommodated through an established hierarchy of safe and attractive streets that have adequate provision for servicing and parking. Although one of the expressed objectives for urban villages is that they are able to serve the everyday needs of those who live within the community, it is also an economic necessity and social advantage for each community to be well connected to adjacent neighbourhoods and districts.

The social dynamic recognizes the fundamental role that a diverse social fabric plays within any successful community. In past decades many planned urban districts created peripheral, mono-cultural and disconnected housing estates that have limited communal facilities, shops, services and public transport. It is essential that new urban neighbourhoods respect and facilitate a complex range of social activities and networks, for much of this provides the lifeblood and vitality of most of our communities. The nurturing of community must go beyond the simple provision of shops, health centres and community buildings to meet the needs of a broad demographic and social structure. In addition to the central role played by schools within the community, the needs of children should be appreciated and met through imaginative and safe opportunities for play and established routes for walking and cycling. Of particular social value is the articulation of public spaces that allow for both spontaneous interaction and organized social activity.

Chapter 4

Neighbourhood design in practice

Andrés Duany

The previous chapters provide an argument for the fundamental role that the neighbourhood plays in the creation of human communities. This chapter sets out the techniques that foster such environments, and although the terminology used to describe them may vary on opposite sides of the Atlantic, the principles for their creation remain the same.

Left:
**The Octagon Café at
Poundbury in Dorchester**

Above:
Many historic towns and cities, including Charleston in South Carolina, provide invaluable examples of good urbanism

Right:
An initial plan for Poundbury in Dorchester sought to articulate the urban quarter with a clearly defined axial structure
Leon Krier

Neighbourhood precedents

Whether placed within cities or extending them, neighbourhoods have similar characteristics. The surviving historical examples have an innate ability to nurture and maintain fruitful communities. As Christopher Alexander suggests, the pattern of the neighbourhood fulfils the social need to find 'an identifiable spatial unit to belong to'. People want to be able to recognize their part of the city as being distinct and to feel a sense of collective ownership and pride.

For reasons that are unclear, since the 1930s the practice of urban design has pursued the social benefits attributed to neighbourhoods while remaining intent on ignoring the physical neighbourhood pattern. Cities have suffered greatly from strategies that segregated functions and privileged vehicular movement. Although efficient and economic in terms of construction and management, the resulting places have a record of dismal social performance over the longer term. It is interesting to note that ecologists have warned that comparable monocultures in the natural world are inherently unstable.

The New Urbanism in the United States and the Urban Village movement in Britain have sought to address these failures by reassessing those places that continue to work well. The role of the traditional neighbourhood, for instance, has been at the heart of this process. It is central to the *Charter for the New Urbanism*,[1] which sees such neighbourhoods as the basis for the human habitat.

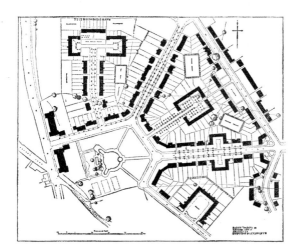

Right:
Part of Parker and Unwin's plan for Hampstead Garden Suburb

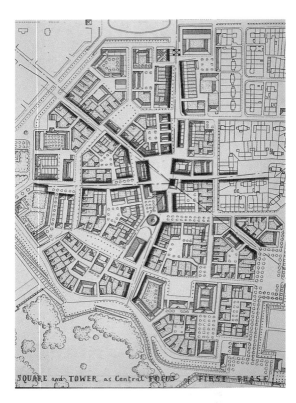

SQUARE and TOWER as Central FOCUS of FIRST PHASE

It has been possible to observe that the neighbourhood has been an empirical component of villages, towns and cities from time immemorial. An early rationalization of the neighbourhood can be attributed to Raymond Unwin, Ebenezer Howard's lead architect of the garden city movement. Unwin's *Town Planning in Practice*, first published in 1909, remains one of the most useful manuals. 'The communities that stand today as a result of its prescriptions are still successful in many ways that matter. This can be said of many places, including Letchworth, Hampstead Garden Suburb and Welwyn in England, and of Coral Gables, Forest Hills and Mariemont in the United States.'[2]

The current theoretical framework that re-establishes this approach to urban planning is underpinned by the writings of Leon Krier and the work of Christopher Alexander. The latter produced an influential series of manuals, including *A Pattern Language*,[3] and the impact of Krier's long-term campaign to reinvigorate town planning cannot be underestimated. It was Krier who refocused attention on the role of the urban quarter, or neighbourhood, as the fundamental urban component.

Below:

The network of thorough-fares is the principle structuring device of the urban pattern

As featured in *The Lexicon of the New Urbanism*/ Duany Plater-Zyberk

At present, government-sponsored urban design guidance in Britain and *The Lexicon of the New Urbanism* in the United States are the primary publications of neighbourhood-based planning.

Town planning in practice

Almost a century has passed since Unwin's *Town Planning in Practice* was first published, yet it still provides a comprehensive response to the requisites of urban design; its techniques optimize urban density and financial return without neglecting function and liveability. Five lessons are provided in the pages of Unwin's book:

– learn from precedent;
– respect the individuality of places;
– promote civic art and life;
– establish a clear urban structure; and
– maintain the harmony of the whole.

Learn from precedent

Study of existing models was fundamental to Unwin's practice, and his book includes copious documentation of established places. Yet he was explicit about the need to interpret them. 'Though the study of old towns and their buildings is most useful, nay, is almost essential to any due appreciation of the subject, we must not forget that we cannot, even if we would, reproduce

SAVANNAH PATTERN

Advantages
Excellent directional orientation
Controllable lot depth
Provides end grain of blocks for fast traffic
Even dispersal of traffic through the web
Straight lines enhance rolling terrain
Efficient double-loading of alleys and utilities

Disadvantages
Monotonous unless periodically interrupted
Does not easily absorb environmental interruptions
Unresponsive to steep terrain
Syn.: **Orthogonal Grid, Gridiron**

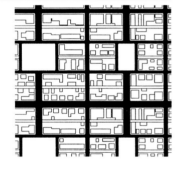

NANTUCKET PATTERN

Advantages
Hierarchy with long routes for through traffic
Even dispersal of traffic through web
Responsive to terrain
Easily absorbs environmental interruptions
Monotony eliminated by terminated vistas
Follows traces on the landscape

Disadvantages
Uncontrollable variety of blocks and lots

Syn.: **Sitte Model, Townscape**

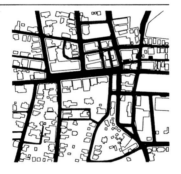

MARIEMONT PATTERN

Advantages
Hierarchy with diagonals for through traffic
Even dispersal of traffic through the web
Monotony interrupted by deflected vistas
Diagonal intersections spatially well-defined

Disadvantages
Tends to be disorienting
Syn.: **Unwin Model, Spider Web**

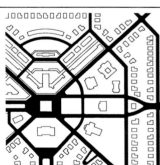

WASHINGTON PATTERN

Advantages
Hierarchy with diagonals for through traffic
Even dispersal of traffic through the grid
Diagonals focus on terrain features
Diagonals interrupt monotony of the grid

Disadvantages
Uncontrollable variety of lots
High number of awkward lot shapes
Diagonal intersections spatially ill-defined
Syn.: **City Beautiful, Haussmann Model**

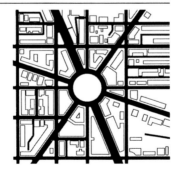

RIVERSIDE PATTERN

Advantages
Monotony interrupted by deflected vistas
Easily absorbs environmental interruptions
Highly responsive to terrain
Even dispersal of traffic through the web

Disadvantages
Highly disorienting
Uncontrollable variety of lots
No intrinsic hierarchy
Syn.: **Olmstedian**

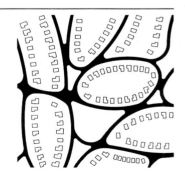

RADBURN PATTERN

Advantages
Good street hierarchy for locals and collectors
Controllable variety of blocks and lots
Easily absorbs environmental interruptions
Responsive to terrain

Disadvantages
Congestion of traffic by absence of web
Syn.: **Cul-De-Sac**

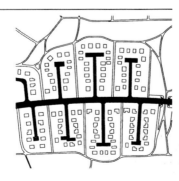

Above:
**Creating a strong sense
of community was the
primary goal for the initial
concept of Seaside, Florida**
Duany Plater-Zyberk

the conditions under which they were created'.[4] Historical places should be assessed dispassionately for the practical lessons they offer to the present, and no more. Planners must be neither nostalgic like traditional architects nor ideological like the modernist ones; urbanism must remain dedicated to whatever works best in the long run.

Respect the individuality of places

Building on the work of Patrick Geddes, who was the first to call for a comprehensive city survey to ensure 'diagnosis before treatment', Unwin states that 'the designer's first duty must be to study the town, the site, the people and their requirements'. Too often masterplans fail to enhance the existing fabric and spirit of the place. Most such schemes are born out of corporate or global economies that favour the standardization of products.

Through systematic observation, Unwin uncovers the personality of each site. 'There are in each certain settled characteristics arising from the nature of the scenery, the colours of the local building materials, the life of citizens, the character of the industries prevalent in the district,

Above:
Diagram of the distribution of public and private buildings at Seaside, Florida
Duany Plater-Zyberk

Above right:
The design of individual buildings at Seaside is guided by an urban code that supports the urban plan

and numerous other circumstances, which taken all together go to make up that flavour which gives to the town its individuality'.

Promote civic art and life

Unwin sought to instil high purpose in town planning; urging that we look beyond the 'mere aggregation of people', to the making of community. This requires a plan that anticipates the evolution of a community. From the outset it is important to allocate places for public needs, even if these may be implemented much later. In addition to the basic elements of dwelling, commerce and streets, the plan should establish public places in the form of parks, squares and civic buildings.

Unwin stresses the need to infuse artistic endeavour into this work. He calls for 'the vivifying touch of art which would give completeness and increase value tenfold'. Beauty, he observes, 'is an elusive quality, not easily defined, not always easily attained by direct effort, and yet is a necessary element in all good work'.

Establish a clear urban structure

Unwin then turns to the process of establishing an overall order. Attention should be paid to neighbourhood boundaries and approaches for the contribution that these make to identifiable character. Although today the definition of boundary is not that of ancient towns, Unwin suggests that 'we take [the] most pregnant suggestions of the value of defining and limiting towns, suburbs and new areas'. Overall urban growth boundaries have become a common tool in maximizing density and land use efficiency; their value at the scale of the neighbourhood is less important. As Krier says, 'A centre is a necessity, an edge is a luxury.'

Unwin then sets out the argument for memorable urban centres. Central public places provided the economic, social and informational focus for the community and the hinterland beyond. Although their practical purpose has been greatly eroded by telecommunications and private transport, central spaces still perform a necessary role in social life. Such centres must be enclosed by buildings that bring activity and a sense of place.

The proportion of enclosure should be carefully considered to provide a sense of completeness and repose; set the buildings too far apart and the space disappears into an unpopulated non-place.

The arrangement of thoroughfares and the planning of each block is the middle scale of detail. Beyond their role in circulation, thoroughfares determine the structure of a neighbourhood. An analysis of network patterns drawn from precedent in the United States show that regular patterns, including the familiar gridiron, offer an equitable division of building plots. These may be progressively modified by the addition of diagonal routes. Then irregular web patterns offer the agility to continuously respond to specific architectural and landscape features, but the resulting lots are irregular. Both have a place in the repertoire of planning.

Maintain the harmony of the whole

Having addressed the plot division, it is important to consider the finer detail of building placement and architectural composition to ensure the compatibility. Today, we often find excessively individualistic building undermining the integrity of the community as a whole.

Maintaining harmony within diversity can be achieved through the adoption of specific codes, and these will be discussed subsequently. Rather than designing all the buildings, which would lead to a 'project' rather than urbanism, codes allow the process of town-building to be a sequential process of development by many hands. The essential thing is that it shall be as little artificial as possible, that it shall be a spontaneous growth following traditional lines of development.

Structuring neighbourhoods

Unwin's treatise proved exceedingly popular throughout the early years of the twentieth century: in just over 20 years *Town Planning in Practice* was already on its eighth edition. And then the influence was lost.

Since the 1980s there has been a marked renaissance of Unwin's practices in urban planning, lead by the New Urbanist and smart growth movements in the United States and by the Urban Villages and English Partnerships campaigns in Great Britain. It was no less a reappraisal of Unwin's original contribution than it was a rejection of suburban practices. An early diagram summarized the alternatives posed by conventional suburban development (CSD) and traditional neighbourhood development (TND). The suburban option, illustrated at the top of the drawing, forces everyone to drive and to do so on the few collector roads. Alternatives for pedestrians, cyclists and even public transport become non-existent. The lifestyle options of such suburban places are severely restricted. Children, for example, have to be driven everywhere for even the most basic activities, such as attending school and playing with friends.

The neighbourhood structure pictured on the bottom half of the diagram includes all the same components but is configured differently. The network of thoroughfares allows flexible access to all uses and activities, since homes are in close effective proximity to schools and shops. Walking and cycling become real alternatives. Such a network encourages a degree of completeness; the ordinary daily shopping outlets, basic health facilities, nursery and primary school, some workplaces, along with recreational and governance facilities, can all be accommodated within its boundaries. The ideal for these neighbourhoods is that they are compact, pedestrian-friendly and diverse in terms of function and tenure.

These principles were summarized by the New York planner, Clarence Perry, in his influential diagram of 1929, conceptualized as the Neighbourhood Unit. Until the post-war period this pattern was the form of urban development preferred by both government and the private sector in the United States. Perry based the numerical size of the neighbourhood on the number of families required to support a primary school. He established the spatial size by the five-minute walking circle of a quarter-mile radius drawn over his diagrammatic plan.

Perry provided six principles for the Neighbourhood Unit: [5]

– the population needed for one elementary school should determine the size of a residential neighbourhood (about 750–1,500 families on 60–120 hectares);
– wide arterial roads that eliminate through traffic to the neighbourhood should form a boundary to the neighbourhood;
– within the neighbourhood there should be a hierarchy of streets, each designed to minimum widths and set out to discourage through traffic;
– streets and open spaces should make up at least 40 per cent of any neighbourhood;
– schools and other communal institutions should be grouped around a central point in the neighbourhood; and,
– shopping areas adequate for the size of the population should be placed at the edges of the neighbourhood, and adjacent to arterial traffic.

Right:
The comparison between low-density sprawl (top) and the design of traditional neighbourhoods (bottom)

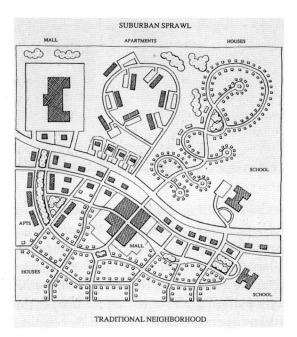

SUBURBAN SPRAWL

TRADITIONAL NEIGHBORHOOD

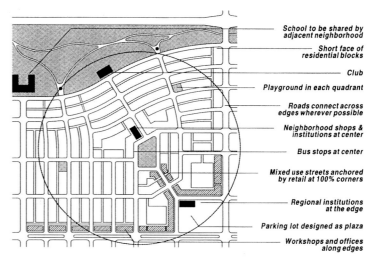

NEIGHBORHOOD UNIT 1927

- Regional institutions at the edge
- Pedestrian shed one-quarter mile radius
- Neighborhood institutions and schools within
- Civic space at center
- High capacity thoroughfares at the edge
- Many playgrounds
- Shopping at traffic junctions at the edge

TRADITIONAL NEIGHBORHOOD DEVELOPMENT 1997

- School to be shared by adjacent neighborhood
- Short face of residential blocks
- Club
- Playground in each quadrant
- Roads connect across edges wherever possible
- Neighborhood shops & institutions at center
- Bus stops at center
- Mixed use streets anchored by retail at 100% corners
- Regional institutions at the edge
- Parking lot designed as plaza
- Workshops and offices along edges

- **Neighborhood Unit:** A diagram and description from the First Regional Plan of New York (1927) which conceptualizes the neighborhood as the fundamental element of planning.

Size is determined by the walking distance of five minutes from center to edge, rather than by number of residents. Density is determined by the market. A community coalescing within a walkable area is the invariant.

An elementary school is at the center, within walking distance of most children. This is the most useful civic building, providing a meeting place for the adult population as well.

Local institutions are located within the neighborhood. Regional institutions are placed at the edges so that their traffic does not enter the neighborhood.

There is a civic open space at the center of the neighborhood, and several smaller playgrounds, one in close proximity to every household.

A network of small thoroughfares within the neighborhood disperses local traffic.

Larger thoroughfares channel traffic at the edges.

Retail is confined to the junction having the most traffic, accepting the realities of the automobile.

- **Neighborhood Development:** A diagram that updates the Neighborhood Unit and reconciles current models.

The school is not at the center but at an edge, as the playing fields would hinder pedestrian access to the center. The school at the edge can be shared by several neighborhoods, mitigating the problem created by the tendency of neighborhoods to age in cohorts generating large student age populations that then drop off sharply.

There are few sites reserved for local institutions at the center and more for regional institutions at the edge. Ease of transportation has made membership in institutions a matter of proclivity rather than proximity.

The shops at the busiest intersections have been modified to accommodate larger parking plazas for convenience retail and extended by an attached main street for destination and live-work retail.

More service alleys and lanes have been added to accommodate the increased parking requirements.

The minor thoroughfares are connected with those outside the neighborhood in order to increase permeability and disperse traffic. This modification, however, increases the possibility of shortcuts.

The thoroughfare types support a transect from rectilinear streets at the urban center to curvilinear roads toward the rural edge.

The traffic along the boulevards at the edges is more unpleasant than originally envisioned. Three mitigating strategies are proposed: the provision of an end-grain of blocks at all edges, a green buffer shown along the bottom edge, and the location of resilient building types, such as office buildings, shown along the bottom edge.

The traffic along the highway shown at the top is assumed to be hostile and therefore buffered within a parkway.

Above:
Perry's Neighbourhood Unit, 1927, and Traditional Neighbourhood Development, 1997
As featured in *The Lexicon of the New Urbanism/* Duany Plater-Zyberk

Although the terminology and detailed characteristics may vary, these principles are currently embodied in a number of models that include Urban Villages, Traditional Neighbourhood Developments, Transit Oriented Developments (TODs), Liveable Neighbourhoods and Leon Krier's Quarter.

Urban Villages

In Britain's Urban Village campaign, community size was seen to be crucial; the village must be large enough to offer the variety of activities that support ordinary life, yet small enough to ensure that all the necessary facilities are within walking distance. Parameters of the Urban Village include:

– a combined resident and working population of 3,000–5,000 people, accommodated in about 40 hectares;

– a range of uses that should be mixed within the neighbourhood, block and building, where feasible;

– a theoretical ratio of 1:1 between jobs and residents able and willing to work as well as the provision of opportunities for individuals who may wish to work from home; and

– a good mix of tenure for housing that would enhance the socio-economic structure of the neighbourhood and accommodate the needs of individuals, families, students and the elderly.

Traditional Neighbourhood Developments

TNDs are seen as the fundamental human habitat, providing a community that satisfies a full range of ordinary human needs.[6] American TNDs reflect the characteristics of British Urban Villages and both

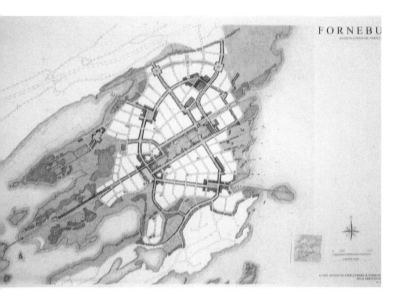

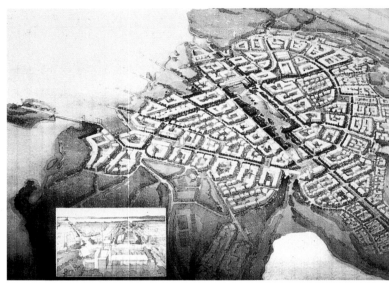

FORNEBU

follow the spirit of Perry's Neighbourhood Unit. TNDs ensure that:

– the size and shape is defined by a five-minute walk from the neighbourhood centre to its perimeter. About 70 per cent of the developed area should be within this 'pedestrian shed';
– local civic and social facilities are placed at the centre of the neighbourhood, while other civic buildings of regional importance and the retail are located at the edge, to be shared by a number of neighbourhoods; and
– schools are at the edge of the neighbourhood so that student population is not limited to the age profile of a single neighbourhood.

Transit Oriented Development

TODs follow the majority of TND principles but focus around transit lines. They are capable of supporting regional commercial and public facilities. The characteristics establish that:

– the size of each neighbourhood should be able to support a walking distance of up to ten minutes from the core commercial area and transit stop, although this will vary with the characteristics of each specific site;
– the needs of the integrated public transit structure at a regional scale supports the detailed elements of specific neighbourhoods; and

– higher density housing and key retail, institutional and social facilities are placed at the stations of the transit network.

Liveable Neighbourhoods

The Western Australian Planning Commission has followed a similar approach for the Sustainable Cities Initiative, which it launched in the mid-1990s. The characteristics of Liveable Neighbourhoods reflect the familiar themes that:

– define the standard five-minute walk from the neighbourhood centre to its perimeter;
– locate neighbourhood centres at major street junctions in support of the retail framework;
– locate large parks and schools between neighbourhoods to ensure that they are accessible on foot from adjacent neighbourhoods; and
– suggest that public transit is set at both the core of the neighbourhood and at the intersection of major streets to support retail activity.

Summary of the model

These principles are now firmly established within the lexicon and practice of New Urbanism. They have been formalized through the Charter and the Congress for the New Urbanism[7] and they are increasingly being adopted within the mainstream

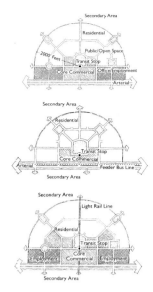

Above:
**Transit-Oriented
Development (TOD)
incorporating feeder bus
routes and light rail**
Calthorpe Associates

planning profession. Under the auspices of the Department of Housing and Urban Development (HUD), for example, the Clinton administration incorporated these standards to the new guidelines for public housing. They are now embedded into the HOPE VI programme by the HUD publication, *New American Neighbourhoods: Building Homeownership Zones to Revitalize Our Nation's Communities*.[8]

Similar official endorsement has taken place in the UK, as described in David Lock's chapter on planning for sustainable communities. The final report of the Government's Urban Task Force clearly supports the virtues of mixed-use neighbourhoods, focusing on the geographic provision of public amenities – shops, schools, community and business facilities – near to neighbourhood centres. The subsequent Urban White Paper reinforced many of these principles and has become a central component of the government's planning policy and guidance.[9]

The framework of the transect

Having addressed structure, one may now focus on the character of the urbanism. Although projects may fulfil the requirements of a particular site and programme, they also have an obligation to the wider urban context. Neighbourhoods must work together, while retaining their character. The framework of the transect offers a declension of possible associations of urban elements.

Familiar to the discipline of ecology, the transect is an ordering system that arranges a sequence of natural habitats. It has proved a particularly useful way to detect transitions and distribution patterns. The transect can be extended to the human habitat as a means of creating a coherent rural-to-urban gradient. In addition to providing a system of classification, the transect is an instrument of design upon which the usually specialized urban components can be correlated.

The earliest presentation of the transect as an intellectual construct can be attributed to Sir Patrick Geddes. His Valley Section diagram,[10] published in 1909, ascribes a series of determined human societies to a simplified geography, distributing hunters, farmers and tradesmen along a landscape section drawn through highlands, foothills and fertile plains to an urbanized coast. The settlement tiers implied by the Valley Section lead from the hamlet through the village and on to the town and city, and present idealized relationships between town and country. The Section provides a useful structure on which to relate economies and ecologies. Urbanism is to be understood as a geographic event as much as a cultural one.

Following re-presentations by in the 1960s, in *Design with Nature*, published in 1969,[11] and in Alexander's patterns in *A Pattern Language* of 1977, the transect is evolving into a comprehensive planning system for the USA, an alternative to the current system of zoning. In the UK, the 1997 Essex Design Guide uses a 'Spectrum of Visual Density', similar to a transect to provide a framework for the relationship between specialized urban elements. In both systems, all such elements can then be placed within a common rural-to-urban continuum: a street is more urban than a road, a curb more urban than a swale, a brick wall more urban than a wooden fence, and a line of street trees more urban than a cluster. Even the character of streetlights can be assigned within the transect according to the materials from which they are

Right:
**Patrick Geddes'
Valley Section as
published in 1909**

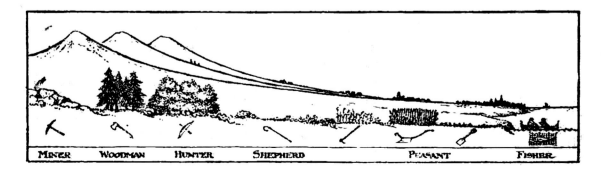

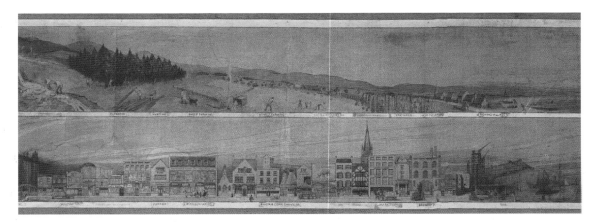

Above:
Celebration, Florida – Disney's version of traditional small-town America includes a large mix of single and multifamily housing

Above right:
The Valley Section and its manifestation in the town, before 1925, from the Patrick Geddes Archive

made: cast iron, extruded pipe or wooden post.

The idealized geographic continuum of the transect can be divided into locally-calibrated tiers that are distributed from Natural to Rural, Sub-urban, General Urban, Urban Centre and Urban Core. In actual application, transect zones are rarely set within a series of concentric circles, for authentic urbanism is often manifested as a mosaic of areas.

Urban Core and Urban Centre

These sections of the community have the greatest mix of uses and the greatest density. Buildings should be larger and flexible in use; they should be attached and their frontages aligned, preferably directly on the footpath. Pavements should be wide enough to accommodate heavy pedestrian flows and activity. Building frontage at the pavement level is primarily dedicated to commercial use.

An Urban Core is at the heart of larger cities, where buildings tend to be tall. An Urban Centre is more common in towns and in neighbourhoods, where the buildings rarely rise above five floors. Core and Centre zones are always located on the busy intersections that tap the energy of the traffic and support public transport.

Open space at Cores and Centres is generally designed in the form of paved plazas and formal squares. Housing tends to consist of flats or terrace houses with densities ranging from 25 to 100 dwellings per hectare. In the Core areas, parking should be accommodated within the centre of blocks in parking structures. In Centre areas, parking lots and garages should be accessed by mews, and on-street parking should be permitted throughout.

General Urban zones

These areas are primarily residential, although there is a measure of mixed use. They are still distinctly urban in character. Streets have raised curbs and sidewalks on both sides. Housing types include a broad range: single houses, semi-detached, terraced and townhouses. Small apartment buildings can be accommodated within this zone, although care must be taken to ensure that they blend with the predominant scale. Smaller businesses that are socially useful are generally in the form of corner shops and cafés. Schools, churches, clinics and other public buildings may also be included. Open space is less formally structured, taking the form of greens and parks.

Setbacks of buildings may range from 4 m to 10 m, and in the United States there will be a preference for porches that should be allowed to encroach on this setback zone. Back alleys/mews should be incorporated so that garages can be located at the rear of the plot. This is particularly important to the narrower plots whose frontage would otherwise be consumed by parking accommodation. Sidewalks should be wide enough to accommodate side-by-side walking, whilst most street trees should be canopied to overlap the front gardens and yards.

Sub-urban zones

The Sub-urban zone once occurred at the edges of cities, towns or villages, marking a gradual transition from the urban to the rural condition. However, as cities expand Sub-urban zones are now captured within the expanded urban fabric,

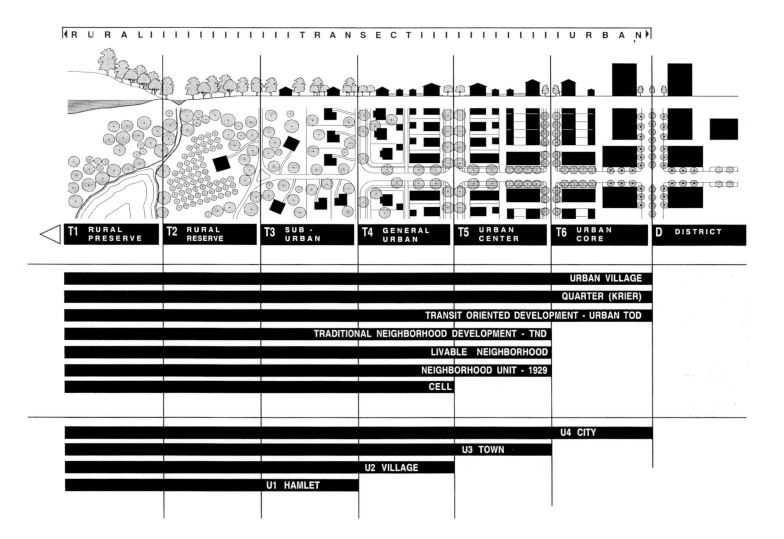

RURAL |||||||||||||||||| TRANSECT |||||||||||||||||| URBAN

T1 RURAL PRESERVE	T2 RURAL RESERVE	T3 SUB-URBAN	T4 GENERAL URBAN	T5 URBAN CENTER	T6 URBAN CORE	D DISTRICT

URBAN VILLAGE

QUARTER (KRIER)

TRANSIT ORIENTED DEVELOPMENT - URBAN TOD

TRADITIONAL NEIGHBORHOOD DEVELOPMENT - TND

LIVABLE NEIGHBORHOOD

NEIGHBORHOOD UNIT - 1929

CELL

U4 CITY

U3 TOWN

U2 VILLAGE

U1 HAMLET

Above:
The Urban Transect
As featured in *The Lexicon of the New Urbanism*
Duany Plater-Zyberk

forming a mosaic of zones rather than the original transition to countryside.

In the USA Sub-urban zones are 'greener' and lower in density than the European equivalents being built today, such as those in Upton in Northampton, and Kirchsteigfeld in Potsdam. The majority of Sub-urban development is dedicated to single-family homes, although the buildings should be available to make a variety of uses, including community and educational activities, possible. Working in the dwelling should be permitted, within specific limits. Plots are larger than in the urban zones, and road patterns tend to be irregular.

Planting is generally informal, with tree clusters. Setbacks are generous and building plots are deeper to accommodate larger gardens. Housing densities may be as low as 10 units per hectare, but only when calculated as an average; some lots are substantially bigger and others smaller. There should be the possibility of increasing density to 30 units per hectare at certain locations.

Rural Reserve and Preserve zones

These zones are beyond the urban edge, on land that should be set apart from development. The Reserve includes land that could be built on in the future, but where development should be delayed to economize on services and infrastructure. On the other hand, the Preserve is to be permanently protected from development and bound by law or purchase to remain as open space. These areas include designated parklands, farmland that has foregone its development rights and environmental areas that have legal protection.

Opposite, above:
**The Poundbury Code
Regulating Plan**

Opposite, below:
**The Urban Code for
Seaside specifies building
type and the spatial
definition of public space**

The role of codes and standards

Many sound urban plans have been compromised by inflexible zoning codes and standards. A new set of design codes should replace the existing ones. Bureaucracies will rarely be dismantled or reformed; however, they will willingly administer new standards.

The New Urbanism now adopts stages to implement a project; from an Illustrative Masterplan with guidelines, to a Regulating Plan with legally binding codes. Such codes provide municipalities with a legal framework to replace an existing standard that precludes the creation of traditional neighbourhoods. These codes are necessary, not to repress creativity but on the contrary to allow buildings to be designed by many hands, for true urbanism requires the sequential influence of many.

Such codes, which have been known as TND Ordinances since 1988, have now come to be called 'smart codes' in support of the popular term 'smart growth'. They still qualify, encourage and entitle TNDs. They may be municipal documents or private covenants administered by the developer or housing association. Conventional ordinances are prophylactic in nature, generally stating what cannot be built, whilst smart codes state what can be built and how to encourage it.

These codes involve a matched set of documents – the Regulating Plan, Urban Standards, Thoroughfare Standards, Architectural Standards, and Landscape Standards. When conceived in support of the transect these provide harmonious environments for each zone of the development.

The Regulating Plan

The Regulating Plan has legal standing and is mandatory (unlike a Masterplan, which is illustrative and persuasive). It comprises a map that: (a) assigns the types of public open space and the thoroughfares; (b) shows the private land subdivided into lots; and (c) indicates the assignment of these lots to transect zones.

Right:
**Regulatory Codes assure
that community
development adheres
to a predetermined
neighbourhood structure**

The Code *consists of five documents used in conjunction:*

REGULATING PLAN
A map precisely locating the various zoning categories. The Regulating Plan also shows the form and location of public open spaces, and the type and trajectories of the various thoroughfares.

URBAN STANDARDS
A matrix of text and diagrams that regulate those aspects of private buildings which affect the public realm. The urban standards vary according to the zoning categories of the Regulating Plan. Theses include the frontage standards which encourage the provision of certain building types and frontage elements that influence social behavior. The urban standards define building function as the uses permitted in each of the zoning categories to various degrees, with emphasis on mixed use wherever possible. Parking needs are correlated to the various uses

THOROUGHFARE STANDARDS
A matrix of drawings, specifications, and dimensions that assembles vehicular and pedestrian ways into types, specialized in both capacity and character. These specify vehicular ways, sidewalks, planters, street trees, and street lights. The combinations range from urban to rural. They are assigned to appropriate locations on the Regulating Plan.

ARCHITECTURAL STANDARDS
A matrix of text that specifies, for private buildings, the materials and configurations permitted for walls, roofs, openings, and other elements intended to produce visual harmony among disparate building types. The standards relate to the vernacular building traditions of the region, thus incorporating a suitable response to climate. Civic buildings are exempt from the architectural standards

LANDSCAPE STANDARDS
A list of plant species with instructions regarding their location and planting pattern. The lists are separated into those pertaining to public areas and to private lots. The planting lists are coordinated toward achieving a coherent landscaping of the urban fabric. The selection and disposition of the planting is intended to support the urban-to-rural transect and to create an ecosystem compatible with the climate and hydrology of the site.

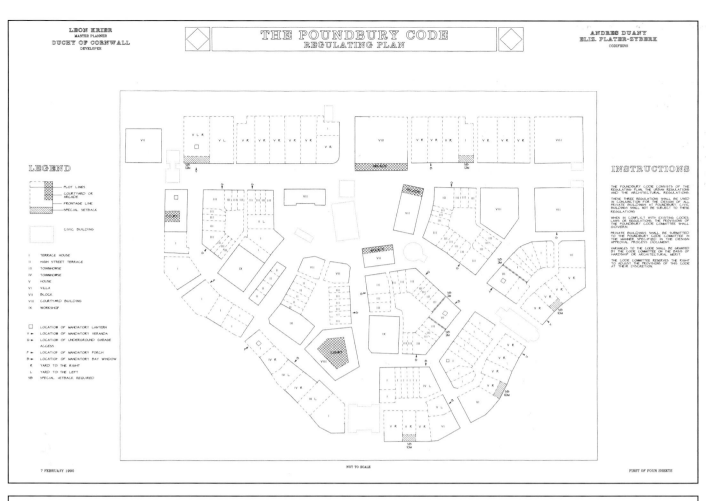

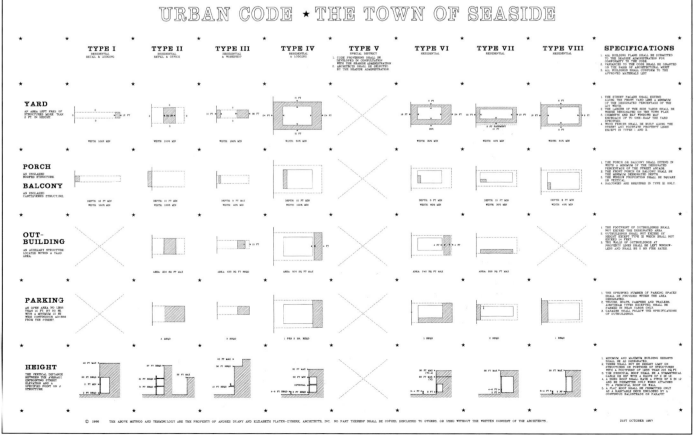

A Master Plan
is illustrative and
compliance is voluntary

*The illustrations are
formulated as guidelines*
▼

Guidelines

are enforceable
by covenant

*The guidelines are translated
to legal language*
▼

A Code
is instructive and
enforceable by
contract

*The Code is enacted
into law*
▼

An Ordinance
is mandatory and
enforced as
municipal law

Urban Standards

The Urban Standards are keyed to the Regulating Plan and describe the parameters of function and disposition of the private buildings. These foster building types that support walkable, compact and diverse urbanism in various intensities, depending on the urban-to-rural character of the applicable transect zone.

Architectural Standards

A set of Architectural Standards encourages a harmonious language for the configuration of the private buildings. The specifications should be derived from the regional vernacular, as interpreted through the local economic and craft practices.

Landscape Standards

These foster private planting compatible with the public streetscape in support of the urban-to-rural transect. The gardens or backyards should remain uncoded, to permit the expression of individual preference.

Categorical Exemptions

Civic buildings should be free from categorization, to ensure freedom of expression and aspiration for the institutions they embody, as well as the full creative freedom of the project architects. Un-constrained civic buildings should be the principal locus for advancing the art of architectural design.

A sequence of design

Urbanism is an intrinsically complex and multidisciplinary activity that by its nature is difficult to summarize succinctly. The following sequence offers one guide to the difficult process. Although some of the techniques are applicable to infill projects, most of them concern larger urban extension and new community projects.

1. Establish the principles of the regional plan

At the outset of a project it is essential that a comprehensive plan at the regional scale be established. Such plans include issues associated with environmental protection and infrastructure provision. The location of development and redevelopment must connect with a regional context that maximizes the potential of transportation and open space.

2. Identify the type of community to be designed

An urban extension should be conceived as a complete TND or its English equivalent, the Urban Village. An entirely new project on a greenfield site may be developed as either a hamlet, a village, or town centre. A hamlet (or cluster development) is appropriate for a location on a simple road, and therefore inevitably destined to have a weak commercial component. A village (or TND) is suitable for busier crossroads locations, and is the programmatic equivalent of a complete urban neighbourhood. A town centre (or transit-oriented development) must be located at a regional transportation nexus that is capable of sustaining the programmatic equivalent of a full shopping centre, with workplaces and civic uses of regional consequence. The regional transportation system, while often car-dependent, should also support rail and buses. Transit options need not be present before the project is complete; transit can follow, as well as lead, development. In all cases, these community programmes should be designed to be compact, walkable and diverse.

3. Locate the site's commercial centre

This should be placed at the thoroughfare or the intersection with the maximum drive-by traffic. This is advisable even if the resulting location is not at the centre of the site. Without traffic, the retail elements will fail to thrive. An exception would be a powerfully attractive location, such as a transit stop or landmark feature, that will draw traffic and pedestrians to itself as a destination.

4. Structure the development pedestrian sheds

A pedestrian shed is equivalent to a five-minute walk from the neighbourhood edge to centre – an area of about 80 hectares. The principal

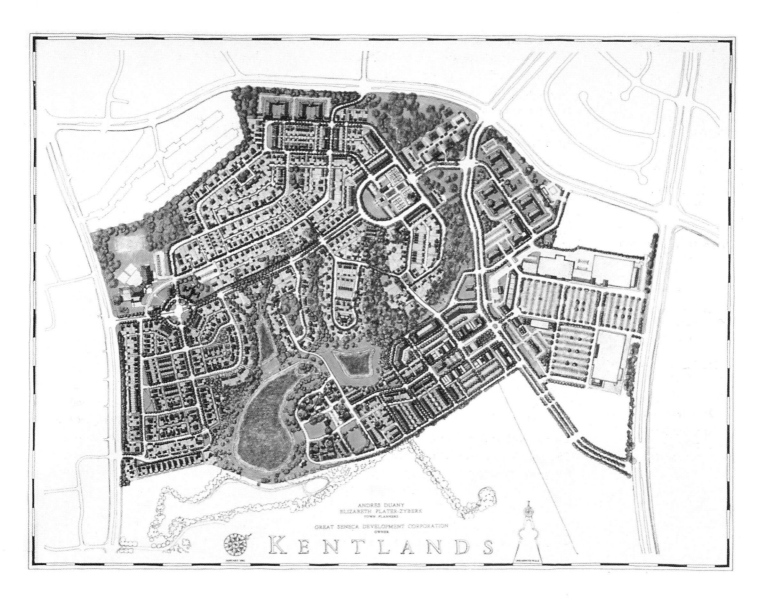

KENTLANDS

ANDRES DUANY
ELIZABETH PLATER-ZYBERK
TOWN PLANNERS

GREAT SENECA DEVELOPMENT CORPORATION
OWNER

Above:
The 356-acre masterplan for the development of Kentlands, Maryland Duany Plater-Zyberk

pedestrian sheds must be pivoted on the previously determined commercial centre. Additional sheds should be arranged to cover the remainder of the development site without substantial overlap. The geographic extent of the pedestrian sheds, rather than a statistically derived density, should define neighbourhood size, which must vary as a function of the housing market.

5. *Incorporate traces of the land, natural or manmade*

Traces must be mapped and assimilated into the plan. Natural traces include ponds, streams and wetlands; these should be kept intact for water management, which becomes critical as the land becomes impervious through development. Wooded areas, specimen trees and ponds should be retained with parks and greens delineated upon them, affording the benefit of mature vegetation from the outset. Hedgerows may provide an initial structure for planted avenues, and vernacular stone walls could provide an alignment for new roads. Existing country paths and lanes embody priceless country wisdom and should influence the trajectories of new thoroughfares wherever possible. A certain innate beauty may result from assimilating such traces of the land, just as they graced pre-modernist communities.

6. Adjust the location of the pedestrian sheds to existing features

This should ensure that, wherever possible, the centres of the pedestrian sheds coincide with meaningful traces of the land. A cluster of specimen trees can be developed as a central green, and a rise or a ford can provide a secondary centre. This process requires a skilful designer's eye as well as a 'lucky site'. Several designers should work on proposals independently, because a single one is less likely to find the key that unlocks an underlying pattern that supports a natural neighbourhood structure. Where traces do not provide a determinant, a public space or a key special intersection should be imposed as the centre of each pedestrian shed.

7. Connect these neighbourhood centres with each other

At this point, the influence of the natural topography and character has been assimilated into the urban network; the main commercial centre has been determined and the pedestrian

sheds of the neighbourhood structure have been outlined. Now, each neighbourhood centre should be connected to the others by larger thoroughfares such as avenues, main streets and high streets. These should be direct but not necessarily straight, as most thoroughfares should follow the natural landform and features.

8. Infill the area between the main thoroughfares

Through the application of secondary routes one should form an efficient and flexible network throughout the urbanized area. This need not be geometrically coherent throughout the entire community and should often take on a localized character. The networks must be adjusted to create a block pattern that is smaller and more permeable when in proximity to a centre, then progressively larger towards the rural edges. The block pattern should then be subdivided into lots that also become larger relative to the buildings that occupy them, to ensure that the ratio of open space becomes progressively more rural towards the edges of the community.

Right:
Kentlands was one of the first new developments to apply traditional neighbourhood design principles

Top:
A group of townhouses at Kentlands, lining the south side of the town commons

Above:
Poundbury's Fleur de Lis building has been designed to respect the visual structure of Krier's original masterplan

9. Detail and code the urban elements in relation to the transect structure

In line with the transect structure discussed earlier, all urban elements should be detailed to support a range of environments from the relatively urban to the relatively rural. The transect provides a system of classification that creates a declension of urban habitats by co-locating the typical elements of urbanism. These provide for a diversity of lifestyles, supporting the needs and preferences of residents. The elements of urbanism allocated by a transect must now be described with the precise language and diagrams that constitute a code. Without a code, a plan remains an illustrated Masterplan to emphasize that it is recommended rather than mandatory, whilst a Regulating Plan is keyed to a code.

10. Reserve sites for civic and community facilities

Civic institutions are as necessary to the well-being of a community as any other element, yet it is often impossible to provide them unless there is public funding or surplus private capital to pay for them. The market generally provides the means to build the private residential and commercial buildings but not the civic buildings that accommodate educational, governmental, recreational, religious and cultural institutions. Sites for local institutions, such as elementary schools, childcare facilities and community halls, should be reserved at the neighbourhood centres. The town centre should provide sites for regional institutions such as secondary schools, government agencies, religious and cultural buildings. If the Regulating Plan preserves such civic sites in perpetuity, it generally proves to be the case that the residents themselves will, over time, bring the civic buildings into being, as and when they are required.

11. Prepare a set of covenants for the community

A community requires local governance to safeguard its long-term character and quality. A set of covenants should be written to be enacted by contract as a condition of the purchase of a lot or a building. Such documents exist, but are usually conceived to protect the prerogatives of the development agency, abrogating all power to itself. Consequently, the community remains restricted, unable to organically adjust to society, culture and economy as they evolve. The covenants should form a community association providing for an elected executive with considerable influence, a role initially played by the developer, balanced by a small deliberative body and an appellate forum. The community association must have the capacity to levy charges that provide for the ongoing maintenance of the public spaces. A small portion of the charges should be allocated in trust for civic improvements, allowing the community over time to decide how such funds are best invested, usually on the reserved civic lots. Such covenants must make reference to the code that guides the ongoing construction of the community.

12. Withdrawal of the planners

At some point during the building-up of the community – after the direction has been firmly set, but while meaningful adjustments are still possible – the original planners and developers should withdraw in favour of a planning office staffed by those who live in the community. For it is only by participating in the daily life as citizens that municipal administrators have standing in the community they govern. Those developers, planners and other professionals who must move on have undergone an apprenticeship in community building, the lessons of which may be applied elsewhere.

Chapter 5

Connectivity and movement

David Taylor

The art of creating successful neighbourhoods must go beyond the physical process of urban planning and architectural design, for in the long term places can only flourish if they are well connected and enjoy a strong and diverse social infrastructure. Creating good patterns of movement must be seen as integral to the complex process of place-making, and should be viewed as much more than simply establishing a basic system for transport and circulation. Good connectivity not only makes a significant contribution to the physical sustainability of new communities, but will also underpin the economic and social vitality of existing neighbourhoods by forging links with adjacent districts and regions. At the macro scale of strategic planning, good connectivity significantly contributes to the release of economic benefits associated with the clustering of activities and commercial opportunities, while well-designed movement patterns at the micro neighbourhood scale will directly make possible the richer social dynamic that is so often undervalued as a component of community.

We have always had a natural desire to move, and the structure of human settlements is directly influenced by the patterns of movement from which they originally evolved. Our towns have become established where people have chosen to stop travelling; they have become nodes on a hugely complex network of routes and they have taken their character from the flow and activity which continues to pass through them. Movement and connectivity, therefore, must be considered the lifeblood of any settlement, village, town or city: without it, these urban centres will surely fail to thrive or even exist.

Left:
Cowcross Street in London's Clerkenwell comfortably accommodates cars and pedestrians and connects with public transport

C. 1800 - 1900   C. 1900 - 1950   C. 1950 - 2000

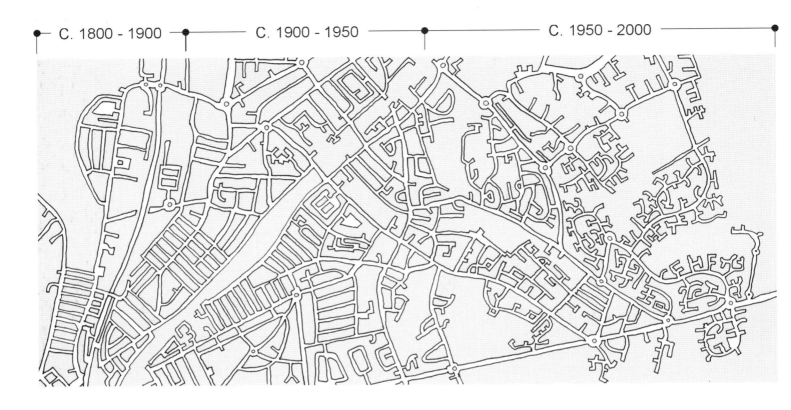

Above:
Luton's oldest streets favoured a permeable block pattern, in contrast to modern layouts that are low-density and poorly connected

Before the dominance of the car, circulation patterns related directly to human scale and pace, with villages, towns and cities created around the movement of pedestrians and horse-drawn transport. Inevitably, the arrival of motor vehicles bought fundamental changes in the scale, speed and form of movement. Today, there is continual pressure to move ever more swiftly and efficiently from one point to another along standardized networks that have been designed exclusively for the use of the car. These routes provide little opportunity for social interaction and pay scant regard to the environment through which they pass. The original multicultural role of the street has been sacrificed by traffic planning that has created urban spaces that almost exclusively serve only the functional needs of the car. Our wealth of traditional and pedestrian-oriented environments, which used to nurture and support social interaction, exchange, walking and even cycling, has been overwhelmed by the needs of the vehicle. Networks of interconnected streets, ideal for easy walking, have been replaced by mazes of culs-de-sac, for the navigation of which a car is essential.

Patterns of movement – putting people first

The pattern of movement is often considered solely as a means of getting from one place to another, a necessary and unenjoyable means to an end rather than as an experience in its own right. Yet, it should not be forgotten that planning and design for movement is not just about making it easy to arrive at the end of a journey; the journey itself should be able to provide opportunities for interest, commerce and human interaction. Well-designed movement patterns, associated with an attractive and functional urban form, should generate good social interaction, which in turn should create a sense of pride and citizenship. The key to success is the ability to establish a harmony between an attractive and functional urban form and human-oriented patterns of movement.

Successful urban neighbourhoods should be designed for people rather than vehicles. Current traffic engineering policies, epitomized in the UK by the rigid standards laid down in the Department of Environment, Transport and the Regions (DETR) *Design Bulletin 32*[1] and the Department of

Right:
In recent decades public spaces have increasingly become dominated by the needs of vehicles

Right:
In recent decades public spaces have increasingly become dominated by the needs of vehicles

Above:
Upton Enquiry by Design – it is essential that the public and local stakeholders participate in the planning of new transport networks

Right
De Strijp, Holland – neighbourhood streets should serve the needs of both pedestrians and vehicles

Transport's *Design Manual for Roads and Bridges*,[2] tend to dominate the urban environment and in particular the public realm. The engineering rulebook, circulation geometry and computer programmes for transport should be tools to assist in the creation of good urbanism rather than prescriptions for the rigid infrastructure upon which all other urban elements have to be placed. It is a sad fact that the practice of urban design and transport engineering all too often end up as confrontational, rather than collaborative activities.

The general public is further divorced from the process as the views and opinions of the end user are rarely sought. The planning and design of transport networks is often seen as a purely technical process, in which public consultation enjoys little recognition. The creation of good places and good transport patterns should be considered as much an art as a technical science, and one that should directly benefit from the opinions and knowledge of citizens familiar with the area. Those with common sense and a willingness to contemplate change are in a position to make a real and significant contribution to the design process.

Consulting with residents, stakeholders and local businesses taps into their unique knowledge of the place, helps to realize their aspirations and engenders a direct and long-lasting relationship with the project. Planning weekends, at which developers can present their evolving ideas to local stakeholders, provide valuable opportunities to identify potential problems, thereby gaining a consensus on the way forward. The sense of collective ownership that can result from such collaborative exercises is often as important to the ultimate success of a project as the quality of the urban design or transport planning solutions.

Above:
Successful streets, such as Cowcross Street in London's Clerkenwell, support a lively mix of activities and uses

Below:
The intimate scale of Cowcross Street successfully balances the needs of pedestrian, shops, offices, apartments and vehicles

Revaluing the diverse role of the street

The street lies at the heart of good urbanism and needs to regain its place as the primary element that affords a good movement structure throughout every neighbourhood. The main task of all urban planning and design should be the physical definition of streets and public spaces as places of shared use. Streets not only provide the framework within which blocks and buildings are placed, but also act as the conduit along which the commercial and social life of the neighbourhood will pass.

Streets must therefore be seen as more than simple public utilities that provide the alignment for sewers, electrical supply and access to properties. As Alan Jacobs has clearly observed in his meticulous appraisal of great streets[3] throughout the world, communication remains their major purpose: 'streets moderate the form and structure and comfort of urban communities … focusing attention and activities on one or many centres, at the edges, along a line, or they may simply not direct one's attention to anything in particular.' In their simplest form, streets allow people to be outside, and thereby undertake a plethora of social activities that contribute to the transformation of neighbours into neighbourhoods.

Although this section inevitably focuses on establishing efficient and effective patterns of movement, it is important to restate the multiplicity of roles good street design should serve. In the opening chapters of *The Death and Life of Great American Cities*,[4] Jane Jacobs chose to focus on the street as one of the fundamental components of authentic urbanism. She observed that:

> Streets in cities serve many purposes besides carrying vehicles, and city sidewalks – the pedestrian parts of the streets – serve many purposes besides carrying pedestrians. These are bound up with circulation but are not identical with it and in their own right they are at least as basic as circulation to the proper workings of cities.

As the planning of towns became segregated into compartmentalized activities undertaken by individual disciplines, the multifarious uses of the street became streamlined and simplified by highway planners and traffic engineers. The Charter of the Congress for the New Urbanism has made a significant contribution to the reappraisal of the street's social value, stating that 'in the contemporary metropolis, development must adequately accommodate automobiles, but not at the expense of the pedestrian.'[5] Streets should be safe and comfortable to use; they should support social interaction and provide attractive opportunities for commercial enterprise. Street design that is established around a clear hierarchy

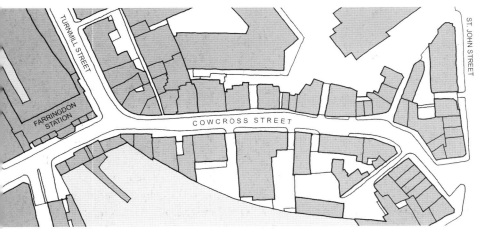

50 Metres

can maximize the commercial benefits that accrue from a well-connected location. The value of our original main streets, high streets, market streets and shopping streets, which provided both the purpose and the commercial and social backbone for original neighbourhoods, should not be forgotten or understated in the design of our new neighbourhoods and urban villages.

Promoting sustainable forms of movement

As we have read, one of the fundamental issues facing the strategic planning of our new urban neighbourhoods is the need to deliver more sustainable and smarter forms of development. Good transport networks lie at the heart of this objective, but if we get it wrong a whole string of negative impacts will result: high energy use, pollution, congestion, degraded environments and a social infrastructure that demands long journey times to function adequately. Get it right, and we have the potential to create healthy environments that are well connected, have a limited need for travel and offer attractive and diverse social opportunities that can be supported by walking and cycling.

This is not just a simple issue of using more energy-efficient forms of transport systems, such as the emerging technologies associated with electrical cars and gas-powered buses. Although these do have benefits in their own right, they will neither reduce journey times nor increase the opportunities for human interaction and exercise. To achieve these goals, we need to create compact and well-connected urban forms that do not need an extensive transport infrastructure to operate

efficiently and effectively. These new urban neighbourhoods need to improve proximities to activities, maximize the number of connections and facilitate movement to allow people to circulate as they want, using the easiest, healthiest, least polluting and most sustainable methods.

Such objectives are far from new and they have focused the minds of planners and designers for at least a century. Ebenezer Howard's attempt was lucidly presented in his 1898 diagram for the 'sociable city', which proposed clusters of Garden Cities linked by a network of rapid transit systems.[6] Copenhagen started to develop its 'finger plan'[7] in 1948, based along a series of five corridors of growth connected by an efficient rail system. More recently, Peter Calthorpe's planning practice on the West Coast of the United States has prepared a number of plans for Transit-Oriented Developments, or TODs, including his 1994 design for the Old Mill Neighborhood, adjacent to the CalTrain commuter rail station at Mountain View, California (illustrated overleaf). A development's success in encouraging more sustainable forms of movement can be measured by setting targets, often as part of a Green Travel Plan.

Creating sustainable movement patterns is far from a straightforward process: no two places are the same, so solutions need to be tailor-made for each place. This requires not only an appreciation of the existing context to ensure that new proposals fit within the wider area, but also the preparation of a clear movement strategy or framework and the delivery of a robustly connected masterplan. The three stages that are required to create an efficient movement network can be summarized as follows:

– Undertake a baseline *audit* that establishes the existing structure of movement and connectivity and identifies the patterns that are likely to be generated by the new community and its defined character.
– Establish a *movement framework* to show how the potential forms of movement will be accommodated and encouraged in the overall concept and how the planning of the neighbourhood will specifically promote walking and cycling, and human interaction. The movement framework should set

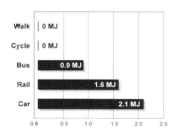

Above:
Individual energy requirements for different forms of transport

Right:
The nature and scale of some impacts of transport on the health of Londoners
Source: *Informing transport health impact assessment in London,* AEA Technology/NHS Executive London 2000/TfL 2001

Impact	Scale
Road accidents, fatalities (2000)	286
Road accidents, total casualties (2000)	46,003
Percentage considering noise from road traffic a nuisance (GB figure, 1991)	63
Calories consumed for 70kg person (kcal/hr), driving a car	80
Calories consumed for 70kg person (kcal/hr), walking at 5km/hr	260
Calories consumed for 70kg person (kcal/hr), walking at 7km/hr (brisk walk)	420
Estimated net life extension, compared to whole population, of those who walk or cycle to work	2 Years

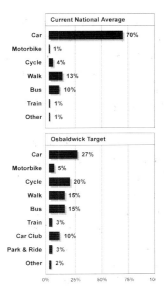

Above:
**Current modes of travel
to work compared with
Green travel plan targets
for Osbaldwick, York**

Right (above):
**A new, transit-oriented,
mixed-use neighbourhood
at Mountain View,
California**
Calthorpe Associates

Right (below):
**Mountain View is sited
next to a new CALTrain
commuter rail station**
Calthorpe Associates

reasonable targets for reducing car
dependency.
– Create *detailed designs* for both the built
and open space elements of the
neighbourhood, to ensure that the principles
of the movement framework are clearly
expressed and achieved.

These principles can be applied as much to tight
urban infill projects as they can to large-scale
brownfield and greenfield developments. Whatever
the scale, the human perspective and the need to
fit into existing patterns of movement remain the
same. For regeneration projects in particular, as we
have seen at Crown Street in Glasgow and Hulme

Above:
The neighbourhood of Beacon Cove in Melbourne is centred on a tram stop, providing a simple commute to the centre of town

in Greater Manchester, there is often the opportunity to restore routes severed by derelict sites; this not only returns movement to the site but also improves the surrounding area, by allowing people to flow more freely. Paying the right attention to movement and connectivity brings out and strengthens the existing character of the whole neighbourhood. Just as there can be no shortcut to the process, there can be no substitute for the imagination that is required at every stage. The key lies in taking a fresh approach to each site, for only in this way will the individuality of each place be harnessed and the human needs of movement be met.

Auditing existing patterns of movement

No place exists in isolation and, as has been made clear, the crucial first stage is to understand an area's context, the existing patterns of movement across the site and the way it connects into the wider regional patterns. The context of the area will have a direct impact on the final form of the place. On a broad scale, this means understanding the local hierarchy of settlement and connections. The structure of the transect, discussed in detail in the preceding chapter by Andrés Duany, provides a useful tool for analysing the character, order and purpose of each place. It illustrates the need for setting a clear hierarchy for connectivity and movement. An urban centre is, by definition, more concentrated than a suburb and can therefore take a higher density, a harder layout and a greater range of services. On moving further away from the urban core the layout often becomes more relaxed, the density lower and the street pattern and open space layout more informal. The structure of the urban layout, the street patterns and sections, should bear a direct relationship to this hierarchy and it is essential that new frameworks and plans establish a direct fit into the wider context of the place.

The same is true of movement patterns, for they form an underlying grain which new development should not simply respect but must actually harness to make a successful place. They will inform the character of the place and

determine the structure and mix of uses that are most suitable. Occasionally such an audit may even indicate that it will be near impossible to link with the adjacent local network of streets and it may therefore not be possible to develop an integrated and sustainable network as first envisaged.

Of particular importance within the initial audit process is the influence of existing urban grain and service infrastructure. Although Britain's towns have few remaining medieval buildings, most still have medieval and occasionally even Roman road patterns that dictate the baseline framework of the place. Once streets become conduits not just for human movement but for water supply, sewers, electricity, gas and telecommunications, it is difficult and often prohibitively expensive to realign them. Large mains sewers and electrical cabling runs can directly influence potential movement patterns. Even the alignment and width of the standard 1.8 m-wide pavement is more often dictated by the alleged requirements of the various utility companies than by the needs and desires of the pedestrian. The baseline audit needs to determine the way in which past history and current services dictate the existing layout of a place, and to identify those elements around which, for logistical reasons, new development must be structured and people must move.

Within the initial movement audit it is essential to have a clear understanding of both the types of movement (where the people are travelling) and the methods of movement (how they are travelling). The precise constraints, objectives and patterns of movement often differ greatly from place to place and, for each one, the patterns of movement can be assessed under three key headings:

Movement within an urban village

If the 'ideal' size of an urban village is in the region of 40 hectares, it should be possible to walk from the centre to the edge in five minutes and cross the entire neighbourhood in around ten minutes. Movement patterns will directly depend on the location and the mix of uses with people travelling to and from home, shops, work and school, as well

◄| R U R A L |||||||||||||||||||||||||| T R A N S E C T ||||||||||||||||||||||| U R B A N |►

- **Highway:** a long-distance, speed-movement thoroughfare traversing open countryside. A highway should be relatively free of intersections, driveways, and adjacent buildings, otherwise it becomes strip development which interferes with traffic flow and human comfort. *Syn.:* **Townless Highway**

  Variants include **Expressway** and **Parkway.** An expressway is a highway with grade-separated intersections. A parkway is a highway designed in conjunction with naturalistic landscaping, including a variable-width median.

- **Drive:** a thoroughfare along the boundary between an urbanized and a natural condition, usually along a waterfront, a park, or a promontory. One side of a drive has the urban character of a street or boulevard, with sidewalk and buildings, while the other has the qualities of a road or parkway, with naturalistic planting and rural detailing.

- **Road:** a local, slow-movement thoroughfare suitable for Edge and Rural Zones. Roads provide frontage for low-density buildings such as houses. A road tends to be rural in character without curbs or striped on-street parking; it may have clustered plantings and paths instead of sidewalks. The degree of rural or rustic character of a road may be adjusted by the manipulation of such elements.

- **Boulevard:** a long-distance, free movement thoroughfare traversing an urbanized area. A boulevard is flanked by parking, sidewalks, and planters buffering the buildings along the sides.

- **Avenue:** a limited distance, free-movement thoroughfare connecting civic locations within an urbanized area. Unlike a boulevard, its length is finite and its axis is terminated. An avenue may be conceived as an elongated square. *Syn.:* **connector** (from TOD usage)

  Variant: **Allée.** a rural thoroughfare, free of fronting buildings, except at the terminus, where only trees in alignment define the space. Over time, an allée may become urbanized, evolving into an avenue.

- **Street:** a local, slow-movement thoroughfare suitable for General, Center, and Core Zones. Streets provide frontage for higher-density buildings such as offices, shops, apartment buildings, and rowhouses. A street is urban in character, with raised curbs, closed drainage, wide sidewalks, parallel parking, and trees in individual planting areas. Character may vary somewhat, however, responding to the enfronting commercial or residential uses.

Above:

The planning of main thoroughfares should address issues of capacity and urban character
As featured in *The Lexicon of the New Urbanism/* Duany Plater-Zyberk

as other local services. Ideally, most of this movement should be readily and enjoyably undertaken on foot or bicycle, although there will be times and activities which will require a car.

Movement into and out of an urban village

The relationship of the village within the larger urban centre is fundamental in the formation of a movement framework. We have seen in both the United States and Britain that at times this has been ignored, to the real detriment of the development. Direct links must be established with areas that support the ethos of the village but

provide additional or specialist facilities, including employment opportunities, hospitals, further learning centres, transport interchanges and cultural attractions. In addition, the servicing of the shops and commercial premises of each neighbourhood need to be adequately supported, and this can often lead to a complex pattern of movement, which needs to be both understood and controlled. Although cycling to other urban areas should be an option, methods of movement in and out of the village will generally be by public transport and car for people and by van or lorry for deliveries. Ideally, there should be maximum permeability between different urban centres that, at best, should be reachable on foot, by cycle or by public transport.

Movement through an urban village

Urban villages should be seen as one component in a network of neighbourhoods, towns and cities. They have often, and erroneously, been viewed as self-contained developments that have little relationship with the surrounding urban area. Internal patterns of movement should directly connect with adjacent districts and the important role of the urban village in providing a stopping point on a longer journey should not be neglected. This element can directly influence the overall layout of the neighbourhood, producing an elongated form along principal routes, rather than the traditionally favoured circular growth around a compact centre. Long-range movement, of both people and goods, should be principally by bus, train, car and lorry, though specialized routes, such as a canal or long-distance footpath, should be considered and exploited where possible.

Establishing a movement framework

In the early stages of preparing a framework for movement the existing baseline connections, discussed above, must be assessed and evaluated. The key issue is to respect and accommodate these existing patterns within a new strategy that can deliver the principles and meet the targets of the urban village model. Existing patterns of movement have to be respected, but there will often be the opportunity to enhance or improve them. For example, a busy road can often be made more cycle- or pedestrian-friendly by improving the crossing points and by widening pavements. New bridges and crossings can make a main road or railway less of a barrier to other forms of cross-movement.

The framework for movement can also have strategic importance in influencing the entire philosophy of the development, directly influencing transport patterns and choices and establishing a cohesive network of links with adjacent areas. A key aim will be to reduce the

Above:
Shared pedestrian and vehicular road surfaces in Duderstadt, Germany

impact of motor vehicles, for although they are and will remain an essential method of transport, they should not be allowed to dictate the overall strategy and pattern of development. Fundamentally, the movement framework must set out to reverse the current implication that people only walk, cycle or take public transport when they cannot afford to own a car.

Charging and restricting transport

One of the simplest ways to reduce the dominance of vehicles is to make it harder and more expensive to get from place to place, by charging for access, restricting parking and introducing traffic calming. But with the stick must also come the carrot. Careful planning can reduce the direct need for vehicle journeys and encourage a range of alternatives including public transport, cycling and walking. Realism and pragmatism are essential: a movement framework, in all but the most urban situations, which attempts to force people to abandon their cars or sets unrealistic targets, will fail. Only when a framework makes it easier for people to get to work, school or the shops on foot or by cycle will a genuine reduction in car usage be produced.

Reducing the need for transport

At the strategic level, the mix of uses proposed within the development framework can have direct impact on the volume of transport that may be generated by the project. Certainly, the benefit of mixed uses, including live/work accommodation and the proximity of shops serving basic everyday needs will significantly reduce the number of journeys made by car. This mix of use can be managed in two ways: in dense urban centres it will be 'vertical', with the potential for shops at street level with office and residential on the upper floors. Elsewhere, where more space is available and the density is lower, the mix of use can be achieved 'horizontally' with the urban blocks.

Increasing density

Density is clearly a sensitive issue and the successful achievement of high density needs very careful handling. At the same time, it is undeniably true that higher densities bring considerable advantages to the movement framework: they

Above:
Frameworks for movement and development masterplans should encourage walking wherever possible

Right:
Streets Unconnected and Connected – new movement frameworks should be highly permeable
Calthorpe Associates

reduce distances and thus should directly encourage walking and cycling as well as achieving the necessary capacity to create viable public transport catchment areas. Precise densities will depend on context: in larger town centres for example, the London Planning Advisory Committee has recommended densities of up to 1,100 habitable rooms per hectare (hrh), whilst on the edges of towns and in suburban locations it can be significantly lower, even as low as 150–200 hrh. The crucial threshold is that required to sustain viable public transport. The accurate way to visualize this is by plotting walking distances that indicate the proximity of suitable user densities and contribute to determining the best layout.

Centralizing uses

Grouping the key elements of the development, including residential, retail, educational and business uses, will ensure more efficient access to the correct movement routes. As Calthorpe has shown in his 'streets connected' diagram, placing the commercial centre next to the arterial road allows deliveries to stay away from residential areas, and allows the centre to act as a buffer to the noise and pollution of a busy road.[8] A mix of shops in a group enhances choice and variety, should provide a real alternative to larger supermarkets, and may encourage the sharing of local delivery vehicles. If the urban village is large enough, the primary school should be seen as a central component. Journeys by parents and children to and from school are one of the principal generators of movement and social interaction within the neighbourhood. Good pedestrian and cycle links should be seen as essential – as is cycle proficiency training for children – and the Government's new 'Safe Routes to School' initiative[9] is beginning to address this need.

Promoting alternative forms of transport

The structure and layout of the framework plan, in addition to the density of the development, will have a fundamental effect on people's choice of transport. Providing direct and safe routes for pedestrians and cyclists, avoiding the use of culs-de-sac, linking into existing transport networks and focusing activity on public transport

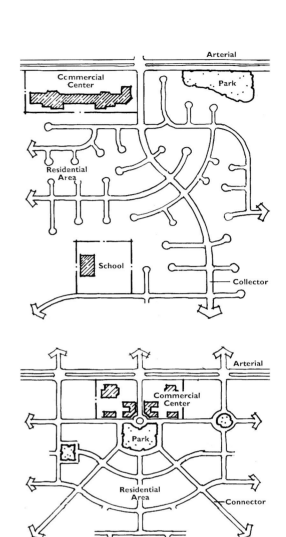

interchanges will clearly have an impact on reducing the need to travel by car. The layout must fit into the local context and have a clear hierarchy of structure that can be illustrated by the nature of the urban transect. In the centre, along with higher density and vertical mixed use, the urban form should be tight and regular. Further out, the movement patterns tend to be more sinuous, and often follow natural topographical lines and environmental constraints. Although a basic grid pattern remains essential to maximizing movement, it should be able to respond to its context, reduce its angularity and increase the

	Option 1	Option 2	Option 3
Car parking provision	High 2.0 - 1.5 spaces per unit	Moderate 1.5 - 1.0 spaces per unit	Low Less than 1 space per unit
Predominant housing type	Detached and linked houses	Terraced houses and flats	Mostly flats

Location	Accessibility Index	Setting	Density (habitable rooms per hectare)		
Sites within town centre 'Ped-Shed' 10 minutes walking distance	6 to 4	Central			650 - 1100
		Urban		200 - 450	450 - 700
		Suburban		150 - 250	250 - 350
Sites along transport corridors & sites close to a town centre 'Ped-Shed'	3 to 2	Urban		200 - 300	300 - 450
		Suburban	150 - 200	200 - 250	
Currently remote sites	2 to 1	Suburban	150 - 200		

- **Accessibility Index** - assessment of a site's accessibility to public transport based on walking and waiting times - 6 being the highest and 1 the lowest

- **Central** - very dense development, large building foot prints and buildings of 4-6 storeys and above e.g. larger town centres and much of central London

- **Urban** - dense development, with a mix of different uses and buildings 3-4 storeys e.g. town centres, along main arterial routes and substantial parts of inner London

- **Suburban** - lower density development, predominately residential of 2-3 storeys e.g. some parts of inner London, much of outer London

Above:
LPAC's sustainable residential quality matrix illustrates the location, car parking and density for large and small sites
Source: GLA/Mayor's Transport Strategy

potential for incorporating an appropriate proportion of green space. Not everyone will want to live in the dense urban core, but there is no reason why suburbia cannot be designed for public transport, walking and cycling.

Integrating servicing within the framework

Establishing an appropriate alignment for the main infrastructure of a project will be crucial. Poor buildings can be knocked down, replaced or relocated, but once a drainage and utility network of services has been installed, streets are then almost impossible to move. It is important to plan services infrastructure imaginatively, perhaps routing it through communal areas instead of continuing the tradition of running it along the adopted highway. This approach has successfully been implemented at Poundbury and allows the infrastructure to serve the place rather than dictate the urban form. It also allows a pavement to fulfil its true function as a public space for people, rather than as a route for pipes and cables.

Considering the impact of technology

At detailed planning level, new technology has an increasingly important role to play. Internet shopping and home delivery, particularly of bulky or heavy domestic goods, has a real potential to reduce the need for multiple and individual car journeys to supermarkets. It should pool transport and delivery needs and encourage local and more specialist shops to be accessible by foot or by cycle within a compact retail core. The establishment of a local supermarket delivery point, where people can collect goods ordered over the Internet, could also act as a magnet for other services. Such local facilities in turn increase diversity and bring life to an area, enhance the viability of further shops and give people the chance to meet and socialize.

In the end, the aim of all these measures is to significantly reduce the number of motor vehicle journeys and in turn to cut down on the levels of car ownership. This should then trigger a series of additional benefits, including an improved quality of the environment, a reduction in the space needed to park and store cars and the potential to increase the volume or the allocation of open space. In parallel, the occasional use of cars for leisure travel or specific transport needs can be accommodated by easy access to a pool of cars, such as a car club, which can provide fast and economical short-term hire. Car pools now running in a number of British cities, including Bristol, Edinburgh and Oxford, show the way forward; certainly the initial statistics are impressive: a single car can be shared by up to 12 people, who might otherwise each have their own. If the decision to include a car club is taken at an early stage, the development can be planned to take maximum advantage of the significant reduction in car ownership.

Improving public transport

In parallel with reducing the number of car journeys, the movement framework must give encouragement to other forms of transport. The key is to ensure that, for each type of movement, the most appropriate method becomes the easiest and most obvious choice. This also entails a shift in public perception of the status of public transport, which often has a poor reputation and is for many

Right:
Required catchments for various forms of public transport
Source: Urban Design Compendium

	Stop Interval	Corridor width Area served	Catchment per stop
Minibus	200 M	800 M	320 - 640
Bus	200 M	800 M	480 - 1,760
Guided Bus	300 M	800 M	1,680 - 3,120
Light Rail	600 M	1,000 M	4,800 - 9,000
Rail	1,000 M+	2,000 M+	24,000 +

considered the last resort. New public transport projects have begun to reverse this image, but this process needs to be given the highest priority to ensure that really good quality alternatives to the car are readily available. New technology has the potential to support such an initiative by providing real-time information on schedules, not just at bus stops but also to homes and shops, even mobile phones. Initial steps to implementing such strategies have been taken, for example by Midland Mainline,[10] but waiting at bus stops will only become a thing of the past when third generation WAP-enabled mobiles become widely available and are regularly used for communication and information supply.

A framework for people

Fundamentally, the preparation of the movement framework should reverse the commonly-held belief that the motor vehicle is the prime dictator of urban form. The ownership of the street needs to be given back to the people. The public realm, including roads, footpaths, cycleways, squares, parks and incidental open space should be primarily designed to reflect all the human activity that may take place in it, and the motor vehicle should not be allowed to

Right:
Bamberg's Red Zone prioritizes streets for pedestrians and cyclists

dominate to the exclusion of all others. Shifting this priority lies at the heart of current government policy and is discussed in detail in *PPG 13 Transport*,[11] which emphasizes the need to integrate transport policies to help achieve sustainable developments. Key recommendations are:

– wherever possible, new housing should be located in existing urban areas, or in areas well served by public transport;
– conversely, development should be discouraged in places where it is likely to generate car commuting;
– local authorities should maintain existing housing densities and, where appropriate, increase them; and,
– mixed-use development should be promoted to enable people to live near their work.

This will continue to require a fundamental change to existing approaches. Currently most roads, and therefore the places around them, are laid out on the basis of Highways Standards. These are usually derived from *Design Bulletin 32*,[12] the design guide for residential streets, and are aimed at keeping the traffic moving. Instead we need to start by defining the place that we want to create and then use technical design methods, including computer-tracking techniques, to fit the road safely into the space.

Adopting alternative approaches

Such an approach to the planning of movement can produce much greater variety, but it needs to draw on imaginative design that goes beyond the standard uniformity imposed by traditional Highway Standards. It is essential that we break away from the 'one standard fits all situations' approach and tailor the design of each space to its specific requirements and particular uses. There are now an increasing number of alternatives that can safely integrate the pedestrian and vehicular realm: Home Zones, School Zones and Residential Zones, now spreading to the UK from Europe, allow the public realm to be equally shared by all users. The increasingly popular 20 mph (30 km/h) speed restrictions should warn motorists that there are other users of equal status. Elsewhere, such as vehicular delivery areas, pedestrians and cyclists

Top:
Improved cycle and pedestrian routes are encouraging more children to walk and cycle to school

Below:
The Government's 'Safe Routes To School' initiative is beginning to increase the number of children using bicycles

Right:
Enforced traffic calming in Eschwege enhances the social life of streets

can share space, whilst vehicles are segregated to ensure safety.

In summary, the establishment of an overall framework for movement will have a key role to play in the form and functionality of urban areas. It must build on existing movement patterns and connections to reduce the need for motor vehicles and should be based on what the inhabitants want rather than what highway engineers deem as standard. This process should reclaim ownership of the street for people and set realistic targets for increasing human movement by cycle, public transport and on foot.

Expressing the framework in the detailed design

Once a clear movement framework is established it is essential that the clarity and creativity of the strategy be reflected in the detailed design. Since the underlying principle is to allow people to move as they want, rather than forcing them into unnatural patterns, the design should be able to work naturally and almost subconsciously. The careful design of each layout, the selection of materials and the provision of planting should encourage an instinctive, rather than enforced, pattern of use. An obvious example is the 'gateway' to a Home Zone, a strong visual sign that a space with different rules has been entered. More often than not, cluttered and complicated designs are indicative of complex and ambiguous spaces and uses. Of particular relevance is the Government's companion guide to *Design Bulletin 32, Places, Streets and Movement*,[13] which places greater emphasis on place, community and context in the detailed design of networks for movement.

Traffic calming and control
The design priority is to make explicit the purpose of the spaces and the hierarchy of movement in them. Adopting a single street level and unifying the surfacing materials can be used to indicate that all users have equal priority in the space, a commonly adopted strategy for Home Zones. Careful design of the space – limiting visibility or narrowing road widths – can introduce traffic

calming measures, without the need for visually intrusive elements such as speed bumps. A common design technique in Home Zones is to ensure that drivers entering cannot see the entire length, so that they do not know whether there is any way out. This makes them move cautiously. Elsewhere, curbs, raised levels and different surfacing materials and colours can serve to define dedicated spaces intended specifically for the use of motor vehicles, cycles or pedestrians. The movement framework must ensure that the servicing access to shops is kept separate from the pedestrian access, but this separation of function needs to be expressed in the design if it is to work in practice.

Accessibility for all
The design stage for the urban village should have as important a role to play in promoting the alternatives to the motorcar as the initial framework stage. The TODs developed by Calthorpe show how the existence of key public transport interchanges can be given emphasis and status by both their location and their architectural quality. This is further expressed in the detailing of the streetscape and public realm. They should be easy to use and fully integrated with other modes of transport – for example, bus and train stops should be linked to residential areas by direct cycle and foot paths; they should provide comfortable shelter and secure racks where cyclists can leave their cycles, or hire facilities for visitors arriving by public transport. Ideally, such integrated thinking should extend throughout the neighbourhood

Above:
**Osnabrück, Germany –
integrated public transport
nodes should provide easy
connections between local
neighbourhoods**

development: the storage of cycles, for example, needs to be addressed in the design of the home to ensure easy alternatives to car use are readily available. Additionally, the needs of the mobility-impaired must be integrated into the detailed design to ensure the creation of fully accessible and inclusive places.

Engendering ownership of the public realm

The public realm needs to be both attractive and secure to encourage its use throughout the day and night. In many European countries, property owners and tenants have a legal responsibility for the street in front of their house. In Britain this is not the case, and we have to rely instead on creating public spaces where people will want to meet and linger. This in turn encourages a sense of community involvement and ownership that encourages people to look beyond their legal boundaries and responsibilities, and fosters pride in the appearance of the public realm.

Appropriateness of design to purpose, as recent guidance for the public realm[14] suggests, is always the key to success. In residential, retail, educational and recreational areas, the design should lead people to appreciate their surroundings and encourage additional social activities and uses. In other parts of the neighbourhood, such as key links to adjacent areas, movement routes may be biased to vehicular transport but should still be designed to accommodate the needs of people. Visual clutter should be kept to the absolute minimum and the inclusion of landscape and green space should be used to minimize the impact of the vehicle – though this should not be undertaken at the expense of safety and functionality.

Ensuring safety and security

The public realm can be both secure and attractive. Attractively designed spaces that integrate with mixed-use development are generally well used and are perceived as being safe and suffer less

Above left:
Car parking areas adjacent to mixed-use buildings in Crown Street, Glasgow, increases security through passive surveillance

Above right:
On-street car parking provision, as shown at Poundbury, can be attractively incorporated within the street pattern

Left:
Swanson Street, Melbourne – efficient tram systems can be easily and attractively integrated within a busy streets

from vandalism. Furthermore, if people feel that they own the space, there is more readiness to maintain, care for and repair it. The urban design of housing blocks and the architectural positioning of windows to limit dead or blind spaces, along with the provision of good lighting and putting movement routes through car parks, as seen at Poundbury in Dorset, are all obvious ways of making a place naturally secure. In parallel to traffic calming measures, creating secure and social spaces at the start of the design process rather than as a residual activity at the end can be an effective way to avoid having to readdress problems at a later stage.

Fundamentally, the design ethos of the urban village should encourage a sense of community and neighbourliness and promote a perceived joint ownership of public spaces that are biased towards pedestrian use. Movement patterns can make a fundamental contribution to this by encouraging people to limit the use of their cars, adopt alternative forms of transport and interact more with their physical and social environment. Getting the movement framework and detailed design right, and ensuring good links with the right networks will contribute powerfully to creating a strong and successful neighbourhood.

A summary checklist

Connectivity and movement is essential to the creation of a successful urban village. Well-handled patterns of movement will:

- provide good links and connections both within the village and with its neighbours and the urban centre;
- build on existing patterns of movement, reinforcing existing and restoring severed connections;
- be planned for a human scale and pace of life;
- ensure that travel is not just a means to an end, by making the journey itself an enriching experience;
- reduce the need to travel long distances by car, by mixing uses and achieving densities high enough to ensure viable, quality public transport;
- encourage walking and cycling by providing good routes and facilities and by creating spaces that are shared equally by all users;
- take account of the views, aspirations and needs of local stakeholders;
- recognize the unique nature of each place and break free from the imposed uniformity of national standards; and
- contribute towards security and a sense of community by providing a richness and variety of movement, and the chance for human interaction.

Chapter 6

The social dynamic

Ken Worpole

The second half of the twentieth century was full of plans and proposals about where and how people should live. Yet as we have seen in cities throughout the developed world – in Amsterdam, Chicago, Dublin, Glasgow, Liverpool, Newcastle, New York, Paris and Stockholm, among many others – the dreams have often turned to nightmares for many of the inhabitants. In many unsuccessful large housing projects, those able to leave, leave behind what sociologists now despairingly call 'residualized communities'. The failure of architecture and planning to recreate forms of urban community and solidarity has come to haunt politicians and planners in cities throughout the world, and in many places residential districts and quarters that were designed and developed only 20 or 30 years ago are being demolished in order to experiment anew. But will we be any wiser 'when we build again'? If not, the world of new housing will quickly polarize between 'voluntary' and 'involuntary' communities, both gated in some form, one based on self-selection by price, and the other on welfare allocation and sheer lack of economic mobility.

Left:
South Bank, Melbourne.
Streets and public spaces
should be designed to
maximize social interaction

Above:

**Many modern housing
experiments have created
'residualized communities'
with poor social facilities
and negligible open spaces**

Disconnected and severed communities

The failure of so many large public housing
projects cannot simply be ascribed to the
architecture, design or quality of the materials
used. Public housing standards have often been
higher than those found in the private housing
market. So what are the key factors that have
resulted in the collapse of those utopian schemes?
In my opinion they are largely geographical and
social. Since this chapter is principally
concentrating on the social dynamics of new
communities, I will only briefly refer to the
geographical factors at work, notably,
peripheralization and *disconnection*. A key element
of housing policy in Britain after the Second World
War was to demolish inner-city slums and decant
residents to new estates on the outskirts of the city.
Whether in Brighton, Dublin or Glasgow (which
are all cities I know well), the immediate effect
was to cut off populations from their long-standing
social, familial and even employment networks,
and leave them struggling to create new networks
all over again. This was Year Zero utopianism.

These new estates, while often well
constructed, were poorly served by transport,
shops, clubs, pubs and other services. Furthermore,
whilst the inner-city housing in which people lived
may have been poor in quality, it was often well
integrated into the 'central place' services of the
city itself – including much wider social,
educational and employment opportunities. Many
such opportunities were severed at the root by the
geographical peripheralization of the new estates,
and the many other forms of disconnection from
the wider horizons and greater life chances that
mixed communities can often embody or represent.
As a result, the new, monocultural estates often
turned in upon themselves, creating tough,
'survivalist' cultures, separate from the mainstream
of society. This has been graphically described by
Bea Campbell in her book about problem urban

areas in the UK, *Goliath*,[1] and by François Maspero in his book, *The Roissy Express*,[2] which describes the terrible plight of the many families now beleaguered on the vast peripheral estates (*banlieue*) of Paris, unconnected to each other, and prey to high levels of unemployment, drug abuse, and gang violence.

Housing – the social foundation

So planning and housing policy cannot go down this route again. If new communities are to be constructed, then the processes of consultation, the wider environmental and social objectives, together with management and long-term maintenance programmes, need to be clear, robust, closely argued, and sensitively delivered. Furthermore, such developments have to take place within the broader economic context of market choice. This is particularly important given that in the UK today, the introduction of market disciplines and greater consumer choice now informs the funding and regulation of social housing, state education, health and many other forms of welfare and amenity provision. People will no longer simply accept what the state wishes to give them, without a large degree of personal choice.

Yet in the UK so far, the process by which the new communities of the future are to be created does not augur well. The Greenwich Millennium Village is a case in point. This was the first of a series of 'Millennium Villages' planned by the New Labour government that was elected in 1997, close to the Millennium Dome on a brownfield site adjacent to the River Thames on the Greenwich Peninsula. The early publicity for the scheme announced that it was to be a pioneering example of environmentally-friendly construction, allied to a mixture of housing types and tenures which would produce a better social mix – and therefore a more sustainable community. Indeed, the government minister responsible at the time, John Prescott, called it 'a template for life in the twenty-first century'. Yet apart from the initial glossy publicity brochures, the whole development has been shrouded in secrecy, except for a flurry of angry public exchanges between architects and

project managers when the chosen masterplanners, Hunt Thompson Associates, quit the project in 1998, alleging that many of the more environmental objectives had been challenged, modified or dropped by the private developers responsible for different elements of the scheme.

This wall of silence became apparent when during this period I was carrying out research on the impact of parental choice on home-school relations in London and elsewhere in the UK. Members of the research team were keen to find out what educational arrangements were being suggested in the Greenwich proposals. All enquiries to the management company developing the site were redirected to the New Millennium Experience Company, the public relations arm of which was adamant that for us to meet the architects, developers or even project planners, would be considered inappropriate at that or any other time. In their view, the project was a commercial undertaking and therefore subject to rules of confidentiality.

One thing we have learned, however: although the Millennium Village has at its heart

Right (above):
Greenwich Millennium Village is one recent government-led initiative to create new communities for the future

Right (below):
The nearest underground station is too far to walk for many residents at Greenwich Millennium Village

one of the finest and most modern metro stations in the world, connecting residents to central London within minutes, initial research has identified that a number of residents considered the station – at ten minutes' walking distance – was too far away, and carried on using their private cars to access schools, shops and even workplaces in the city. Furthermore, although the village itself is walkable and relatively resource-friendly in its construction and energy requirements, it has been swamped by a vast out-of-town retail park, hotel and 16-screen multiplex planted right next door to it, which breaks every guideline in the environmental and community-building rulebook. Issues of scale and integration into the wider urban fabric have simply been ignored.

Compare this process with that of the 'European Village' constructed for the Bo01 exhibition in Malmö, Sweden in 2001, and featured as a case study at the end of this book. This was constructed on a brownfield waterfront site rather similar to the Greenwich Peninsula, on land that was previously used for harbourside industries. This was a village of permanent homes, shops, restaurants and two permanent parks, accompanied by various temporary exhibitions of model landscapes and public art works, but it was open to the public for six months, and many

conferences, debates and seminars were held on site, at which issues of architecture, planning, landscape design and community-building were regularly discussed. Tens, if not hundreds, of thousands of visitors came to the site, from all over Sweden and beyond, to explore and discuss what kinds of homes were best suited to modern lifestyles and environmental concerns. This kind of openness to public concern, interest and debate is essential if the communities of the future are to be embedded in the aspirations and social and environmental needs of modern urban populations. Doing good by stealth, which appears to be the hallmark of the New Labour administration in the UK, does not guarantee long-term viability: all social experiments need to be tested by rigorous public debate.

Consider children first

So what are, or might be, the social underpinnings of the New Urbanism and its villages and communities? It is salutary to remember the example of the young Dutch architect, Aldo van Eyck, in this regard. In the crucial years following the end of the Second World War, modern architecture had an unprecedented opportunity to demonstrate a new, socially-minded, urban flair, yet the consensus today is that in many places it failed. Aldo van Eyck was one of the most scathing critics of the mechanistic approach taken by some of his modernist architectural colleagues to urban reconstruction, claiming that its 'blank-sheet-on-the-drawing-board' approach rode roughshod over existing social networks and the seemingly parochial loyalties of pre-war neighbourhoods.

Van Eyck believed that architecture could help in other, less direct, ways. In 1947, at the age of 28, he went to work for the Office for Public Works in Amsterdam, and as his first project chose to construct a small playground (*speelplaats*) on the Bertelmanplein. While many of his colleagues were keen to start with a housing development or a new street plan, he had been encouraged to think seriously about play provision by Jacoba Mulder, who along with Lotte Stam-Beese, were the first two prominent women planners in the

Below:

Bo01 – The 2001 European Housing Expo was held in Malmö, Sweden, on a brownfield site in the former docklands

Right:
**Van Hogendorpplein,
Amsterdam, in the 1950s**

Right:
**A child-friendly Van
Hogendorpplein,
following the addition
of a playground by
Aldo van Eyck**

Netherlands, and who had already completed the popular Beatrixpark in Amsterdam before the war. Delighted with the popularity of the playground, Van Eyck designed over 700 more such play areas throughout the city over the next 30 years.

The connectedness and playfulness of the city that architects and planners so often failed to achieve, was, Van Eyck noticed, inadvertently

Right:
A van Eyck playspace introduced into a vacant building lot in Zeedijk, Central Amsterdam
Mural by Joost van Roojen, 1958

Above:
Creative opportunities for children to play should be an integral part of any neighbourhood

Below:
A children's festival at the Horseshoe Square in Kirchsteigfeld, Potsdam

sometimes brought about by the weather, especially a heavy fall of snow – which allowed children to become 'temporarily lords of the city' once again. In a memorable phrase he asked architects to conceive a way of designing city spaces that would give children a freedom that was 'more permanent than snow'. The network of play spaces and street corner havens, which he designed in Amsterdam, still shapes the layout of the residential areas of the city even today. This tradition has been revived with the *woonerf* (play street), a Dutch word and design concept that has become part of the vocabulary of planning departments throughout the world in recent years. Visiting Rotterdam in the summer of 2001, I was shown many similar play streets and play areas in that city, often with paid workers operating out of huts and toy stores adapted from ship containers, organizing games and activities for children after school and at weekends, and making them feel very much part of the urban street culture.

Few will surely disagree that where people grow up and play in early childhood and adolescence creates one of the most attachment-forming experiences they are likely ever to have. This deep sense of emotional loyalty to the 'familiar landscape' of childhood – whether in the form of local parks, playgrounds, streets, alleys or derelict land – recurs again and again in all autobiographical literature, yet it still too rarely features in the design guides, and even less in the models of urban morphology promoted by traffic engineers.

Schools – the social forum

It seems obvious to suggest, then, that if new communities are designed and planned to put the safety and mobility of children at the heart of the design, they will also work for almost everybody else. This is of course a complete reversal of much post-war planning thinking, which has put the needs of the motorist at the heart of urban design. This also brings us to the crucial role that the primary or elementary school is likely to play in securing the success of any new urban community. I agree with Todd W. Bressi,[3] who in a recent set of essays on the New Urbanism wishes to reclaim the 'Victorian notion … that the functional and literal centre of a neighbourhood should be an elementary school.' This was also true of post-war new town planning policy in the UK: that the primary school was the symbolic heart and embodiment of future ideals in any new community.

This key role emerged in Ben Jupp's detailed research study, *Living Together: Community Life on mixed tenure estates*,[4] which has already cast helpful light on a very complex subject. Jupp's study for the UK think-tank, Demos, was based on 1,000 personal interviews with residents on 10 new mixed-tenure estates developed in the UK in recent years. He concluded that residents themselves showed little concern for differences in tenure in the new communities where they now lived, and believed it to have little connection to how they felt generally about their new neighbourhood. Interviewees still maintained their other social networks, and continued to draw most of their social life from these wider networks. Where people did occasionally mix with people in other forms of tenure, it was much more likely to be at street level. While neither the pub nor the local shops were thought by interviewees to be places where they met new people, Jupp concluded that it is local schools and nursery schools alone that *'are by far the most important local amenity for meeting other people'* (my italics).

Yet the important role that the primary or elementary school plays in community-building – acting as the hub of new social networks – is today threatened by the increasing use of the car to

Top:
Open-air concert held in school playground, Delfshaven, Rotterdam, 2001

Above:
The defensive stockade around the Greenwich Millennium Village primary school restricts out-of-hours use of the large playground

chauffeur children to local schools, leading in many neighbourhoods to congested streets and empty pavements. In 1971 seven out of ten seven-year-olds in the UK made their own way to school. Today it is less than one in ten. Over the past decade, 'escort education' trips have risen by 52 per cent (and mileage by 90 per cent), and now outnumber business trips in the UK. The increase in the use of cars to take children to and from school is now responsible for 20 per cent of road traffic in urban areas during the morning peak period in 1995/97, compared with 14 per cent in 1989/91.[5] Parents and carers are driving children to school because they fear dangers from traffic (which, paradoxically, they exacerbate), and 'stranger danger', the graphic phrase now used to describe deep-seated parental fears about their children being abducted in the street or abused by predatory adults (which, statistics show, is much more likely to occur in the home).

As a result, children in the UK and North America (in particular), are now subject to enormous forms of parental and civic over-protection, chauffeured to and from school each day, to buildings and campuses which resemble stockades, compounds or even prisons, with their high walls, entrance gate security procedures, CCTV cameras and other forms of defensive design. An architect recently told me that she had entered a competition to design a new primary school in an existing residential community in the south east of England, and had been horrified to discover that the brief included the instruction that

the playground should not be visible from any of the surrounding flats or houses. Even the primary school at the Greenwich Millennium Village has been designed by architect Edward Cullinan to resemble a wooden stockade. While wholly admirable in the design of its inner spaces, the extensive playground and grassed arena serving the school is locked throughout the school holidays, so that local children have to play elsewhere – which some do by using the vast car park of the nearby shopping centre. The integrated management and maintenance of public open space – which surely, according to classic Noilly principles, should include school playgrounds – is a precondition of neighbourhood renewal.

Belatedly, but thankfully, some private developers and house builders are picking up this message. John Callcutt, chairman of Crest Nicholson, has recently argued that today companies need to 'shift the emphasis from building houses to creating communities'. In order to do this, he now realizes, we need 'to create towns that are safe for children, and therefore desirable for families, and that put schools and homes for older people in the centre, rather than on the edge'.[6]

Enhancing social networks

Generally, though, one is forced to look abroad for better practice in this regard. Compare the spatial isolation of the Greenwich primary school's playground with that of two primary schools I visited in 2001, one in Rotterdam and the other in Malmö. In both cases the playground/park was an integral part of the community's open space, accessible at all hours of the day and week to anybody who chose to use it. The playground at the Malmö school was busier at weekends than during school hours. There is now some movement in the UK on such issues, notably through the organization, *Learning through Landscapes*.[7] They have argued that, 'in the rush to install expensive features such as intruder alarms, security lighting, fencing and closed-circuit television, and to clear the grounds of trees and bushes, we are in danger of frightening the very children we wish to protect,

and of creating sites which give negative messages: "go away", "not welcome" and "keep out".' They go on to claim that redesigning playgrounds in consultation with children, staff, parents and members of the wider community, including allowing community access out of school hours, can not only improve playground behaviour, but reduce vandalism as well.

The question raised by such impermeable spatial and territorial boundaries is, how can we continue to think of education as a 'thing apart' from the life of the community, in a world where the home is likely to possess as much information technology as the school, and in which learning about people and how to live together is as important as learning how to succeed at exams and tests? Integrating formal education processes with the daily life and activity of the community ought to be a key challenge for urban villages. For as Manuel Castells has argued, 'Networks constitute the social morphology of our societies, and … the new information technology paradigm provides the material basis for its pervasive expansion throughout the entire social structure.'[8] In the communities of the future, providing children with access to networks – whether of educational resources, social contacts or

employment prospects – is likely to be as important as sitting them in a building for so many years and filling them with useful facts. Sooner or later the walls have to come down.

The provision of leisure facilities also provides opportunities for greater gregariousness and social mix. One of the early planners of the new towns in Britain, Don Ritson, when asked what his message was to other planners when designing new communities, answered, 'start with the park!' Even today, despite years of diminishing funds, parks are not only regularly used by about 40 per cent of the population, but surveys throughout Britain show that over 70 per cent who use parks actually walk to them. Thus parks are great generators of local pedestrian activity, and pedestrian activity is surely

Top:
Lewisham Public Library Café provides an important community meeting place for all ages

Above:
Public realm improvements to Nyhaven, Copenhagen, have created an extremely popular meeting place that is used throughout the year

one sign of a secure and potentially thriving neighbourhood and community. Likewise public library services in Britain claim between 35 per cent and 50 per cent local membership and regular use, though the current trend is away from the local provision to the development of larger, more centralized library and information buildings and services in town centres. Yet some neighbourhood libraries have reinvented themselves as Internet-access and homework centres, in addition to the loan of books, records and videos: so opportunities do remain for local information and library provision, if it is tailored to meet specific local needs and interests (and demographics).

Nevertheless, it would be foolhardy to equate community with geographical locality alone, as the story of post-war housing policy failure – recalled at the outset – seemed to demonstrate. Spatial segregation and isolation can lead to an imprisoning sense of ghetto-like failure, where facilities are poor and there is a sense of having been abandoned. Connections to opportunities further afield need to be encouraged; there is no reason why people cannot be loyal to a particular geographical area whilst at the same time developing a more independent personal identity and set of life-chances as well. What is needed is a more nuanced definition of community (and indeed, urban village), not *gated* but *variegated*, offering a sense of local identity and belonging as well as access to opportunities further afield.

I have largely concentrated on the needs of children in the new urban neighbourhoods because, while there is no reason to assume that all new urban developments will be exclusively for families with young children, it would be difficult to develop a viable urban village based on replicating the national household structure in the UK at micro-level as it stands today: 30 per cent pensioners; 25 per cent male and female adults with children; 16 per cent childless couples; 13 per cent adults-only households; 12 per cent single households; 4 per cent single parents.[9] Some of these groups will either be happily settled in existing housing and neighbourhoods, others will, if given the choice, opt to move out of cities altogether, while others will prefer to live in parts of the city where single lifestyles are either

encouraged or more accepted. We have to assume, in the near future at least, that new-build urban residential developments will be largely focused on family housing.

Public space for social interaction

Nevertheless, not everybody will have children or be able to use local schooling as a meeting-point for developing new social and community ties and responsibilities. Given that we know, from Ben Jupp among others, that many people's familial and social networks will extend well beyond the neighbourhood, what else is there in the urban village which can help underpin better local forms of identity and belonging? Rather obviously, the street plays a crucial role here. This is where people meet and cross paths, as they gain access to other key nodal points of the public domain such as shops, bus stops, railway stations and parks.

We know that traffic levels can have a severely inhibiting effect on public interaction at street level, not just for children but for many adults as well – as the well-known research by Appleyard and Lintell into the relationship between traffic densities and neighbourhood interaction in a residential area of San Francisco, published in 1972, demonstrated.[10] A fast, straight, trunk road can divide a community as effectively as a steel fence or high brick wall, in much the same way that suburban railway lines once often used to symbolically divide towns and villages into the 'right' and 'wrong' side of the tracks. Getting the balance right between 'movement space' and 'exchange space' in the network of streets, footpaths, car parks and other public routes and corridors in the urban form, needs to be considered much more than is currently the case. Already experiments with 20 mph zones in residential areas in the UK – in advance of an even more ambitious experiment with Dutch-type Home Zones, already mentioned earlier – appear to have reduced child pedestrian and cyclist accidents substantially, and have been described by the participating authorities as a 'resounding success'.[11]

Streets, pavements and public spaces must not only be safe, but they must also look cared-for and

Right:
Pedestrians take precedence over vehicles within Bamberg's Red Zone

Right:
Copperfield Street Community Garden in Southwark has been converted from a derelict churchyard

well maintained. The quality of the 'public realm' has in Britain become a new political theme for New Labour since the Prime Minister, Tony Blair, devoted a whole speech to the subject of 'Improving Your Local Environment' on 24 April 2001, setting in train a 'Cross-cutting Review' of public space by the Treasury. Politicians have belatedly realized that uncollected rubbish, graffiti, broken pavements and bad street lighting not only have physical ill effects on the environment but also have deep psychological effects on communities too. In short, poor maintenance sends out the simple but graphic message that 'nobody cares'. There seem to be two major strands to policies designed to reverse this neglect: first, connect up the proliferation of different agencies

variously responsible for the maintenance of the public realm (utilities, traffic engineers, street lighting, street cleansing, policing, grass cutting) and make them work in a more coordinated way; and, second, create local employment opportunities for people to undertake local public maintenance programmes, thereby creating jobs and solving dereliction at the same time.

An exemplary model of this kind of activity is the Bankside Open Spaces Trust, a charitable organization that seeks to improve parks, play areas and public spaces in the Bankside area of Southwark in south London. The Trust works with communities to raise funds, and employs local people as well as using volunteers, to refurbish neglected sites. It has achieved an astonishing level of success in raising money from local businesses and charitable trusts to upgrade local parks, play areas, derelict sites and even neglected cemeteries, and has even set up a local plant-growing nursery in conjunction with a local hostel for the homeless, in which those previously homeless grow plants and maintain some local parks and gardens. Issues of improved lighting, wardening and enhanced safety through greater local involvement in management and maintenance have all been to the fore.

A successful street and walkway pattern not

only increases opportunities for people to meet, but also helps increase levels of trust locally through the frequency of face-to-face encounter and negotiation. A sense of trust – the belief that others, even strangers, are basically helpful and considerate – is essential to the social life of urban communities, and to local economic life as well. In fact, much local trading of goods and services would not be possible without a large degree of trust on all sides. There is now beginning to be some serious research done, notably by the New Economics Foundation, into the relationship between local levels of trading activity and levels of social cohesion, based on the unsurprising idea that people who meet regularly to exchange goods and services – whether babysitting, childcare, house cleaning, car repairing, gardening, home-care or house decorating – are more likely to develop a sense of familiarity and trust with other local people, than those who buy services in other, more distant and commercialized ways.[12] For some time a number of people have been arguing for a closer relationship between economic development and welfare policies at the neighbourhood level, in order to capture the network-creating capacities of local mutual aid.

The interest in how to regenerate trust, not only between people, but also between people and institutions, has become a key theme of modern political discourse, as it is widely believed that levels of public trust have been eroded in recent times. One example of this has been the growing fear of crime and dangers to children in the public domain – fears that are rarely borne out by the actual crime levels themselves. Another is the declining rate of participation in local elections. Even more worrying is that increasing levels of public mistrust can result in a self-fulfilling prophecy, as people protect their children and themselves by using private cars to travel everywhere, leaving the pavements and walkways increasingly empty, and therefore more conducive to opportunistic crime (as there are fewer opportunities for the 'natural surveillance' of passers-by).

Such views are thought romantic, if not regressive, by those who argue that the private car has done more to improve than harm people's mobility and life opportunities. Like many arguments, the debate about the positive and negative aspects of very high levels of private car ownership on community life cuts both ways. There is no doubt that the private car allows many more opportunities for individuals, families with children, and especially people with disabilities or infirmities, to travel more easily and comfortably, and has to be regarded as a great social good. But it should also be remembered that the benefits of car ownership are not equally distributed to all sections of the population, and neither are the disadvantages. Most of the children injured or

Above right:
Schouwburgplein, Rotterdam, provides a new civic social space in the heart of the city

Below right:
Formal public spaces should also be capable of supporting informal and spontaneous recreation

Right:
**Great Northern Square, Manchester –
an adjacent mix of uses brings additional life to public spaces**

killed in traffic accidents belong to non-car-owning families. The spatial geography of traffic congestion, pollution and accidents is also a social geography of the modern city. Appropriate and inappropriate patterns of car use, as described in the preceding chapter, can be a focus for neighbourhood discussion, planning policy and action; indeed traffic calming and street safety campaigns are now often a focus for community solidarity.

Finally, it is time again to review the classic distinction between public space and private space that has hallmarked twentieth-century thinking about life in the modern city. Jane Jacobs insisted that the distinction was essential to a vibrant street culture. 'There must be a clear demarcation between what is public space and what is private space. Public and private spaces cannot ooze into each other as they do typically in suburban settings or in projects.'[13]

Jacobs was writing before the modern media made such an intrusive encroachment into the modern home, turning many homes into media portals with telephones, TV monitors, sound systems and web connectivity in every room, the dining room displaced into the TV lounge, and individual family members working flexible shifts

at the evening school, the office, the leisure centre, and of course at the telecommuting workstation at home. The ordered world of mid-twentieth century family life has been stretched and sundered. Of all the lessons I learned from the research project into urban parks in the UK which I directed in 1994, the most significant was that for many people, a visit to the park was a way of escaping from the intensely communicative and public nature of the modern home, and restoring a degree of intimacy and privacy into their lives. In short, the public park had become a private sphere, and the private home a public setting. We are likely to see more of these reversals, as well as an increasing degree of fluidity between domestic and public, intimate and social acts, roles and settings in future. Just think of the way in which the mobile phone has reconfigured intimate and public space in a matter of a few years. The design of the houses, public spaces, and local institutions of the new urban villages, will have to reflect these fluidities and flexibilities. Even the 8 a.m. – 10 p.m. school has already emerged in some UK communities, offering everything from breakfast clubs to late-night computer classes and gym sessions.

Such urban villages or new communities will

need to develop a new kind of local political structure. The continuing decline in local voting turnout indicates that many people feel a loss of involvement (or representation) in local government as it is presently constituted. As a result, the neighbourhood is likely to regain some of its historic 'parish council' power over decisions which affect the immediate community. Rather than allow a new generation of urban villages to be designed and built with minimal engagement in issues of local decision-making, it is essential that we make such an engagement an integral part of the design and development process.

Summary lessons

Focus on housing, schools and children as a priority.

Housing
- Design dialogue and consultation must be inclusive and extensive.
- It is essential to address wider environmental and social objectives and concerns.
- There must be clear management and long-term maintenance programmes.
- A broader economic context of market choice must be established, even within programmes of social housing.
- New housing must be able to adapt to modern lifestyles.

Children
- Ensure that safety and mobility of children is at the heart of the design.
- Value connectedness and playfulness.
- Promote urban street culture.
- Provide children with access to educational, social and employment networks.

Schools
- Recognize the crucial social role of the primary or elementary school in neighbourhood life.
- Respect the value of local schools and nurseries as a local amenity for meeting.
- Integrate formal education with the daily life of the community.

Commerce, employment and leisure
- Local trading of goods and services is more likely to enhance local networks than 'bought-in' services.
- Economic development and welfare polices should be more integrated.

Social networks
- Ensure a balance between movement space and exchange space.
- Appreciate and elicit a sense of trust.
- Capture network-creating capacities of local mutual aid.

Public spaces
- Establish key nodal points of the public domain, such as shops, bus stops, railway stations and parks.
- Promote the social role of the street and underpin local forms of identity.
- Integrate management and maintenance of public open space and include school playgrounds.
- Understand that in the communities of the future, public and private domains are going to be increasingly fluid.

Part Three

Implementing urban villages

Having established the strategic context and explored the technical, aesthetic and social aspects of neighbourhood design, we now turn our attention to the implementation process. It is at this stage that issues become real, significant investment is made and vast resources are expended over a long period of time. To limit risk and maximize the potential for success it is essential to have a clear and collective understanding of this process at the outset of any new development and regeneration project. This section looks at the techniques and complexities associated with the implementation of urban villages in three distinct stages: project identification, procurement and management. In reflection of the multidisciplinary approach that is required during this process the three contributors to this section, Mike Hollingsworth, Ben Denton

and Chris Brown, have collaborated on all three chapters during their preparation.

Project identification describes the initial phases that need to be undertaken at the beginning of the process. An analysis of Britain's great diversity of urban neighbourhoods highlights many of the challenges and opportunities that will be faced at the outset of any neighbourhood creation and regeneration project. It is common for these initiatives to be led at the outset by the public sector, which is often in the best position to marshal the significant resources required to initiate and guide the implementation process. Subsequently, consultant teams and technical experts are often commissioned to undertake an initial audit and baseline appraisal for the scheme, and to coordinate the preparation of a collective vision that will guide the future development.

Project procurement defines the set of inter-connected activities that leads any project through to the point of construction. As a means to simplify many of the complexities of procurement, the process is described through six key topics: the preparation of a design; issues of statutory planning control; consultation and public participation; the assembly of all the necessary land for development; financial assessment and the securing of the required funding; and the establishment of suitable development partnerships that are capable of delivering a final project.

Project management takes the scheme on through to construction and long-term management. The chapter explores the various choices that are available for implementation and describes the growing role of project partnering during this process. Once the first phases of an urban village are complete it will be essential to put in place a comprehensive neighbourhood management system. All neighbourhoods are in a continual state of long-term change and it will be important to ensure that comprehensive maintenance and future development are carefully managed in a flexible and considered manner.

In conclusion, the *Afterword* reflects on many of the successes that the urban village movement has achieved to date and identifies a number of important issues that urban policy must continue to address. One thing is certain: there are many significant challenges that must be faced as we continue the process of making lively, popular and sustainable urban communities of the future.

Chapter 7

Project identification

Mike Hollingsworth, Ben Denton and Chris Brown

The implementation process for an urban village begins with the initial identification of a potential project. This requires both a pragmatic and a visionary assessment of the needs, opportunities and physical realities for a specific area. The process may at first appear relatively straightforward: the physical, social and economic needs of a neighbourhood are often clear to see; existing land ownerships may easily define a specific area; and distinct physical and geographical boundaries can often delineate particular sites. However, as this chapter highlights, to maximize the potential benefits from mixed use, neighbourhood-based projects, it is essential to undertake a rigorous and analytical assessment of the nature, scope and context of the project at the outset.

Although the starting point may differ, it is possible to identify a number of common characteristics with particular types of neighbourhood. For example, the approach for an inner-city infill project will be different to that for a major brownfield redevelopment or even a new urban extension. This chapter begins by identifying the common types of neighbourhood that can provide a starting point for urban village projects, then considers the roles and skills that the public and private sectors can bring to this process and examines the range of information that is needed to assess the potential for a project and define the vision on which the subsequent development framework can be established.

Left:
Brindleyplace in the centre of Birmingham at the outset of regeneration

Below:
**Glasgow's Crown Street
has been one of the most
successful housing-led
urban renewal schemes in
the 1990s**

The initial context

As with many large-scale urban regeneration
schemes, the implementation process can be a
complex and challenging. The original Urban
Villages Campaign established an initial framework
for delivery, and a number of these principles have
been successfully applied to various ambitious and
successful mixed-use developments, including the
regeneration of Hulme in Manchester, West
Silvertown in London's Docklands, Crown Street
in Glasgow and Poundbury in Dorset. Research by
Cardiff Universiy[1] into the tangible achievements
of over fifty so-called urban village developments
continues to highlight the difficulties and
complexities associated with the delivery of such
schemes. Many projects continue to fall short of
the ambitious vision of the original campaign, but
there should be confidence that with time,
experience and practice the ability to deliver truly
mixed-use communities will continue to improve.

Neighbourhood-based strategies

Whilst respecting and anticipating the enormous
challenges and difficulties associated with such
schemes, the neighbourhood remains a central
component for area-based development and
regeneration. As we have read earlier, it is at the
neighbourhood scale that many of the most
important social relationships, either as friendships
or mere acquaintances, are established. And it is
common that at this local level the collective desire
to bring about change initiates both political
activity and the implementation of strategic policy.

In Britain, the neighbourhood political unit is
formalized into the Ward, or Parish, which is the
smallest electoral unit in the country, and one can
identify parallels of this in all democratic societies.
On an intuitive level, a 'good neighbourhood' is
somewhere that is valued for both its facilities and
its social relationships. Frequently one
neighbourhood will simply lead into another
imperceptibly, with people living next to each other
often indicating affiliation to two different places,
and occasionally to both. Established urban
villages are essentially good neighbourhoods, and
truly mixed-use neighbourhoods provide a wide
range of commercial, social, educational,
employment and leisure facilities, and remain a
central focus for community-based initiatives.

Such a picture suggests that neighbourhoods
are relatively stable entities, but it will be seen that
most have been subject to enormous social and
economic changes that have often undermined the
whole basis on which they were originally
established.

Neighbourhood-based strategies can be traced
back to nineteenth-century social reformers who
sought to re-establish the importance of satisfying
a wider range of human needs – employment,
education and social welfare – in addition to the
provision of housing. The strategic planning of
many of our towns and cities focused on the role of
the neighbourhood and one need only turn to the
work of Patrick Abercrombie and his 1943 County
of London Plan to see the capital subdivided into a
series of neighbourhoods. These were to provide
the basis for planning and service delivery. This
framework continued to form the structure for the

Right:
Abercrombie's 1943 County of London Plan worked with the existing structure of urban neighbourhoods

Right:
Abercrombie's 1943 County of London Plan worked with the existing structure of urban neighbourhoods

new town masterplanning of the 1960s and early 1970s, but much of this thinking was subsequently rejected.

There were several reasons for this. The neighbourhood model was seen as an artificial construct that often did not correspond with the actual pattern of communities on the ground. People viewed neighbourhood-based planning as a form of social engineering and it often evoked resistance from local residents. Older neighbourhoods in particular witnessed major in- and out-migration that changed the social and ethnic composition of their population; much of this was triggered by central government's urban clearance programme that demolished vast areas of sub-standard housing, transforming these neighbourhoods out of all recognition. Post-war slum clearance was followed by the mass-production of housing and the creation of monotonous new housing estates. Many homes were constructed using non-traditional methods, which generated numerous long-term maintenance problems. The lack of choice and variety in the poorly-performing housing stock became increasingly unpopular.

Many neighbourhoods were ill-adapted to the wider changes that were taking place in society. Old shopping and service centres found that their trade was moving out to new, purpose-built shops and offices that were often located in the suburbs and beyond. Many of these changes occurred because older neighbourhoods were poorly equipped to cope with private cars and service vehicles. Roads became congested with through-traffic, and parked cars and delivery vehicles further reduced highway capacity. Changes in the pattern of retailing, driven by improved transport and the increasing role of the multiple retailer, have led to the segmentation of urban districts into single-use retail, residential, commercial office and industrial locations.

Another problem was that, whilst neighbourhoods were originally intended to form a 'template' for all local authority service providers and utility companies, this rarely, if ever, occurred in practice. Such companies tended to be driven by their own internal and individual functional requirements, which rarely permitted any linkage to ensure a more coordinated delivery.

Finally, attempts by planners to impose crude land-use zoning have often been seen to fail. Urban neighbourhoods require a far more complex set of management policies than are currently available.

It is important to note that many of our traditional urban neighbourhoods have maintained their popularity into the twenty-first century, while the anonymous estates that were so popular just 20 years ago are now struggling to retain their viability. As earlier chapters have stated, there is an urgent need to re-establish the art of making good neighbourhoods that can be maintained over the course of many, rather than single, generations. This has been achieved in the past and there should be no reason why it cannot be achieved again.

Project complexity and uniqueness

It is acknowledged that no two neighbourhoods are alike, but one can identify common themes in seemingly disparate places. It has been clearly stated that the physical process of design is an essential element in creating, or re-establishing neighbourhoods, yet such physical development strategies should generally be undertaken in parallel with other programmes. These should include economic development programmes, educational, social and health initiatives and local security plans.

Truly sustainable development should seek to address a whole complex of social, economic and environmental objectives. In respect of this, urban village projects should initially focus on regenerating and reusing existing urban areas, including a wide variety of brownfield sites, before expanding into new greenfield locations. The complexity of such reuse and mixed-use projects increases the level of financial risk, thereby compounding the difficulties in their delivery. It comes as no surprise that many mixed-use neighbourhood regeneration strategies are in danger of floundering at an early stage.

An important objective at the outset is to minimize the level of uncertainty and risk. As the series of case studies at the end of this book will show, markets do react well to the security and predictability that a well-planned and comprehensive approach to development and regeneration can offer. Conversely, markets often shun situations where there is uncertainty in the strategy and policy for an area. All projects have to operate within the requirements of some element of the property industry, even if it is a specialized or niche market, although it should be recognized that markets can, in certain circumstances, be led by innovators.

All projects must start with an appreciation of the specific circumstances found within each neighbourhood, and this must include a detailed understanding of the prevailing market forces. It will also be important to project future trends in the market through an assessment of the commercial potential that a successful scheme may have. Successful neighbourhoods are those that can adapt to change, or which are of sufficient quality to induce property owners to invest in adapting their properties to modern requirements. Conversely, neighbourhoods that lack momentum and fail to respond to change also fail to attract people who would wish to live, or conduct business, in them. This stagnation can be triggered by a number of reasons: the neighbourhood may have insufficient quality or variety; the environment may be poor or badly managed; bad neighbours may drive good neighbours out. It can be a complex process to identify the particular qualities that lead to the success or failure of a neighbourhood. The following section attempts to provide an initial overview.

Neighbourhood types

Much has been written on the structure of British towns, which show a remarkable diversity in the way they have developed. In addressing a neighbourhood approach to both development and regeneration, it is important to understand the context and characteristics of specific districts to assist in establishing an appropriate implementation strategy. Taking the structure of

Right:
The urban transect
can identify the location
of both existing
neighbourhoods and
potential urban village
projects

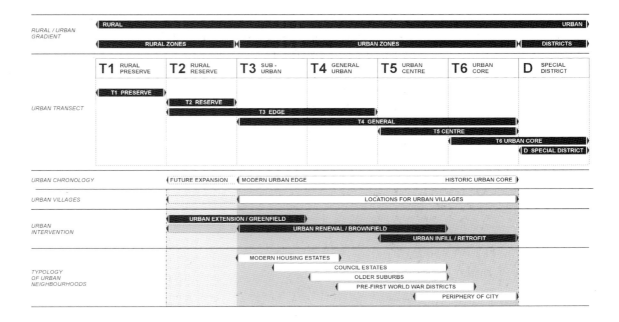

Right:
The urban transect
can identify the location
of both existing
neighbourhoods and
potential urban village
projects

Fight:
Local shopping facilities
in modern housing
estates have often failed
to compete in current
commercial markets

the urban transect discussed in Andrés Duany's chapter, it is possible to locate three varieties of urban village and mixed-use neighbourhood projects. Close to city centres *urban retrofit* strategies, such as that used in Birmingham's Jewellery Quarter, work at infilling and rebuilding the existing historic neighbourhood fabric. Further out, larger-scaled *urban renewal* projects are undertaken where failed neighbourhoods, or redundant industrial sites, have to be completely reworked, as seen in the regeneration of Hulme in Manchester. Towards the edge of existing urban areas *urban extension* projects, like Poundbury in Dorset, connect with adjacent neighbourhoods and provide new urban quarters. Such categories can be useful, but it is important to appreciate that the reality can often be more complex.

In many towns and cities it is possible to identify a generalized chronology of neighbourhood development growing outwards from the central urban core. These include inner urban neighbourhoods, modern suburbs, major brownfield sites and urban extensions. At the outset of any new urban village project it will be useful to identify and appreciate the particular characteristics of these neighbourhood types.

A1 Inner urban neighbourhoods: districts on the periphery of city and town centres

Whilst some of these districts remain successful residential areas, in most places these areas have a significant proportion of older, and obsolete, residential and commercial property. The adjoining town or city centres have, over time, placed great pressure on these areas as locations of secondary commercial uses, along with parking and service functions that have been driven out of the centres. Such neighbourhoods are prime candidates for urban village renewal projects, but issues of high residual value can be problematic.

A2 Inner urban neighbourhoods: pre-First World War districts

The rapid urbanization of the late Victorian and Edwardian periods has created a legacy of older neighbourhoods. These are generally located in a

ring around the centre, but can be found in other locations, including former villages on the edge of the town or city. They were generally built near major employment complexes such as railway sheds and mills, although most of these industrial buildings have now disappeared. In many of the more prosperous towns and cities in Britain these neighbourhoods have become very desirable locations in which to live, with values to match. In such situations, intervention is simply designed to retrofit these neighbourhoods and incorporate modern requirements, such as schools, car-parking areas, the closure of streets to create environmental zones and limited pedestrianization for shopping centres. In less prosperous parts of Britain, such as Scotland, Northern England, Wales and parts of

the English Midlands, many of these older neighbourhoods have gone into a significant decline, and many provide opportunities for mixed-use redevelopment and renewal. Such opportunities depend crucially on there being sufficient development land, either in large consolidated parcels or distributed throughout the area, to achieve significant transformation through the quantum of redevelopment taking place. Essentially, this is what is happening in the Jewellery Quarter in Birmingham and Crown Street in Glasgow.

There are instances where certain of these older neighbourhoods have, in effect, ceased to function. These are characterized by a collapse in house values, problems with drugs and crime, a flight outward of a significant proportion of the original residents and a high turnover of new residents. Such places have such deep-seated problems that cannot be solved by physical renewal and restructuring alone, but will require an additional raft of social and economic initiatives. It is vital to achieve a level of security, safety and renewed confidence upon which a 'normal' neighbourhood can be re-established.

A3 Inner urban neighbourhoods: older suburbs

Between the First World War and the early 1960s extensive suburban development was created in Britain. Many of these new suburbs were designed with reference to the garden suburb and garden city movements. They have planned retail centres, formal and informal open spaces, a limited range of social and educational facilities, and semi-detached (and later detached) housing that was introduced on a large scale. Some of these estates have matured now and fulfil a valuable social and sustainable role in our urban fabric. However, some of these older estates are in need of attention and plainly many have had difficulties coping with the demands that universal car ownership has brought. Essentially the approach is one of retrofitting these suburbs so that they meet modern living requirements. This includes improving social and educational resources, providing for car parking and loading facilities for heavy goods vehicles, improving infrastructure (particularly telecommunications) and restoring public open spaces.

B1 Modern suburbs: council estates

Significant provision of housing by local authorities had begun by the start of the twentieth century, and major suburban-style estates were built between the 1930s and the early 1950s. These were succeeded by a much greater proportion of mixed high- and low-rise development throughout the 1960s and 1970s. Such council estates, including the Leigh Park Estate in Havant, present some of the most challenging problems in Britain. The right-to-buy has helped to stabilize neighbourhoods to a certain degree where it has been exercised by a significant proportion of the tenants. In other cases, however, the combined impact of the right-to-buy and an exceedingly weak property market has resulted in accelerated levels of decline. This was clearly observed by the House of Commons Select Committee on the legacy of housing degeneration in the New Towns.[2]

The drive for efficiency in spending by local authorities has caused under-investment in housing stock, while a reduction in the level of long-term environmental management has caused a significant deterioration in the quality of these housing estates. Furthermore, public housing no longer forms the majority of the property tenure in the Britain, but with increasing affluence and choice, public housing is now predominantly occupied by those families in greatest need, resulting in a high density of low-income households. This in itself means that the income levels in an area are often insufficient to support a range of social facilities. It will be necessary to diversify income levels, tenure and choice of homes in order to break out of the cycle of under-investment and the creation of social exclusion ghettos, as witnessed with some council estates. The government has been progressively creating companies and trusts to administer the stock, but this has not necessarily altered the problem of what to do with these types of estates. Selective demolition of the worst housing and the building of private sector residences along with new retail units and workspace have successfully renewed many areas. Hulme in Manchester is perhaps the best example where a high level of investment and significant intervention seems to have worked. This diversification of tenure and use, along with property remodelling to foster regeneration, is now being attempted on a number of other estates in Manchester.

B1 Modern suburbs: modern housing estates

Surrounding most of our towns and cities are modern housing estates based on the principles set out in the Department of Transport's *Design Bulletin 32*.[3] Essentially, these estates are based on distributor roads without direct frontage from houses, and culs-de-sac off which almost all properties gain access. The movement to establish urban villages and sustainable urban neighbourhoods can be a useful way to remedy some of the failings that these estates suffer from. The increase in design variety, choice of tenure and social integration has helped achieve a higher-quality environment. However, delivering a mix of facilities is still a challenge and because these estates are all fairly recent developments, there are at present limited opportunities to remodel them.

C Major brownfield sites

These can be defined as sites of at least 20 hectares in a single freehold ownership where the existing buildings and structures have been, or will be, cleared. They have arisen in all cases because the original use has ceased. The most common examples are docks, railway goods yards, steelworks and other large industrial complexes, hospitals and defence establishments, including airfields, army and naval bases.

Such sites occur in a wide variety of urban and rural locations. Docklands and major industrial complexes tend to be close to city or town centres and are generally adjacent to pre-First World War districts. These were the focus for much of the regeneration work led by Urban Development Corporations in the 1970s and 1980s. Larger hospital redevelopment opportunities, in contrast, are more likely to be in the centre suburbs or on settlement boundaries, whilst almost all defence establishments are beyond the limits of urban areas.

D Urban extensions

In essence these are the new neighbourhoods currently being planned on the edges of existing built-up areas, or on major brownfield sites adjacent to an established urban district. These are important neighbourhoods in the making, and it is anticipated that they will accommodate at least 30 per cent of new development in the next 20 years. They offer the opportunity to plan afresh and avoid the mistakes of the recent past. By understanding the principles that have made many of our inner area neighbourhoods so successful, and adapting them to the requirements of modern living, it is hoped that we can create places that will remain popular for many generations to come.

Defining project boundaries

A key issue in the early establishment of an urban village will be the definition of its boundary. It is often the case that residents of towns and cities have the most acute sense of which neighbourhood they live in, and also what the boundaries to these neighbourhoods are. Obviously this view will never be unanimous, and there will always be people who will wish to detach themselves from an area that is less well regarded and link themselves to a more fashionable place. This is often done for no other reason than to elevate the value of their property. Establishing where people's neighbourhood loyalties lie is most effectively achieved through surveys, interviews, workshops or using mass-observation techniques. This latter method is based on formalizing discussions with people in the places where they congregate, for example in pubs, clubs or even outside school gates at the end of the school day.

Historically, urban planners and other professionals have taken a physical rather than social view of the extent of neighbourhoods, defining them by such features as railway lines, rivers, main arterial highways and large, non-residential uses such as hospitals and large factory developments. It is also possible to define schemes around key social objectives and to frame project boundaries around areas that are suffering similar problems. This emphasis is becoming increasingly popular through the work of the government's Social Exclusion and Neighbourhood Renewal units.

Work by University College London's Space Syntax Laboratory[4] on the connectivity of roads and streets reveals that there is often a great deal of sense in using features which are barriers to movement as boundaries to neighbourhoods. The exceptions to this are major roads, which may have developed over time as barriers to cross-movement, but nevertheless maintain very good connectivity. They also persist as retail and service centres despite the many conflicts between through-traffic, drivers wishing to park to use the commercial and service facilities within them, and truck drivers wishing to make deliveries.

The economic base of communities provides one of the most important components for the definition of projects, and this is particularly so where there are few employment opportunities in a locality. The government's social exclusion agenda, which includes various local training initiatives, provides a useful guide for the social and economic boundaries of a project. It will also be important to appreciate that the area of impact for a project will often extend well beyond its physical boundaries to adjoining neighbourhoods, or even the urban area as a whole. This issue is often forgotten in the procurement process.

One of the great difficulties in planning on a neighbourhood basis is that the provision of services and utilities undertaken by public agencies and statutory undertakers is rarely undertaken in a common form. The reason is that they are driven by the need to satisfy the requirements of their own policymakers, and so they establish the framework that best matches the requirements of

their own organization rather than those of a common coordinating body. School catchments are a perfect example, in that a primary school with, say, 360 pupils, will try to identify with an area that has a similar number of primary schoolchildren. The result of this mismatch between service-delivery areas is that it is very difficult to achieve either a coordinated policy or the day-to-day provision of services such as health, education, social services, security, welfare, recreation, economic development and transport. This failure is now perceived by government as a key element in perpetuating social exclusion and is one of the main reasons why many worthwhile area-based initiatives are not as successful as they might otherwise be.

As presented earlier in this book, one of the more popular approaches to defining neighbourhoods is by establishing the walking

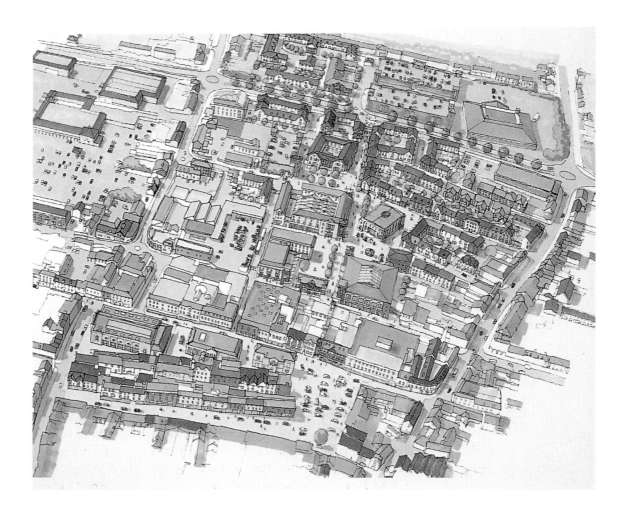

Right:
Bury St Edmund's Cattle Market will 'retrofit' a mixed-use urban neighbourhood within the town
John Thompson & Partners

distance from the residential areas to the centre – the so called pedestrian shed or 'ped-shed'. It is of particular value in urban areas where it defines the accessibility of people to the public transport system, but is now acquiring wider relevance through schemes that are focusing on car reduction and greater pedestrian accessibility. Home Zones, traffic calming, traffic management, and limited high-cost parking, as well as government policies to limit private car use and reduce CO_2 emissions, are all serving to re-enforce the value of a pedestrian-oriented neighbourhood boundary.

The role of the public sector

Project identification and initiation generally require the involvement of both public and private sector teams and partnerships. Where the complexities, cost and duration of suitable neighbourhood projects are particularly high, the early stages are often led by the public sector.

It is generally the case that key public sector organizations in the UK are best placed to

encourage urban villages. These include the Regional Development Agencies (who are tasked by government with securing the urban renaissance), English Partnerships (which has specific skills in regeneration and significant land holdings from its previous life as the Commission for New Towns) and local authorities (and in particular those major urban authorities with skilled in-house regeneration teams).

Within a supportive planning framework, the public sector should establish those areas they wish to prioritize for urban renaissance. These will usually be areas with a combination of need and opportunity. Public sector resources are limited and must be used to best effect, both in delivering beneficial change and in targeting the advantages of those changes on more needy communities.

Once the public sector has identified a potential scheme, but before its boundaries are defined, it is important to carry out a preliminary financial appraisal. This will incorporate outline costs and values of the scheme initially using a discounted cash flow methodology that sets out the costs required for the duration of the project and the level of return. This will identify what shortfalls may occur over the life of the project and what potential there is for grant support. The value of this tool is that it can rapidly be modified to assess what impact the inclusion, or exclusion, of additional sites will have on the scheme. It can also be employed to examine the robustness of market assumptions as far as rental levels, yields, receipts and rates of site disposal are concerned. It is also possible to model the impact of property recessions, such as that which occurred in the early 1990s, on the economic prospects of a project.

Undertaking such an appraisal process is essential if a proposed scheme is to draw in private sector partners or investment by financial institutions. It will be important to undertake this process a number of times before the final boundary is fixed. Demonstrating the fact that an initial appraisal has been undertaken will certainly enhance confidence in the credibility of the scheme at an initial stage and should make the task of attracting investors very much more straightforward.

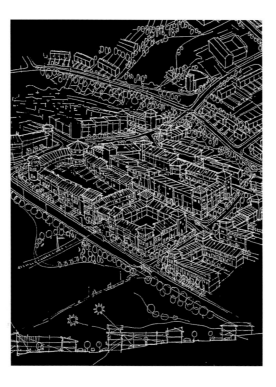

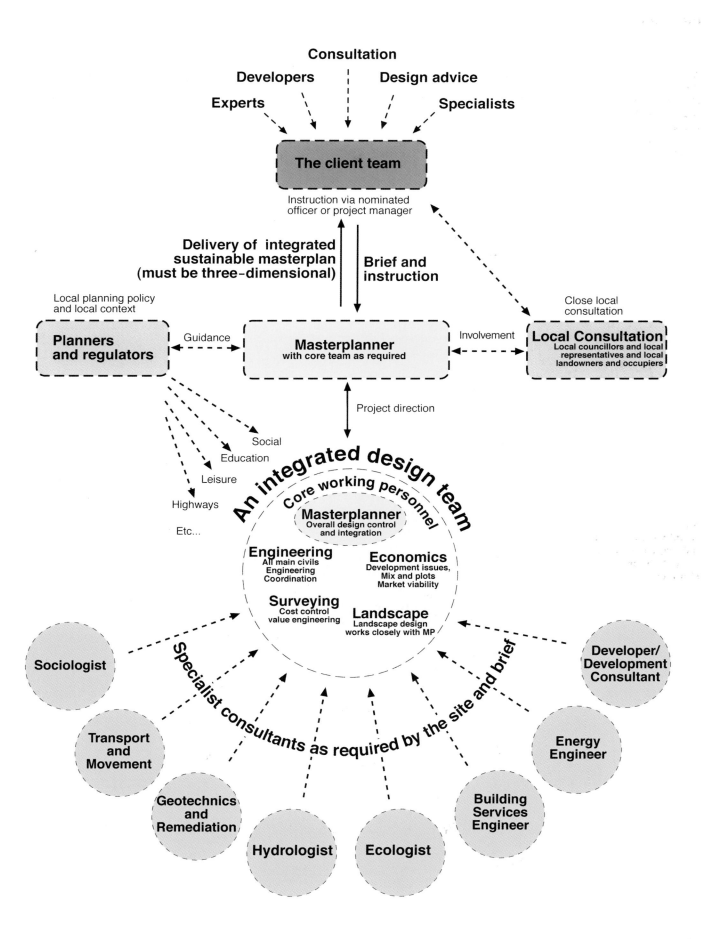

Consultant teams and project briefs

The complexities of urban village projects require a wide range of technical skills to deliver the vision and concept for the scheme. Key to this delivery will be the appointment of a multidisciplinary consultant team who will be responsible for preparing the masterplan, project-managing the various activities to ensure they are properly coordinated, and providing the diverse technical and financial information that will be required for the project.

The selection process is generally undertaken though a process of competitive tender – particularly where this is a statutory requirement. To comply with European Community legislation on the procurement of public sector contracts above a set value, a formal notice must be placed in a specific format in the *Official Journal of European Communities*. This is commonly referred to as an 'OJEC notice'. Alternatively, teams may be short-listed or directly invited by private sector clients on the basis of their particular expertise or track record.

Depending on the characteristics of the project, consultant teams generally include the following skills:

– urban design and planning;
– architecture and landscape architecture;
– transport planning and engineering;
– economic development and commercial property analysis;
– public consultation and collaborative working;
– quantity surveying; and
– financial analysis and funding.

Often, projects require additional specialist and technical skills in at least one of the following fields:

– ecology and landscape assessment;
– geotechnical investigation, infrastructure and structural engineering; and
– heritage architecture and archaeology.

The project brief prepared for the appointment of the consultant team provides one of the most important documents and points of reference for the entire project. It is commonly prepared on behalf of the client team and establishes the context, the overall objectives, programme and scope of work for the project. It remains the main point of reference during the early stages of the project delivery process, and adequate time and expertise should be assigned to its preparation. Common elements in consultant team briefs include:

– project context;
– explanation of terms and key requirements;
– purpose of the brief;
– objectives for the neighbourhood-based framework;
– the study area;
– policy background;
– key issues;
– the management of the study;
– consultants' key tasks;
– required outputs;
– programme and timescales;
– budgets for the study;
– selection procedure for the consultant team.

Baseline audit and analysis

Establishing the baseline condition of a project is the first major activity that is undertaken following the appointment of the consultant team. Much of this work focuses on the physical parameters of the project and provides the foundation on which the masterplan is subsequently prepared. In parallel to the physical baseline, specific data on the social, economic and planning contexts to the project should also be compiled to ensure a balanced and rounded audit. This will be particularly important for urban village projects that are working within, or alongside, existing communities. In such situations redevelopment has to go beyond simply improving the physical fabric of the neighbourhood; it must also rebuild or strengthen the existing social and economic structures.

Information should be collected for both the site and the surrounding area and should include an appropriately wide catchment to ensure connections with local services, transport facilities and utility networks. Information from local organizations, experts, councils and statutory consultees often proves invaluable and should be sought at the outset. Much of the data should be collated on a set of plans that are accurately referenced, dated and supported with a descriptive text. For larger projects these spatial baseline plans can be coordinated within a geographic information system to facilitate future reference and comparative analysis.

Although certain criteria, such as ownership and land use, will need to be collected for all projects, the comprehensive list of baseline criteria should be refined to meet the specific characteristics of each project. Clearly, much of the baseline information required for the renewal of an inner urban neighbourhood will be different to that needed for a major brownfield redevelopment or a new urban extension.

Collecting background information should not be seen as an end itself and should be compiled to establish the potential strengths, weaknesses, opportunities and threats (SWOT analysis) of candidate projects. This should ensure that the technical feasibility of a project is adequately assessed at an early stage to avoid abortive and costly work in future stages. SWOT analysis is a common technique used to establish the realistic potential for the site and its surroundings. It provides a composite of various disparate pieces of information that are drawn together to assess the potential success of a scheme. The analysis for the regeneration potential for the Western Waterfront in Gloucester provides a useful example.[5] Such SWOT exercises should include a wide variety of organizations and individuals, and can be held during public consultation events and enquiry by design exercises, to ensure that a measured assessment of the project is made during this initial stage.

Inner urban neighbourhood analysis

An analysis of inner urban neighbourhood projects must start by understanding the key strengths of the area, including social cohesion and the existence of established commercial and community facilities. It should also determine clear weaknesses, including changing patterns of social and demographic structures within the area. One of the key signs indicating rapid decline is the flight of families out of an area, with a collapse of house prices, a significant rise in vacancies and an increase in rented bedsitter properties. A commercial assessment may identify the loss of traditional retail businesses that have been replaced by low-rent discount operations with a target market that has become city- or town-wide. This can be a strong indication of decline and is particularly the case where such operations work out of semi-derelict properties or even cleared sites. Edge-of-town or city-centre neighbourhoods

Information required for the Baseline Audit	A - Inner Neighbourhoods	B - Residential Suburbs	C - Brownfield Redevelopment	D - Urban Extensions
Physical Context				
Site Topography	■	■	■	■
Land Ownership	■	■	■	■
Patterns of Land Use	■	■	■	■
Vehicular Movement	■	■	■	■
Pedestrian Movement	■	■	■	■
Public Transport	■	■	■	□
Services and Utilities	■	■	■	□
Ecology & Landscape	□	□	■	■
Hydrology	□	□	■	■
Ground Contamination	□	□	■	□
Archaeology	□	□	□	■
Property Condition	■	■	■	
Vacant / Derelict Land	■	■	■	
Townscape Audit	■	□	□	
Public / Private Opens Space	■	■	□	
Social Context				
Demographic / Census Statistics	■	■	■	□
Social Exclusion	■	■	■	
Levels of Employment	■	■	■	□
Economic Activity Levels	■	■	■	□
Patterns of Crime	■	■	□	
Health Facilities	■	■	□	
Education Resources	■	■	□	
Community Facilities	■	■	□	
Recreation Facilities	■	■	□	
Economic Context				
Existing Trading Levels	■	■	■	
Commercial Rents	■	□	□	
Information on Tenure	■	■	□	□
Employment Centres	■	□	■	□
Retail Strength	■	■	□	□
Residential Market	■	■	■	■
Rental Market	■	■	■	■
Policy Context				
Government Guidance	■	■	■	■
Regional Guidance	□	□	■	■
Structure Plan	□	□	■	■
Local / UDP	■	■	■	■
Design Guidance / SPG	■	■	■	□
Development Briefs	■	□	■	
Site Specific Policies	■	■	■	■
Designation / Protection	■	■	■	■
Agreements / S106's	■	■	■	

■ Essential information
□ Supporting information

Right:
Information required for the baseline audit of existing sites should be adapted to the specific needs of the scheme

can be a particularly serious problem. They often become the location for retail and service uses that have been displaced from the centre because they cannot afford the high rents being achieved there. These operations can, however, afford higher rents than local businesses and are therefore capable of outbidding more local enterprises even though they have no connection with the area in which they are located. Such operations frequently generate high volumes of heavy goods traffic and often utilize vacant lots as part of their sales operation and for parking commercial vehicles. Second-hand vehicle sales and commercial parking lots are classic examples that are located in, but do not contribute to, the life of these neighbourhoods.

The opportunities presented in these inner-city neighbourhoods arise from the quality of the housing stock, the residual tight structure of the urban fabric, and the redevelopment opportunities offered by the existence of derelict buildings and vacant or under-used land. In addition, such neighbourhoods are usually well connected within the wider urban network, have good public transport and good utility services, and often have established community assets such as parks.

The weaknesses are usually centred in the collapse of local housing markets and the failure of the local retail sector either to compete with larger units outside the neighbourhood or to adapt to a new role within it. In areas where security problems are significant, small and medium enterprises often choose to move away because of the very real fear of vandalism and theft. This genuine concern is usually matched by high insurance premiums that only serve to increase the financial problems of businesses in the area. Ultimately, insurance companies may even refuse cover, forcing firms to leave.

Older residential suburb analysis

As far as the older residential suburbs are concerned, the main aim is usually to restore the quality of the environment alongside a rationalization and modernization of shopping facilities. Often there are few significant development or redevelopment opportunities within these areas and the main focus of data collection should concentrate on the quality of the built fabric. This will include an assessment of existing public spaces and the quality of the hard and soft landscape elements within the public realm and on private property. An analysis of pedestrian circulation, through-traffic movement and the provision of off-street parking should also be undertaken. There is often the need to accommodate larger and more modern commercial units within the existing urban fabric, or to meet an increasing demand for more comprehensive social and educational facilities for residents.

Modern suburb analysis

The needs of modern suburbs tend to focus on the quality of the building stock. Although many council estates were constructed to a high standard, poor maintenance and repair have often resulted in the asset value being severely diminished. An assessment of the quality of the residential fabric should be undertaken. An assessment of the quality of the residential fabric should be undertaken. Whilst it is often found that the scale of internal space is often very high – particularly in dwellings built to Parker Morris standards, which set a mandatory benchmark for public sector housing in the late 1960s – the same cannot be said for the external areas. There is usually no provision for off-street car parking, other than within garage courts that are frequently vandalized. The level of community, social and retail provision is generally limited. Standard parades of small shops often find it difficult to compete with larger and newer out-of-town developments. They can also suffer from burglary and vandalism. An assessment of market demand for new housing should be made, and an audit of the existing mix of tenure should be undertaken. A robust marketing and design strategy will often need to be put in place in advance of attracting private sector builders and registered social landlords.

Major brownfield redevelopment analysis

A different approach should be taken to data collection for major brownfield projects. These include the redevelopment of large industrial sites, docks and steelworks that have previously been located within or alongside existing neighbourhoods. The great advantage of such sites

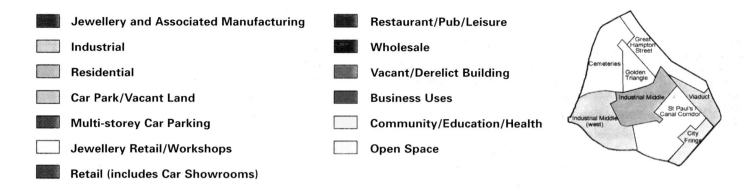

Jewellery and Associated Manufacturing

Industrial

Residential

Car Park/Vacant Land

Multi-storey Car Parking

Jewellery Retail/Workshops

Retail (includes Car Showrooms)

Restaurant/Pub/Leisure

Wholesale

Vacant/Derelict Building

Business Uses

Community/Education/Health

Open Space

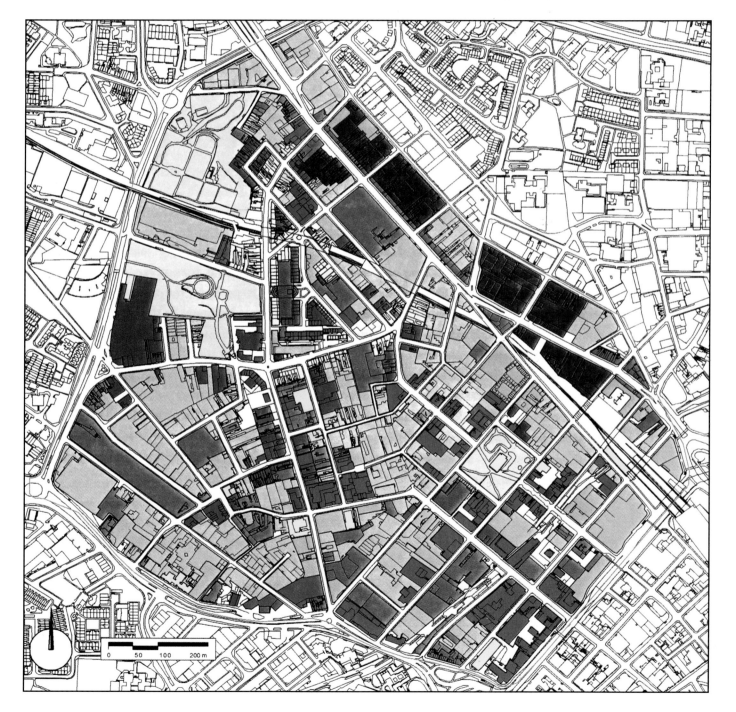

Left:
The regeneration of King's Cross will include a detailed analysis of existing infrastructure and built heritage
Argent St. George Ltd.

is that they are often well located but there may be very high costs associated with remediation, ground preparation, removal of existing legal constraints and the provision of adequate access and services. Such sites often have poor pedestrian and vehicular links to surrounding communities and, when developed, can generate high traffic volumes. Due to the nature of their size, redevelopment can have a significant impact on the physical, social, recreational and educational infrastructure of surrounding communities. Data collection must provide both a physical on-site analysis and an inventory of off-site facilities that would be available for use by the new community.

Urban extensions analysis

In comparison to the complications encountered with inner urban and brownfield sites, the clear attraction of greenfield development relates to the limited number of constraints to development. It will be essential to understand the planning context to the scheme to ensure that the proposals meet with regional guidance and the objectives of both structure and local plans. An initial audit should swiftly assess the impact of designations and planning restrictions associated with the specific site and safeguard key environmental assets, including areas that may have a rich ecology. It is important not to develop such projects in isolation; a baseline analysis should include a wide context to establish good connectivity with adjacent communities. The potential to develop public and private transport provision should be assessed, along with possible pedestrian links to surrounding districts. The collation of social and economic data will depend on the specific characteristics and needs of these surrounding districts. Some of these adjoining areas may suffer from the poor provision of health care, education and other social facilities. Any new development will need to compensate for this shortfall by providing additional and supporting amenities.

The project vision

To conclude the initial identification and inception stage it will be important to establish a collective vision for the project. This should precede any framework and masterplanning activities and provide a succinct objective for the entire enterprise. It should remain a central focus for all subsequent design, implementation and management activities throughout the life of the scheme. A vision should be both evocative and realistic and should:

–   provide clear directions and goals;
–   establish commitments and allocate resources; and, above all,
–   define agreed aspirations for the future.

For example, the vision for Little Germany Urban Village is 'to create a safe, vibrant, well-populated area with a strong sense of identity based around a lively range of local amenities'.[6] The Little Germany Urban Village Company provides the resources and commitment to the vision through a partnership of stakeholders who have established three key strategic aims to underpin the vision. These are to:

–   provide an attractive place to live, work and visit so that Little Germany becomes a sustainable extension of the city centre;
–   safeguard and protect the valuable built heritage of Little Germany to ensure that it plays a full part in the regeneration of the area; and
–   develop a sustainable, diverse and integrated residential and business community.

It is important to avoid a common pitfall during the early stages of a scheme by losing the focus and purpose of a project. At this stage significant amounts of energy and expenditure are about to be committed to the project and it is important that these are spent wisely. At the outset there should be a collective agreement and understanding as to what the project is really about and what the overarching objectives and aspirations should be. Although detailed elements will inevitably change as the project develops, it is important that the central vision remains clear. It is all too easy for schemes to lose their focus and momentum in a morass of bureaucracy and disputes over commercial realities and uncertainties.

Chapter 8

Project procurement

Mike Hollingsworth, Ben Denton and Chris Brown

Once the scope of the urban village project has been identified, the neighbourhood context analysed, the baseline condition established and the collective vision prepared, extensive work on the scheme can really begin. The process of project procurement requires the coordination of a complex set of activities that run in sequence with one another. During this process the level of certainty for the scheme should grow, and confidence in the scheme should increase. At the outset, only the context and vision may be clear, but by the end of the procurement process the detailed elements and implications of the scheme should be fully understood. Beyond establishing an attractive and robust masterplan, it will be important to build a high level of certainty for the scheme in terms of its fundability, community support and deliverability, and to put in place all the necessary planning and legal requirements. The procurement process includes:

– preparation of the design;
– fulfilling all necessary statutory processes;
– establishing a project partnership;
– agreeing relationships and responsibilities for all the implementation parties;
– defining control and management arrangements for the construction and for long-term control;
– setting out the financial parameters;
– securing the necessary financial commitments; and
– completing the preliminary tasks required to start the construction phases of the project.

Left:
A mixed-use, high density urban block developed by the Homes for Change housing co-operative contributing to the regeneration of Hulme, Manchester

Although each urban village project will have some unique characteristics there is real value in following an accepted and recognized procurement methodology. This provides a collective framework within which all organizations and individuals can operate. Establishing a clear management programme determines the purpose and timing of each activity within the overall process. Each recognized stage for the project should refine the detail of the proposals and reconfirm the financial and technical feasibility of the scheme. Six key elements for procurement can be identified:

- design procurement;
- planning control;
- consultation and community participation;
- land assembly;
- financial assessment and funding; and
- establishing development partnerships.

These are cyclical and sequential processes that are commonly spread over several years. It will be important to maintain reference to both the baseline context for the scheme and the vision for the project. This should provide a firm foundation for the urban village and ensure that the basic principles and viability of a project are established before significant resources are committed to the enterprise.

Design procurement

The design-led element of the procurement process takes the initial design proposals through a set of key stages that bring an increased level of detail to a project. The stages are:

- the strategic framework;
- the masterplan;
- design control mechanisms; and
- detailed design elements.

The strategic framework
At the outset a strategic framework should be prepared for the project. This, the preliminary design activity, provides an initial spatial, or three-dimensional, framework that builds on the vision and is in line with the fundamental objectives set by the project brief and vision. It begins to focus attention on the physical realities and provides an initial design structure on which preliminary financial and technical assessment of the scheme can be made.

The masterplan
Further detail for the project is established during the masterplanning stage. This provides a more comprehensive framework upon which detailed funding, market assessment, consultation and negotiation activities can take place. At this stage confidence should begin to build and the physical reality of the future project should be clearly established. The masterplan has illustrative, technical and legal roles: it confirms the principle spatial image of the project, provides a technical base for evaluation and outline approval, and establishes an initial foundation for future development and financial investment. The final masterplan should be supported with a design statement or design rationale that affirms the primary design objectives of the masterplan and sets out the key design elements of the scheme. This is an important document that will be used to evaluate the structure and quality of the subsequent detailed design elements.

Design control
The third stage in the process establishes guidance for the design of individual elements of the project and articulates the quality that should be achieved from the outset. Design control will include: design guidelines that establish the principles of the design, and which direct and lead future development proposals; design codes that set out specific technical principles and standards that are used to regulate the design of specific elements of the scheme; and supplementary planning guidance that provides a vehicle, via formal adoption by local planning authorities, to ensure that design guidance and codes are endorsed within detailed design elements of the project.

Detailed design
The detailed design stage of a project is essential in establishing the final appearance of the built scheme. It addresses both the design of specific

in Keynes Planning Weekend 24m. to 29m October 1996

elements – be they buildings, streets or open
spaces – as well as the critical details that are to be
used in the construction of each element. The
process is iterative and leads from initial, to
interim, and then final details; these are refined
through an established dialogue between the
design team and a design review panel.

This process ensures that the detail of a project
can be built up through a series of logical stages. It
should ensure collective agreement and ownership
of the project at an early stage, and limit the amount
of abortive work during the latter stages. Establishing a clear masterplan and supporting design
rationale should instil confidence in the scheme in
those who will be affected by the development and
those who will invest in it. Furthermore, adopting
comprehensive design guidance and coding should
make the process of securing detailed design
approvals easier and more efficient.

Many of these stages are used by a number
of professional organizations that have established
a set of recognized stages for project design
and management. The Urban Design Group has
published useful guidance on urban design
frameworks, development briefs and masterplans.[1]

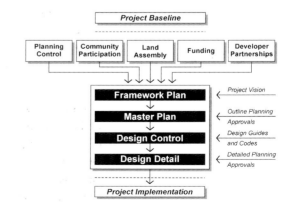

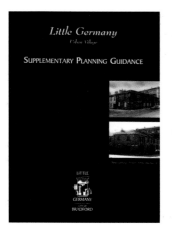

Above:
Supplementary Planning Guidance has been prepared for the Little Germany Urban Village to safeguard the character of the area

Planning control

A critical step in the designation of a urban village will be to establish a clear planning framework for the proposals. In England it is not uncommon for the planning system to take a decade or more to reflect government policy on the ground – which provides plenty of time for government policy to change. Fortunately, however, urban renaissance appears to have all-party support in England and can be respected as a policy with some longevity. This provides a constructive planning policy platform for the implementation of urban villages that are closely aligned with many the objectives for an urban renaissance.

As highlighted in Peter Hall's chapter, brownfield land in the north of England should accommodate all the new development required according to current forecasts of demand. The planning framework therefore must both prevent greenfield development in the short and medium term and proactively seek opportunities to assemble large enough brownfield sites to give the market confidence in its ability to move values upwards in a particular neighbourhood. In southern England, while it is hoped that most development will be on brownfield sites, there is the need for a limited number of town extensions on greenfield land, which must be accessible to public transport.

Such a proactive use of the planning system should create public benefit through improved, and environmentally sustainable, urban environments that are attractive to the expanding knowledge-based and service industries and employees. It is essential not to lose these opportunities because of the inherent inefficiencies of the planning system or delays resulting from an occasionally erratic and cyclical economy.

It is also essential to achieve policy alignment at all tiers of government. If one region or one local authority seeks to gain short-term economic advantage by favouring significant greenfield development over reusing brownfield land, then the urban renaissance is likely to fail. This has been seen on many occasions in the past with, for example, the development of out-of-town shopping centres on greenfield sites and the consequent long-term social, economic and environmental impact on our smaller town centres.

Working with the planning framework
As with any large-scale development proposals, a partnership with the local planning authority should be established at an early stage. The planning principles that underlie urban villages

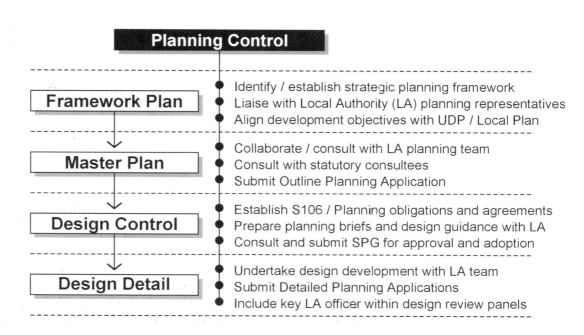

will need to align with the policies and objectives of the local planning authority. It will be essential for each scheme to have active support from planning staff and to be fully integrated within the plan-led local planning system.

Local Plans and Unitary Development Plans provide an essential framework for guiding and controlling development, and act as the foundations on which all planning and development proposals are assessed. They:

–   provide a vision for the area;
–   identify the main objectives that must be achieved in order to realize that vision;
–   define the local context of people and places;
–   set out the overall design policy framework, amongst other considerations, against which the local authority will assess development proposals; and
–   provide the policy foundation for supplementary planning guidance.

It will prove invaluable to have active and constructive representation from the local planning board within the development team throughout the entire development process. Designations for urban villages should go beyond simple planning approvals and 106 agreements (see 'Planning applications and approvals', below). Potential schemes should be clearly identified within Local Plans as sites for urban villages created primarily through brownfield regeneration and additionally by greenfield urban extensions. Research from the Department of Environment[2] states that new schemes should address:

–   the role that new settlements should play in the urban structure of the district;
–   housing and employment mix;
–   phasing and timescale;
–   planning gain;
–   attributes required of the masterplanning team;
–   the scope, scale, form and content of the necessary development framework or flexible masterplan;
–   arrangements for quality control;
–   arrangements for public consultation and participation throughout the development process;
–   arrangements for the involvement of the local

planning authority;
–   design standards, where applicable;
–   contribution towards sustainability; and
–   management and maintenance regime of the public realm.

Such an arrangement gives the local planning authority assurance that the development required for the urban village would be capable of meeting the preliminary planning consent and agreements. In turn this would give the development team long-term planning support, a basis for detailed valuation and, if necessary, the use of compulsory purchase powers.

Development briefs and Supplementary Planning Guidance

Urban design frameworks, design briefs, development briefs and design guides provide a number of vehicles for local authorities to establish clear design objectives for specific urban areas and sites. They are also valuable in stating the potential for an urban village development. In practice, the terminology surrounding these tools is somewhat inconsistent. As a general rule, design guides should focus on areas or issues, whilst the various development briefs should offer detailed guidance for specific sites. The Royal Town Planning Institute (RTPI) has prepared a practice note on development briefs[3] that defines them as 'a summary statement of the author's policy position on development matters relating to the site and/or premises'. The practice note clarifies the terminology thus:

–   planning briefs should deal with planning, land use and transportation matters;
–   developers' briefs address financial and land management aspects; and
–   design briefs cover townscape and other design aspects and aesthetics.

Additional guidance for areas and sites can be adopted as Supplementary Planning Guidance (SPG), which can directly influence design and the outcome of planning applications. Initial urban design principles associated with urban villages should be established as policy within the development plan, whilst the various ways that this can be achieved should be set out within the

SPG. Such guidance can play a valuable role in reinforcing and articulating the policies set within Local Plans, and can provide useful material in support of planning applications. It should be noted that only policies in the development plan should be used to determine planning applications, although SPG can be taken into account as a material consideration. It is important that SPG be prepared in consultation with the public, businesses and other stakeholders to ensure that a wide body of opinion is taken into account before the guidance is finalized. It may also need to be reviewed and when necessary updated in the light of subsequent experience and changes in policy and regulations. Following council resolution, the SPG should be formally adopted.

Council officers, developers and all those concerned with the development will find the SPG easier to use if it has a clear, consistent format and familiar process of preparation. It may prove helpful to publish summary brochures or leaflets on the SPG to enable a more general message on the principles to be put across to a non-technical audience. SPG will only be effective if it expands on the principles of the development plan. Where it is used to support the principles of an urban village, the design objectives must be realistic in terms of the prevailing economic conditions and the conditions of the site and its setting.

By Design, prepared by the Department of the Environment, Transport and the Regions (DETR) and the Commission for the Built Environment (CABE),[4] reiterates the point that the effectiveness of design guides, development briefs and supplementary planning guidance will depend on:

- the degree to which all relevant departments of the council are committed to it;
- the vigour with which council members and officers support it;
- the effectiveness of public participation in preparing it; and
- how logically it is structured, how clearly it is written, and how well it is illustrated.

Planning applications and approvals

Local Plans and Unitary Development Plans provide the context for urban villages and mixed-use schemes within a local planning authority's district. Subsequent stages for securing consent for development will need to be discussed with key members of the local planning staff, who should ideally have direct representation within the development team. Ensuring support from local planning officers is essential in maintaining confidence in the scheme, and will be a prerequisite for any public grant funding. The local planning authority should be able to provide strategic advice on the preparation of planning briefs and supplementary planning guidance before outline planning applications are prepared.

Establishing outline consent for a project will be an important stage in the process of securing the statutory approvals that will enable the scheme to proceed. This may be a relatively simple application showing little more than an outline for the development and a description of the scale of the proposed uses. Nearly all the specific details may be treated as reserve matters or left until a detailed application is made for individual projects. In negotiating outline consent, planning officers will often focus on the terms of any Section 106 Planning Agreements established within the Town and Country Planning Act 1990.[5] These agreements focus on the on-site and off-site infrastructure, phasing, tenure mix, community facilities, design quality, and any commuted sums for management and maintenance. Public consultation on the application will be a statutory requirement and should be seen as an integral part of the long-term consultation strategy.

Application for detailed planning approval will be made for individual buildings or groups of buildings, rather than for the project as a whole, and in most cases individual developers will make these. Application will also need to be made for all infrastructure works including roads, parks and other open spaces; these are generally made on behalf of the development team. *By Design* provides a useful checklist of the information that will be required for such planning applications. Adequate detailed information should be given to ensure that planners, councillors, residents and amenity groups understand the detailed implications of the scheme.

Above:
**Crown Street, Glasgow.
Public consultation
strategies should engage
all sections of the local
community**

Consultation and community participation

Consultation with key stakeholders – statutory authorities, local community organizations and individuals – is an essential requirement within the planning and statutory processes. Since the first Town and Country Planning Act in 1947, varying degrees of public participation have been incorporated in the UK planning system, although it was not until the Skeffington Report of 1969 that widespread public participation became embedded in the process. The 1980s marked a growing awareness of the need for communities and individuals to have a more direct role in the regeneration process. The New Deal for Communities, established by New Labour in 1998, and coordinated by the Neighbourhood Renewal Unit, now spearheads the Government's commitment to coordinate a broad base of community issues in partnership with a programme of physical regeneration initiatives.

There is often confusion about the processes of consultation and participation, and it is essential that the difference between the two be understood at the outset. *Consultation* involves seeking the views of individuals and organizations, but not necessarily involving them in decision-making, whilst *participation* implies direct involvement and influence in the decision-making process.

An urban village project should go beyond the minimum levels required by the statutory process by actively encouraging the public and stakeholders to participate in the design and decision-making process. If local residents and future users of a new community are not supportive at the outset, the scheme is unlikely to succeed in the long term. Establishing an inclusive partnership between all the stakeholders, including local authorities, government agencies, the private sector and the surrounding community organizations, is now seen as crucial in establishing successful and inclusive development and regeneration projects.

Initially identifying the 'community' can be problematic. Urban infill projects and regeneration initiatives tend to be located within existing communities where there are key stakeholders, including residents' groups, civic societies and religious organizations. Greenfield and urban extension projects will rely initially on the involvement of adjacent organizations and individuals until a new residential community is established. Through their elected status, district, county and parish councillors will often play a key leadership role and it is important to establish a constructive working relationship with them at the outset.

If a new project is to foster a real sense of belonging it is essential for the community to be

DUCHY of CORNWALL
POUNDBURY PLANNING WEEKEND
THURSDAY 15 TO MONDAY 19 JUNE 1989
HOW SHOULD
DORCHESTER GROW?

Come and give us your ideas !

THURSDAY 15 JUNE : 19.30
TOWN MEETING : COUNTY MUSEUM
- David Landale: Duchy of Cornwall
- Councillor John Lock: Setting the Scene
- Derek Boyt, WDDC: Forward Planning
- Richard Belding : MAFF
- Leon Krier: Master Planning Objectives
- John Thompson: Weekend Preview

FRIDAY 16 JUNE : POUNDBURY FARM
OPEN DAY 1 : NEEDS OF DORCHESTER
How can the Poundbury development best meet the needs and
aspirations of local people ?
10.00   **Session 1 - History and Planning**
- Roger Peers,County Museum, Dorchester
- David Hall, Town & Country Planning Assoc.
- Leon Krier: Urban Planning
  Open Forum
11.30-   **Session 2 - The Needs of Dorchester**
- Jane Raimes, Community Council for Dorset
- Phil Hodges, Area Director, Social Services
- Glen Bengough, WDDC Housing Officer
- John Wicks, WDDC Economic Development
  Open Forum
13.00   **Lunch**
14.00   **Session 3 - Employment and Training**
- Anthony Horrocks,Facility for Access to
  Creative Enterprise
- Len Carslake, Rural Development Commission
- John Varley, Dorset Crafts Guild
- Don Brierley, Weymouth College
  Open Forum
15.30   **Session 4 - Special interest workshops**
  1. Housing and Special Needs
  2. Education
  3. Community Development and Healthy Cities*
  4. Employment and Training
  5. Arts and Recreation
  * including a presentation by Ros Tennyson,
    Marylebone Centre Trust.
17.00   **Plenary Session - Workshop Reports**

SATURDAY 17 JUNE : POUNDBURY FARM
OPEN DAY 2 : MASTERPLANNING
*To explore how the Poundbury develpoment should take place, both
physically and socially.*
10.00   **Session 1 : Masterplanning**
- David Oliver, Architect WDDC:
- Leon Krier:Masterplanning:
  Open Forum
12.00   **Session 2 - Use Procurement**
- Robert Davis, Seaside DevelopmentCorporation:
- Petra Greenwood, Housing Corporation:
- Sherley Short, Woolwich Building Society:
  Open Forum
13.00   **Lunch at Poundbury**
14.00   **Session 3 - Development Process:**
- John Turner, Right Livelihood Award 1988:
- David Cadman, Fellow of Wolfson College
- Stephen Lloyd,Bates Wells &Braithwaite:
- David Liggins, Coopers & Lybrand:
  Open Forum
16.00   **Session 4 - Present and future trends**
- Tony Gibson,Neighbourhood Initiatives Foundation
- Phil Bixby, Constructive Individuals
- Annabel Jackson,London Industrial
- Andrew Page,Protocol - Telecommuting
  Open Forum

SUNDAY 18 JUNE : 14.00 - 18.00
MONDAY 19 JUNE : 10.00 - 16.00
EXHIBITION AT THE COUNTY MUSEUM

MONDAY 19 JUNE : 19.30
TOWN MEETING : TOWN HALL
Report back from the Duchy of Cornwall's Team on the
weekend proceedings and review of future options.

*If you would like to come to the Open Days at Poundbury Farm,
please ring Andrea Norris in advance at the Duchy of Cornwall
(0255 874194) to see if space is still available. All other events are
open to everybody to attend. Poundbury Farm is 1/2 mile to the
West of Dorchester on the North side of the Bridport Road (A35).*

Above:
**The Poundbury Planning
Weekend was held at the
outset of the project**

process in action. It requires experts with significant experience as well as theoretical qualifications.
They should have extensive skills and specialist
practice in establishing a strong community
commitment to a project through regular consultation
and participation. Achieving the right balance of
action and consultation is always difficult and
brownfield development can often produce a
NIMBY reaction every bit as strong as that
provoked by proposed greenfield development. It
tends to be the case that the more inadequate the
consultation, the more violent the reaction.

Collaborative design techniques
There are numerous techniques and examples of
collaborative and participatory processes and it is
essential to choose the correct one. *By Design*
defines the factors that contribute to successful
collaboration:

- the process is tailored to local circumstances;
  everyone who is involved understands their
  role, rights and responsibilities from the
  beginning;
- where appropriate, the process is open to
  everyone who has a stake in the area;
- the flow of information is managed to match
  the needs of all participants; and
- participants have appropriate access to skills
  and professional expertise.

The plethora of techniques may initially appear
confusing. There are Planning Weekends, Planning
Days, Community Planning Forums, Open House
Events, Street Stalls and Interactive Displays, to
name but a few. It is essential that the most
appropriate technique be adopted for each specific
project. There is only space here to outline four of
the most useful techniques; a collection of the
more common approaches to consultation and
participation are presented in detail in the
Community Planning Handbook.[7]

Future Search and *Open Space* are techniques
for consulting groups of people – as few as five or
as many as 800 – over a period of between one
and five days in order to identify common
interests, discuss ideas, share information and
experience, and organize individuals into ongoing
working groups focusing on specific topics. Here, a

actively involved from the outset. All too often,
projects have failed because the initial consultation
was haphazard and participatory exercises were
undertaken after key development decisions had
been made – by which time developers and planners
had ceased to have open minds. The art of
successful community consultation and participation
has much improved in recent years and there are
now several valuable guides that outline the
process and techniques that can be adopted.[6]

There are many examples of the consultation

cross-section of community members or stakeholders creates a shared vision for the future, although this tends to deal with general issues rather than specific sites.

Planning for Real enables residents to use a model of their area as a tool to help them determine priorities for the future, with technical experts available 'on tap but not on top'. The use of simple models helps people to focus their ideas and to put forward priorities on how their area can be improved. It is a highly visible, hands-on community development and empowerment tool, which people of all abilities and backgrounds find it easy and enjoyable to engage in.

Design Workshops or *Enquiries by Design* (sometimes known as *charrettes*) bring a wide range of participants together to explore design ideas for a particular area. These are generally hands-on sessions run over a day, week or weekend, allowing small groups of professionals and non-professionals to work creatively together developing planning and design ideas.

Action Planning, Community Planning Weekends and *Urban Design Action Teams* involve collaboration between local people and an invited team of professionals to explore design ideas for a particular area. They allow people to produce plans of action at carefully structured sessions at which all those affected can work creatively together. They can be used at any stage of the development process and provide a viable alternative to having to rely on bureaucratic planning processes.

Consultation stages

It is essential to match the consultation process and technique with the appropriate stage of the project. There is a danger that raising individual desires and single issues of minor importance at the outset can confuse the overall vision; equally, strategic issues that have a fundamental impact on the initial scheme should not be allowed to confuse the design of the detailed elements at the latter stages of a project.

The strategic aspirations and a vision for project will need to be established at the outset. It is often an advantage to show community leaders examples of best practice, which may include

examples of appropriate development projects from abroad. Future Search and Open Space techniques provide useful ways to establish initial aspirations for the area without needing to address some of the more complicated issues of technical detail. Often this process will become part of a wider dialogue that covers other needs of the local community, including issues of health, education, and crime. It is important to establish these issues at the outset so that the parameters of the physical development can be understood and appreciated within the wider needs and aspirations of the community.

Very few public and private sector clients and their associated design teams can do this work well, and much education is still required to improve this process. One approach is to use one firm initially, to facilitate the community engagement, and then, in partnership with the local community, select an urban designer for the project. The RTPI-award-winning Smithfield Neighbourhood in Manchester adopted such a process and a guide to this can be found in the booklet and website produced to accompany the project.[8]

Planning for Real provides a valuable way to establish outline objectives for the physical project that will cement the vision and in turn drive the masterplanning process. It is important to ensure that the key priorities are established and agreed by the community before embarking on significant design work. The emerging framework and masterplan should be seen as the vehicle that will enable the community to realize their aspirations, not presented to the community as a fait accompli at the outset.

Enquiry by Design offers an increasingly popular participatory technique to establish collective ownership of a preferred masterplan. Held as an intensive *charrette* or workshop, the process can run for up to a week and brings together a wide range of stakeholders, including councillors, local community representatives and developers. During the process a framework or masterplan is prepared – in real time – to provide a basis upon which shared interests and conflicts of interest between the stakeholders can be aired and addressed. At each stage of the design new questions are raised and, in the process of answering them, design modifications are made.

Consultation should be seen as a long-term process that occurs throughout the life of the project. Open discussion with appointed individuals should inform the development of design codes and infrastructure and plot layout to achieve urban design and building styles appropriate to the local vernacular and the aspirations of the community. Building new neighbourhoods on any significant scale is fraught with difficulty, as the mistakes of the 1960s and 1970s have taught us. Maintaining a collaborative approach through to the detailed design stage affords the opportunity to focus on smaller components of the masterplan and allows projects to grow more organically, thereby minimizing the risk of large-scale errors.

Land assembly

The condition and control of the land in terms of both its physical and legal status is fundamental to the initial feasibility and the long-term management of a neighbourhood. At the outset of the Urban Villages Campaign the need to have such ownership and control was seen as a crucial requirement for the success of a scheme. Only rarely is this achieved through a single organization or individual. For example, much of the success of Poundbury in Dorset has been attributed to the single ownership of the Duchy of Cornwall, whilst difficulties in establishing Ancoats Urban Village in Manchester have been caused by the mosaic of individual landowners.

Large-scale land assembly, to reduce risk and increase certainty, is a fundamental requirement for any urban village scheme and is generally made possible by the public sector. The land necessary for the project and the essential surroundings should be under the control of an agency dedicated to achieving the prescribed objectives. Common sense dictates that without ideally contiguous ownership – or at least collective control – of the land, the project is exposed to significant risk. It tends to be more common for larger brownfield urban renewal and greenfield urban extension projects to fall within a single ownership, whilst tight urban infill or retrofit projects often are complicated by a myriad of small ownership and tenure arrangements.

The condition and quality of the land resource should also be assessed at an early stage. This is usually undertaken during the initial baseline audit and assessment of the scheme, and can be

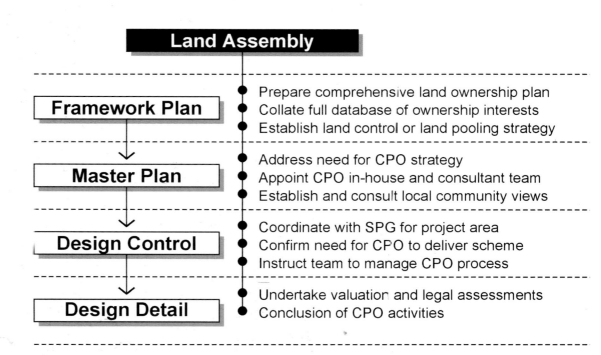

Right:
A proactive approach by the public sector has protected key historic buildings within Ancoats Urban Village

ROYAL MILL

ERECTED 1797

VISITED BY THE KING & QUEEN 19TH NOVEMBER 1942

RE-BUILT 1912

achieved initially though local knowledge and desk studies, although a more comprehensive assessment can only be accomplished through geotechnical investigations on site. Land contamination, particularly on post-industrial brownfield sites, can pose the single greatest threat to the technical and financial feasibility of a project, because it may dictate what is acceptable and affordable as a future use. Full costs for remediation need to establish the true value, or liability, of the land at an early stage so that the costs to purchase and construct the project can be defined.

Currently the system by which land is assembled by the public sector is not at its most dynamic in England – although the government has recognized this and is intending to make the changes necessary to facilitate the process. As yet, we are a long way from the sophisticated guidance operated by the Urban Development Corporations or the resources of the new towns but we are slowly moving in the right direction of balancing the rights of the individual with the needs of the wider community to secure the future of their neighbourhood.

The ideal is for the land to be owned by a single entity or organization that can also act as the promoter or key partner in the enterprise. This is a common scenario for many projects that have been initiated by English Partnerships. Alternatively, the single owner may act as strategic partner in the project, either during the initial masterplanning stages or, as with the case of the Duchy of Cornwall, throughout the entire life of the project.

More often, the situation is complicated by joint or multiple ownerships throughout the entire landholding of the project. In this situation, key owners have to form a collaborative partnership or pool the land resource into a single holding, to ensure the initial feasibility of the project. If this is unfeasible or cannot be achieved within a realistic timeframe, the promoter may have to resort to compulsory purchasing the land. With these options in mind, it will be important to confirm at the outset of a project that:

– all the landowners, or certainly the key owners, are willing to make their sites available;
– there is key landowner support for the proposal in principle at the outset;

– a land control strategy can be put in place that includes the capacity for landholdings to be 'brought out' if a party in the venture no longer wishes to be involved; and,
– there is strong evidence that the key landowners are prepared to dispose of their land to the promoter, or participate actively and constructively in the development of the emerging scheme.

Land pooling

When the situation dictates that single ownership cannot be achieved, an initial option is to seek to pool the different ownerships into one control in advance of having to compulsorily purchase the land. Pooling is generally very difficult to achieve and relies on the logic that the total value of the individual land holdings is less than the value of the same land pooled. Pooling will necessitate a strong and binding agreement, to reduce uncertainty, and this in itself may be unattractive to landowners. If there is willingness to pool, there still remain several problems that are common to joint development on sites in multiple ownership. For example:

– how does one allocate future uses between individual owners?
– How does one allocate value between uses and sites?
– How is a differential infrastructure cost burden allocated?
– When can each partner take its return from the joint development?

Land pooling agreements that have worked have been drafted on a similar basis to shareholding agreements. The land is vested into the project based on an agreed valuation basis. This gives partners 'shares' in the venture. Third party funders and other organizations may qualify for shares if they have invested in the venture. Cash may be geared into the venture to pay for infrastructure works. Land may be sold, or buildings developed and sold, and after repaying borrowings, returns will be distributed in accordance with the shareholdings. The financial operations of the venture may also allow for one party to offer its shares to another and, if it wishes, to exit wholly or partly from the venture.

Voluntary pooling is notoriously difficult to achieve and may therefore need to be underpinned by a strategy of Compulsory Purchase Orders (CPOs). The justification for a CPO would be that it is in the public interest and that it would not be in the public interest to allow existing ownership boundaries to frustrate the creation of an urban village.

Compulsory purchase

If necessary, a determined Local Authority or Regional Development Agency (RDA) can acquire land compulsorily. The process is relatively straightforward: having identified an appropriate location, the agency or authority should first establish a compulsory purchase team. Many public sector organizations lack the necessary in-house resources to undertake a full CPO. As a minimum, they should have the necessary staff capable of acting as a well-informed client for a private sector team. A CPO team will usually comprise:

– a referencer experienced in identifying ownerships and producing the required plans and schedules;

– a valuer experienced in the compensation system and able to negotiate and financially close pre-Inquiry acquisitions; and
– an experienced CPO lawyer.

The first task of the CPO team is to undertake a preliminary analysis to establish the CPO strategy. This will include the precise boundaries of the CPO, the planning strategy, the approximate number of owners and occupiers and a broad estimate of likely cost and timescale. It is important to be able to demonstrate that the CPO area is an essential component of the regeneration initiative. The CPO area should be sufficiently large to generate private sector investment confidence in the scale of the initiative, yet not so large that individual owners could defeat the CPO at the Inquiry stage by demonstrating that without their individual landholdings the wider regeneration scheme could still take place successfully.

The strategy should have a planning component. It is usually impossible and undesirable to submit and approve a planning application, even in

outline, as this will create land speculation and, in conservation areas for example, may take many months to resolve. A better process is to undertake consultation with the local resident and business community and with statutory and non-statutory consultees. Planning for Real exercises can be used to support the production of SPG founded on a Local Plan, regional planning and Planning Policy Guidance. At the point of adopting the SPG the agency or authority must also resolve to use CPO policies if necessary to secure the regeneration in accordance with the SPG. This falls short of the need to produce blight notices requiring the acquisition of small business premises, but is sufficient to inhibit the more intelligent speculators and gives some confidence to early phase developers.

Early developers, where they exist, can be encouraged to invest by offers of grant aid and by excluding them from the CPO process on the basis of a signed development agreement with the public authority. These may represent some of the first agreements reached by the valuers in the CPO team. At the same time, the public authorities may also undertake the selection of a lead developer, or a series of developers; the decision about which route to take will primarily revolve around the extent of available public sector skills and financial resources. If the public agency has limited funds it will wish to secure financial backing from the private sector. There may be circumstances where the Day One value for development (the residual development value) is positive; the private sector should be prepared to underwrite this amount, subject to an agreement with the public agency for early purchases should the CPO fail.

The decision on whether to find one, or more than one, private sector underwriter will be determined by the scale of the project, the relative compensation and redevelopment land values, and the availability of private sector investors. It will also be determined by the availability of financial and staff resources in the public sector to play the role of master developer. At a minimum, the public sector will need to act as an intelligent client to negotiate and police the development agreement. This will be particularly true for activities, including project managing, accountancy or quantity surveying, that may be perceived to reduce short-term profits by some private sector partners.

Alternatively, the public sector may choose to set up an urban village delivery team but it is essential to ensure that this is properly resourced. It must be recognized that the people who can lead these teams well are few and far between, although increasing education and training through the regional centres of urban excellence is expected to increase their numbers in time.

Public sector finance for the CPO will usually come from the RDA. These bodies have a public sector agreement target, set by government, to deliver the urban renaissance. The government has made clear their view that delivering the urban renaissance is likely to be critical to the regions' economic success in the knowledge economy. The RDAs and English Partnerships are able to finance these acquisitions through the Brownfield Investment Grant mechanism, which allows them to buy land, service it and then dispose of it to the private sector with the minimum grant necessary to make the development viable.

Once the lead team, the SPG, the acquisition finance and the CPO strategy are in place, the public agency can commence detailed referencing and proceed to make the decision to issue a CPO. This process can take from four to 18 months, depending on the complexity and quality of the forward planning. A dedicated project management function is indispensable in ensuring that the planning and the delivery are effective, as delay should be avoided during this critical phase.

The view will often be expressed that CPOs take too long, yet experience shows that avoiding them often means that regeneration may not happen at all. The best approach is to assume right at the beginning of the process that a CPO will be needed. If it is not the last piece of the implementation process to fall into place, speculators should be discouraged and the delivery of the urban village should be achieved smoothly and effectively.

Financial assessment and funding

In parallel with the assembly of land, the process of securing finance is critical for the design development and implementation of a mixed-use scheme. Two distinct costs and benefits can be derived from urban villages and mixed-use developments: those that relate to the development industry and specifically address the financial return from expertise, investment and risk-taking; and those that concern others in the community, the residents, businesses, local authorities and all who have some form of financial stake in the health of the community.

Whilst most people understand the value of their own financial resources, the complex ways in which money can be manipulated and used to make more money are less well understood. Like many professionals, financiers like to wrap simple concepts in complex explanations and confusing acronyms and abbreviations. Delivering the economic components of a mixed-use scheme requires a complex set of skills, including financial planning, taxation, corporate structuring, property and legal expertise. This section provides but a simple précis of the principles and key stages that are required to finance an urban village project.

The funding of mixed-use neighbourhoods is generally seen to be more difficult to structure than single-use developments because:

- mixed-use projects are often seen to be messy, requiring many players with a spread of skills and expertise to deliver the solution;
- they tend to be located in urban regeneration areas where the costs for land assembly, reclamation, infrastructure and building construction are generally higher than average, whilst the demand for property is often low;
- mixed developments incorporate a collection of local facilities, including community buildings, parks, schools and health centres, that may have to be financed by the development value of the rest of the scheme or through direct public funding;
- most financial institutions focus their expertise on single specific uses and are therefore not set up to work across the boundaries of different activities; and
- mixed uses bring a more complex mix of financial risks; speculative residential projects tend to have lower associated risks than speculative commercial projects.

That said, there is a small but growing body of research that has identified the value added by good urban design in a number of successful of mixed-use developments, including Brindleyplace in Birmingham and Great Notley in Essex. The research arm of the Royal Institution of Chartered Surveyors (RICS) commissioned a study of the involvement of private property decision-makers in urban design, which highlighted the need to adopt a longer-term view on the financial return.[9] Public funding for good quality urban environments should be allocated and managed in a manner that recognizes the interdependence of different spending programmes and the varying components of projects. Another report, *The Value of Urban Design*,[10] commissioned by CABE and the DETR, quantifies the commercial and social benefits of a number of mixed-use schemes. Mixing uses leads directly to higher user and occupier satisfaction and is fundamental to the social, economic and environmental value in the most successful case studies reviewed in the report. Specifically, good urban design is seen to add economic value by:

- producing high returns on investments;
- enhancing the competitive edge of schemes at minimal additional cost;
- supporting the 'life giving' mixed-use elements in developments;
- creating an urban regeneration and place-marketing dividend; and
- opening up investment options, raising confidence in development opportunities and attracting grant monies.

Identifying the borrower

The characteristics of the 'borrowing' organizations will drive the availability and variety of finance. Lenders will put their faith in people and organiz-ations with track records in using their money safely, and returning it with a healthy dividend. Conversely, where the borrower has a history of abuse or misuse of lenders' funds, the borrowing terms may be more stringent or restrictive. Public bodies' ability to borrow is generally controlled by central government, so they will tend to look to the private sector to fulfil this role.

The private sector may use its own funds, or may borrow, but will usually use a blend of both sources. The private sector will want to see some sort of security over the project before it spends significant sums of money. Such security may be land or buildings; for large and complex projects it can also be in the form of a legal agreement. This is often the case where the public sector may be holding the land but will not wish to have a securing charge raised against it, or may not have the powers to grant a charge against it. There may also be indemnities required by the lender or the investor, such that if one party unilaterally pulls out of the project, the remaining partner, or partners, are pro-tected against the potential financial consequences.

Key principles of finance for mixed-use projects

In line with many other activities involved in the delivery of mixed-use urban village projects, the process of financially structuring a project and securing commitments on long-term funding can be complex and tortuous. Although it is impossible to explain all the complexities of the process in a few pages, the following six principles attempt to establish the fundamental rules that govern the process of project financing.

Principle One: Integrate financial planning at the outset of a project

Design, delivery and financial viability go hand-in-hand in assessing the feasibility of a project. It is a common mistake to consider project finance at too late a stage of the design development, when commitments to masterplans have already become established. All three elements should be used in parallel to inform one other.

Another common error is to believe that only when one has a scheme to fund should financial planning commence. An initial financial analysis should be used to define the opportunity. This usually includes an assessment of outline, or simplified, costs and values, and an assessment of how a project can be put together and cash-flowed. Only once it can be established that an opportunity can be considered 'bankable' should the project team be granted the necessary resources to go through a preliminary framework design, costing and valuation exercise.

Principle Two: Understand the funders' position
It is vitally important to understand the relative
positions of both public and private sector funding
organizations and investors. The conditions that
govern their financial commitment to a project will
have a significant impact on their long-term commitment to the scheme. Developers and property
owners, no matter where in the world they
operate, will have to finance their projects using
equity finance, debt finance or a mixture of both.

The finance of a property or project is ultimately
a derivative of the net income flows it is expected
to produce. The perceived quality of that income
will guide property financiers in relation to: the
amounts of money they will make available; the
price at which they make it available; the terms on
which they make it available; the degree of security
they seek; and the freedom they give to the users
of the money.

Consider three different providers of funds: an
institutional investor; an equity investor, and a
bank. The institutional investor will be using
pension funds, private equity and corporate funds.
The investment decisions it makes need to be on
the basis of safety (i.e. not losing any of its
investors' funds) and getting some capital growth
with the ability to realize an income either as a
capital sum or revenue, when the fund so requires.
Such an investor might be looking for a return on
the investment in the medium to long term; it will
seek to balance its risks, but will tend to favour
low-risk projects and investments.

The equity investor will favour investment
projects that bear a higher level of risk but
generate returns in a shorter time. It will be willing
to back opportunities where the return is likely to
be high. However, the term of investment means
that long-term development projects do not
necessarily meet the financial requirements of
equity providers. A bank will not expect to
participate in the capital growth of the scheme, but
will expect to see all of its debt repaid, with
interest, however badly the project performs.

*Principle Three: Mixed-use projects are more
complicated to fund*
A mix of uses leads to an associated mix of
financial risks that will in turn provide both short-
and long-term yields. As we have seen, mixed-use
projects tend to be messy and to require many
players with a spread of skills and expertise to
deliver the solution. The financing of urban village
projects primarily relies on techniques of property
finance but due to their mix of uses this will
require a more tailored approach than simple
financing techniques. In addition, some of the less
commercial aspects of a scheme may have to be
subsidized or entirely funded from public sources.

The public sector investment may be
introduced in three ways: as a commercial
investment alongside those of the other funders in
the project, as grant support to offset the costs of
the project which the private sector cannot bear,
and as a subordinated investment – to share the
perceived levels of risk associated with a project.
The public sector is sometimes in a better position
to take risks on its investment, given the economic
benefits that flow in the short term (i.e. jobs
attracted, derelict land and buildings brought back
into use) and the potential for the public
investment to be returned in the longer term.

*Principle Four: Longer projects tend to be
higher in risk*
Longer-term projects are generally exposed to
higher levels of risk than short-term projects, due
to greater economic uncertainty over long periods.
Long-term projects will therefore need to be more
profitable than short-term projects. One way to
overcome part of this problem will be to package,
or phase, a long project into shorter phases that
still yield the same benefits and outcomes. Levels
of risk will be fundamental to the funding of a
project. Risk is not necessarily about sensitivity
testing; it is about understanding the confidence
with which certain outcomes are assessed. It will
be assessed on the level of confidence that funders
feel, having calculated the expected financial
outcome of entering into a project.

Complex financial models are available, which
steer the financier towards understanding where
resources and time should be spent in assessing a
project. It may be necessary to provide further
market evidence to reduce the amount of
uncertainty in a project or to structure a contract
financially, or to ensure by other means that risk is

either managed or transferred to another party. To reduce diversifiable risks, insurances may sometimes be used in funding a project. Such insurances might be used to improve funding rates and hence project viability. Bonds may also be used to reduce the perceived risk to one party entering into a contract.

Principle Five: People are as important as projects

Inevitably, public and private sector funders prefer to invest in good projects. Time and again it can be seen that 'significant funds follow great people'. Funders not only invest in projects but also make a significant commitment to the team whose responsibility it is to deliver the project. During the initial stage the quality of the team and the individuals within the team will be a particularly important consideration for the fundability of the scheme.

However good the project may be, people are just as important in the process of attracting funds. Investors expect to have confidence, not only in the projects they are investing in, but also in the individuals running those projects. Good projects incorporate good design and well-considered development, and generate a high level of demand. The promoters of such projects will design their financial structures appropriately, and this will ensure that private finances are attracted into projects.

Principle Six: A good track record instils confidence

Investors' willingness to fund projects is based partly on assessing numbers but also requires a 'gut feeling' of confidence. All projects require a certain leap of faith in moving from feasibility into implementation. Where there is significant market uncertainty, or where information is incomplete or unsure, the leap of faith required will be far greater than in a project that is not exposed to such uncertainties. An analysis of the success of similar schemes undertaken in the past should help to promote confidence in the current opportunity, and thus ensure that the projects can be funded. In addition to these principles a set of key funding stages establishes the financial clarity of a project and helps to instil confidence in the long-term viability of a scheme.

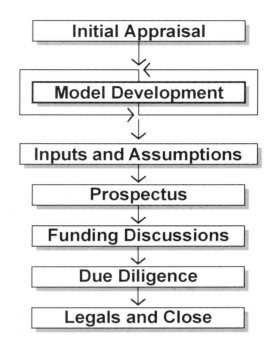

Initial appraisal

The initial appraisal is usually a coarse 'back of the envelope' calculation to assess the initial feasibility for the urban village. This will help to determine the overall viability of the project and how the initial financial structuring might be achieved. Although simplistic, this is an important process for it allows the team to consider how, for example, infrastructure and up-front costs might be phased and funded. This should endeavour to minimize the risk and exposure associated with the project, and maximize the prospects of the scheme being implemented.

Model development

The financial model should be developed and refined over a period of time alongside the framework and masterplanning process. This should be seen as an iterative process that is run alongside the design development team to ensure that what is being designed is financially feasible.

Finalization of inputs and assumptions

At this stage, the final costings for the proposed masterplan should be 'frozen'. It is important to document all the input assumptions and provide data on the financial model to enable third parties to appraise all assumptions for the project. The most financially sensitive elements of the scheme are run, and a risk analysis undertaken to help the promoter determine how best to financially manage the project. At this point a summary will be made of the relative risks and financial returns that are anticipated.

Preparation of the prospectus

Whether the project is a public or private sector scheme it is normal to develop a prospectus document. If public funding is involved this would include financial and economic appraisals in accordance with HM Treasury's *Green Book*, Single Regeneration Budget (SRB) Guidance, New Deal for Communities (NDC) Guidance and other associated public funding requirements.[11] Where private funding is involved, the document would normally be in the form of an information memorandum. This provides all the data necessary for an investor to decide whether to invest in the project.

Funding discussions

This is nearly always a tricky process. In holding discussions with potential funders it is essential to clearly state the project's investment attraction and potential; it is equally important not to mislead investors by overstating such opportunities. The most important issue will be to convey to the potential funder clearly and concisely: the opportunity, the balance of funding required, the risks, the market potential and the timing of the investment. A number of alternative funding organizations may be approached at this time and it will be important to maintain the fine balance between keeping all of the potential funders on board and at the same time not offending any of them and creating a loss of confidence.

Due diligence

Having secured agreement in principle, heads of terms will be prepared and due diligence procedures undertaken. This exercise normally includes a review of the project by a professional team employed by the funders to ensure that there is confidence in the scheme and that the project is ultimately deliverable.

Legals and close

The legal process normally involves a long, and at times drawn-out, process of negotiating the terms; at this stage of the process one may only be half-way through the process of securing funding. Legal expertise is brought into the process, which – due to the inherent complexities of mixed-use projects – may well give rise to numerous funding and legal documents. All legal requirements have to be addressed before any of the funding can be drawn down.

Clearly, the funding process can take a significant amount of time and it is therefore prudent to start the process early to ensure that other aspects of the project's development are not delayed.

Project phasing

Careful project phasing and profiling of expenditure can help to maximize project profitability and, therefore, the potential for a scheme to secure partners and finance. For example, two projects may have the same expenditure and income profiles, although one project is spread over two phases. The two-phase project generates a greater return to the investor than the single-phase project.

In the case of the illustrated chart shown opposite, cash profitability can be higher for a single-phase scheme, but the internal rate of return (IRR) for the two-phase scheme is greater.[12] The important issue is that the IRR is the best indication of return on capital invested and therefore most investors should be more likely to support a two-phase scheme rather than a single-phase development.

Risk-sharing and gap-funding mechanisms

Public organizations including RDAs, central government funding and regeneration departments and local economic development initiatives can all help to share the risk and cost on major schemes.

Joint ventures may be established by development agencies where no single private organization has the necessary resources to carry out the project. These may be used for complex mixed-use developments where the local authority initially assembles the site, and particularly where public sector funding is needed to reclaim the land and establish the initial infrastructure. The arrangements should be structured to enable all

Right:
Careful project phasing
and the profiling of
expenditure can help
to maximize long-term
project profitability

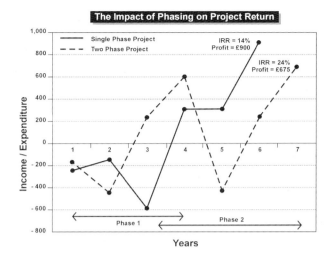

parties to share both the initial risks, profits and future increases in the value of the scheme.

Rental guarantees can be an important way to fund specific elements for a mixed-use scheme. These may be appropriate where a scheme has good long-term prospects but initial rental returns are more uncertain. Rental guarantees can form part of a support package but should be taken into account in grant funding and profit sharing.

Gap funding provides a common mechanism to kick-start a project where the projected returns are expected to be much higher than the cost of the initial investment. Public investment is limited to the initial grant, and all further risk is borne by the other private sector development partners. This is particularly relevant for land reclamation and for uses that will not generate any direct land value. Public agencies generally give preference to schemes that will share any profits that may be generated between the public and private sectors.

Public sector funding

The availability of public funding is often a prerequisite to securing the successful development of a large-scale mixed-use scheme. Historically, the public sector had two general options to initiate and assist in the delivery of large-scale schemes: it could own the site and masterplan the scheme, then either directly or indirectly develop the infrastructure and sell off individual sites – or it could 'gap fund' the development of a scheme by bridging the difference between the construction

costs and the value of the completed scheme.

More recently, and particularly with directives from the European Commission relating to the concern that gap funding represented a form of state aid or subsidy to the private sector, new approaches have had to be identified and promoted. Some of the alternatives now include:

- the public sector appointing development managers on a fee basis to take projects through to a stage where self-sustaining investment activities can be made;
- strategic partnering and risk-taking ventures, where land is used as security to attract investment that can deliver the infrastructure. Land is then sold on through arrangements between the public and private sectors to minimize levels of risk;
- joint venture contractual and corporate ventures; and
- the public sector providing assets that the private sector can use to generate cash flow that can part-fund the development of the project.

All of these approaches use either public assets, or cash, or both. Public funding is used in all of these examples to reduce the risk to the private sector to manageable levels. It will also be used to encourage the project to progress to a stage where it is 'bankable', or deliverable by the private sector, either inside or outside a continuing direct partnership with the public sector. It is important, therefore, in the financial structuring stages, to understand the benefit that public sector financial support can provide, both in the timing and the scale of the public sector assistance.

The promoter of such a venture needs to be careful from the outset to follow EU and UK procurement rules. Careful planning, including assessing the nature of the private sector's involvement, should ensure that the various implementation stages of the project do not involve activities that contravene these legally established procurement routes and methods.

Finally, public sector assistance is usually invested on the basis of the economic and social benefits delivered, although a local authority or an RDA may also invest as a commercial venture.

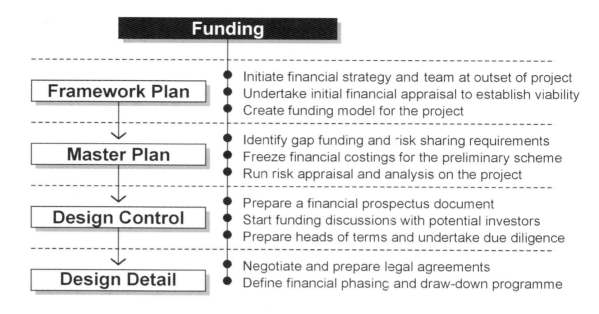

Funding

Framework Plan
- Initiate financial strategy and team at outset of project
- Undertake initial financial appraisal to establish viability
- Create funding model for the project

Master Plan
- Identify gap funding and risk sharing requirements
- Freeze financial costings for the preliminary scheme
- Run risk appraisal and analysis on the project

Design Control
- Prepare a financial prospectus document
- Start funding discussions with potential investors
- Prepare heads of terms and undertake due diligence

Design Detail
- Negotiate and prepare legal agreements
- Define financial phasing and draw-down programme

When drawing-in such participation, it is important to understand the basis on which funding is awarded, to ensure that the entire project, or any individual element of it, is eligible to benefit from the particular funding regime. It is important to understand any conditions, such as the continued use of the project, outputs and selling restrictions, that may come with the award or use of public funding, to ensure these conditions do not adversely affect the ability of the project to incorporate private finance at a later stage.

Although it is clear that it can be complicated to structure appropriate funding strategies in the early stages of mixed-use schemes, such schemes can also benefit from their inherent potential to draw on a wide variety of financial support.

Establishing development partnerships

Because, as we have seen, urban village projects are complicated, and because many schemes are in economically depressed or environmentally degraded areas, some form of public and private sector partnership will generally be required for their implementation. The role of a project promoter may also emerge as the most efficient means to deliver, over a long period, socially sustainable neighbourhoods.

The private sector

It is important to understand the commercial objectives of residential property developers and how their objectives are sometimes at odds with the aims of an urban village project. The financial parameters are such that developers are not attracted to the responsibility for delivering the entire scheme, unless they have an unusually philanthropic business ethos. To date, few developers have been persuaded to deliver all the components necessary for a comprehensive urban village because it requires the ability to implement both commercial, residential and community uses. The best organizations have evolved into specialist residential or commercial developers, each structured with skills, experience and financial arrangements to optimize their financial return, for the risks involved. Often developers even specialize within these broad sectors, perhaps concentrating on up-market detached 'executive' housing, retail warehouses, offices or shops.

Critics claim that many house-building companies are short of influential people with an appreciation of good design. The house-builder's response is that they produce designs that people buy, at a cost-effective price. In addition, critics will suggest that the private sector has a limited understanding of the need to achieve non-financial, long-term, social and environmental

Above:
The Millennium Communities Programme is beginning to create new forms of consortia for mixed-use development

goals. The private sector will argue that they must maximize their short- and medium-term returns to shareholders. Some will argue that the structure of private house-builder organizations in particular are unconnected with the team that buys the land, the team that designs the buildings and another team that sells them, which results in a dislocation between the project's inception and how it is finally put into practice.

There is a need for clarity and understanding between parties, if these differences are to be reconciled, agreements reached and projects delivered. Without such an understanding the future development of urban villages may be limited. To change either the views of the critics or the housing developers may be too difficult to

achieve; hence the need for a master development partner who can finance and deliver the scheme over a long period, and can marry the long-term objectives of the public sector with the business and financial constraints of the house-builders. Where the cash flow constraints of a project may be too difficult for a private sector partner to bear alone, it may be necessary for the public sector to lead, participate in, or assist with the implementation stages by taking an umbrella role.

Mixed-use, long-term projects provide both the public and private sector with considerable challenges, and this is certainly true in the early years of an urban village development. Some individuals and some companies on each side are gradually coming to understand the individual aims of all those involved in the process. Generally the volume house-builders and the specialist commercial developers are not able to respond well to briefs for urban villages and they are being displaced by developers who are either entrepreneurs, or from a broader commercial background. A limited number of larger house-builder developers are starting to meet this challenge, although the motivation in this sector is still largely philanthropic. Specialist developers, project management companies and promoter-development management teams are also beginning to be established. The drive for these new organizations still comes from particular types of projects; initiatives such as the Millennium Communities Programme have created consortia capable of responding to specific market needs. However, in relation to the Government's target of creating 220,000 new homes per year the impact of these new organizations on the marketplace is still limited.

The high-profile millennium village competitions were specifically designed to encourage the industry to hone its skills in this type of mixed-use development. Unsurprisingly, the early attempts were not without difficulty and certainly have yet to achieve the highest standards aspired to for urban village forms of development. However, they do represent a welcome step forward and provide lessons for both the public and private sectors of the industry. What is clear is that the development and implementation of government-initiated pilot projects is useful in creating examples on the ground and in helping new organizations to be formed in response to such opportunities.

The public sector

The public sector's objectives will include the creation of a balanced, cohesive community, long-term environmental and economic sustainability of the neighbourhood, financial value for money and timely development. There has been a tendency, now recognized as short-sighted and counter-productive, to seek the highest financial bid. This has been driven by the traditional audit processes and the concern that deviating from this standard approach carries significant risk for the accountable officer. For local authorities, this has often been

due to a misinterpretation of Section 123 of the Local Government Act 1972, which requires local authorities to achieve 'best consideration'. This does not mean 'the highest cash sum today for the site' but risk-averse property professionals have often interpreted it this way. Clarification of this by government is long overdue.

The latest millennium village to be procured by the Government is the Cardroom area of East Manchester, where the choice of developer has been based on their understanding of the issues and their approach in advance of a masterplan or a financial offer. These selection criteria, combined with a good understanding of the risk and reward approach the developer is proposing, may have significantly better results than the traditional approach of seeking the highest financial offer at the outset. There are many uncertainties to be dealt with over a long time in mixed-use development and, as with any partnership, alignment of interest is crucial. It will be necessary to forge an approach that sets minimum environmental, financial and social targets and provides a financial reward when these targets are exceeded, as well as offering the opportunity to share in long-term value growth.

Alternative procurement methods still need to be tested, such as setting 'affordability' thresholds (i.e. the amount of public funding available for a project) and then inviting bids to achieve pre-defined outcomes, the final selection being made on the basis of quality.

The role of the promoter

At this stage it is necessary to understand what the developer does and to introduce the concept of the promoter or enabler. There are various ways in which rewards can accrue and a number of risks that must be taken by the parties.

Initially there is the need to add social, economic and environmental value to the land and the neighbourhood through assembling the land, energizing the community, securing planning approval and disposing of land to achieve the required development. This may be paid for with a fee, which may be performance-related. There is a small but growing number of organizations potentially equipped to do this. These include

Right:
Project promoters are capable of delivering greater long-term benefits for projects than traditional developers

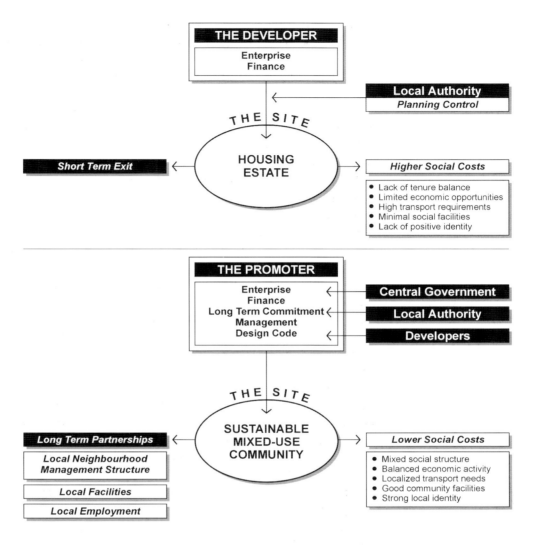

project management companies, development management specialists, various individuals with development management experience and the occasional former City Challenge or Single Regeneration Budget management companies. There is a significant potential benefit to the public sector in encouraging the growth of this type of company but this can only happen if a continual stream of opportunities is generated.

Whilst the Private Finance Initiative (PFI) has emerged to deliver public services and projects, it has forced designers, builders, financiers and property managers to come together to provide joined-up solutions for neighbourhoods. The positive procurement benefits of PFI-type solutions are starting to flow through into mixed-use regeneration and neighbourhood-based projects. In some cases, this will require investors to collaborate with public authorities for 20–30 years to fully establish an urban village project.

More frequently, developers who choose to speculate with both their time and – occasionally – their capital, undertake this process. Their reward is only achieved through an increase in land value so they will tend to be risk-averse; they will seek to minimize their capital investment and generally they will not be motivated to deliver social and environmental objectives. Organizations that specialize in this function, which is most frequently seen as a greenfield activity, will seek to undertake development themselves having enhanced the land value. Their rewards finally accrue through the

difference between the total cost of development and the revenues they receive on its sale. The short-term profit motivation of this type of organization is clear.

An alternative type of organization is the investor-developer, which often includes development expertise and can favour more innovative niche developments. The funds in such cases are generally structured and driven towards capturing the longer-term increase in value of the property. Such organizations may also have fairly strong social and environmental goals as part of a socially responsible investment policy.

As all these groups are developing their capability slowly at present, it is not yet possible to identify a preferred option. It is clear that each project has a number of particular and unique challenges and the selection of the most appropriate developer and funder will need to be adapted to these requirements. Some schemes will be served best through a public sector promoter; some will require a fee- and incentive-driven private sector promoter; and some will need a traditional investor. Procurement Option Appraisal can help to tease out the best procurement route by identifying the project delivery objectives and matching them with the organizations that are best

placed to meet them.

Where a public sector-led promoter is chosen, individual developers will be brought in on a site-by-site basis with detailed development briefs to collaborate with the public sector. Other schemes will be best served with a single developer who will commission different architects in the context of an overall masterplan and design guides to create the diversity necessary for a sustainable neighbourhood.

In addition, organizations such as development trusts and registered social landlords (RSLs) can be involved in urban village projects. Trusts have a potential role but may lack the power to raise equity capital in the markets, although it should be possible for a trust to raise charitable capital. They may also lack the risk-taking culture or the ability to pay profit-related remuneration to their management teams. That said, such trusts could be in a position to recruit qualified management teams, supported by a combination of financial and philanthropic motives, and compete in the market as long-term urban village regeneration promoters and developers. They could then reinvest a significant proportion of the profits back into the organization, the community facilities and other long-term investments. Such organizations seem possible in theory but are more problematical to form in practice.

Registered social landlords, despite their ambitions, are also heavily regulated and therefore may lack the capacity and resources to take significant development risks. In partnerships with other organizations, they may combine consortia in order to deliver and manage mixed-use projects. In particular, their skills and resources enable them to undertake area management activities. In addition, there is a small number of private sector-led organizations that are moving into the neighbourhood management market: these organizations can play an important role in helping to prevent neighbourhood decline. Over time, RSLs may play an increasing role in such projects and their objectives are ideally suited to this task. Indeed, it could be argued that the pressing need of the day is to invent the 'urban village association', the modern equivalent of the housing association capable of addressing the pressing problem of the day – which is not housing the poor, but creating sustainable neighbourhoods for all. We must, however, be alert to the very real risks that this new role presents for RSLs, should they choose to take it on.

Partnership arrangements

The first decision for the landowner or the public sector body undertaking the land assembly is to decide which type of partnership arrangement is most suited to the parameters of the project. A partnership should enable organizations to come together and combine the required resources to make a project happen. As a simple example, a landowner may be willing to make available its land but may not wish to use its own money to fund the project; accordingly, a funder may be invited to joint the project team. The funder may believe that neither it nor the landowner has the appropriate development skills to manage the risks so a developer partner may be introduced. The risk that each party is exposed to, will determine the return that it might expect on its investment. Each party should assess its investment as an 'opportunity-cost' so that the value of the respective input is recognized. This requires a clear view on the availability of financial and human

resources. If the partner has neither the people nor the money, it will require a partner who has both. This might be a developer, either with his own money or backed by a fund, or a development manager backed by an investor.

At the other end of the scale, a public sector promoter with a large and experienced in-house team and sufficient finances to acquire and service the site would probably seek individual development partners for individual buildings or streets. There are currently few organizations in this position, so most promoters will seek a partner, or partners, who share the objectives of the public sector and can bring skilled expertise and financial strength to the project.

An important issue that is rarely appreciated is that as the project progresses the balance of skills in the delivery team will need to change. In the formative stages of the project masterplanning and market assessment skills might be needed, whilst in the later stages of the project the skills might include construction management, project management and development management. The balance of skills in the promoting party will need to change in accordance with these changing aspects of the project.

Where the landowner is a public sector body with goals that are wider than simple profit maximization, finding a compatible partner can be difficult. An investor with declared socially responsible investment goals can be an answer and in the future it seems likely that some development companies will emerge for whom short-term profit maximization is not the only objective.

The structure of the relationship will also tend to vary from scheme to scheme. The legal profession have tended to argue against the possibility of standardized agreements in this area. However, experience on a number of projects shows that the same issues arise again and again, and that significant efficiencies could be achieved by adopting standardized guidance. In other areas of procurement, as is the case for PFI projects, such standardization has significantly speeded up the procurement process and has helped to reduce costs. Standardized guidance could also help to overcome the shortage of skilled people competent to negotiate these agreements.

The basic agreement will allocate the responsibilities of the parties. The public sector should acquire the land, provide financial support, and secure related social and economic regeneration initiatives. The private sector should procure the design and the finance, implement the physical regeneration and secure a long-term management structure. The agreed objectives need to be set out, along with the method of sharing any financial returns and any reasons for termination should the project not succeed.

Such relationships have to be for the long term; Albert Dock in Liverpool, for example, was the subject of an unprecedented 25-year development agreement when it was conceived in the early 1980s. It is inevitable that circumstances will change over such a long period and will be particularly influenced by fluctuations in the condition of the economy and property market. Multilevel agreements can help to deal with the long-term uncertainties such projects need. A framework agreement, or cooperation agreement, may suffice in the developmental stages of a project. As it progresses, development agreements for phases may be entered into, with the scope for review at the end of each phase, subject to the terms of the framework agreement.

Finally, this requires an arrangement that is flexible and which does not transfer risks to a party that cannot manage them. A typical mistake by the public sector is to transfer market risk to the private sector. This is only possible in the short term and therefore cannot be used in long-term development agreements. Thus the agreements should provide the private sector with a base return on its capital and the opportunity to share in any profit. It should also allow for timescales and economic circumstances to change – in times of a recession there is no point in insisting that a developer build a building that will stand empty. Agreements should ensure that the developer is responsible for managing elements, including the construction cost risk, on a building-by-building or phase-by-phase basis.

Coordinating procurement activities

The central task for the project managers who are leading the development of urban village projects will be to coordinate the various activities taking place during the procurement process. The approach that has been described in this chapter has purposefully adopted a design-led methodology that focuses on the preparation of frameworks, masterplans and detailed designs. These provide valuable and commonly-recognized elements upon which assessment, discussion and decision-making can be based.

Timescales associated with this process are guaranteed to vary from project to project and will be dependant on a complex mix of factors, over which the project team may have only limited control. An overview of this entire process has been compiled within a single table, shown opposite, that provides a useful structure to cross-reference many of the key activities associated with procurement. Within this, it is also possible to plot the various skills and roles required by individuals and organizations throughout the life of the project, and thus establish an indicative programme for the various activities.

As with all projects, success is particularly dependent on the skills and judgement of the individuals involved. In addition, it is equally important to ensure that there is a collective understanding of the entire delivery process and a clear appreciation of the purpose, and interconnected nature, of each individual role and activity.

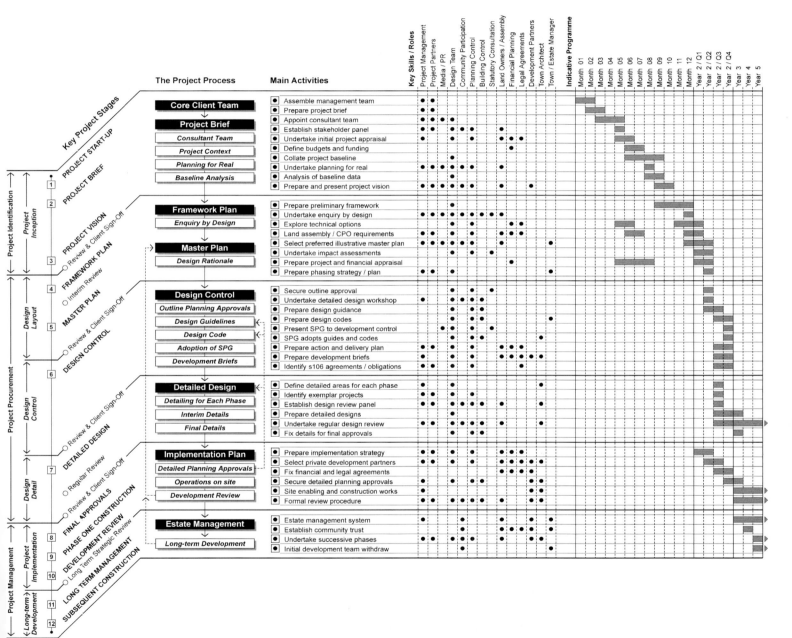

The Project Process — **Main Activities**

Key Skills / Roles: Project Management · Project Partners · Media / PR · Design Team · Community Participation · Planning Control · Building Control · Statutory Consultation · Land Owners / Assembly · Financial Planning · Legal Agreements · Development Partners · Town Architect · Town / Estate Manager

Indicative Programme: Month 01 – Month 12 · Year 2 / Q1 · Year 2 / Q2 · Year 2 / Q3 · Year 2 / Q4 · Year 3 · Year 4 · Year 5

Key Project Stages (left):
Project Identification · Project Inception · Project Procurement · Design Layout · Design Control · Design Detail · Project Management · Project Implementation · Long-term Development

PROJECT START-UP · 1 PROJECT BRIEF · 2 · PROJECT VISION · 3 FRAMEWORK PLAN (○ Interim Review) · 4 · MASTER PLAN (○ Review & Client Sign-Off) · 5 · DESIGN CONTROL (○ Review & Client Sign-Off) · 6 · DETAILED DESIGN (○ Review & Client Sign-Off) · 7 (○ Regular Review) · FINAL APPROVALS (○ Review & Client Sign-Off) · 8 PHASE ONE CONSTRUCTION · 9 DEVELOPMENT REVIEW (○ Long Term Strategic Review) · 10 LONG TERM MANAGEMENT · 11 SUBSEQUENT CONSTRUCTION · 12

Core Client Team
- Assemble management team
- Prepare project brief

Project Brief
- Appoint consultant team
- Establish stakeholder panel
- Undertake initial project appraisal

Consultant Team
Project Context
- Define budgets and funding
- Collate project baseline

Planning for Real
- Undertake planning for real
- Analysis of baseline data

Baseline Analysis
- Prepare and present project vision

Framework Plan
- Prepare preliminary framework
- Undertake enquiry by design

Enquiry by Design
- Explore technical options
- Land assembly / CPO requirements

Master Plan
- Select preferred illustrative master plan
- Undertake impact assessments

Design Rationale
- Prepare project and financial appraisal
- Prepare phasing strategy / plan

Design Control
- Secure outline approval
- Undertake detailed design workshop

Outline Planning Approvals
- Prepare design guidance

Design Guidelines
- Prepare design codes

Design Code
- Present SPG to development control
- SPG adopts guides and codes

Adoption of SPG
- Prepare action and delivery plan

Development Briefs
- Prepare development briefs
- Identify s106 agreements / obligations

Detailed Design
- Define detailed areas for each phase

Detailing for Each Phase
- Identify exemplar projects
- Establish design review panel

Interim Details
- Prepare detailed designs
- Undertake regular design review

Final Details
- Fix details for final approvals

Implementation Plan
- Prepare implementation strategy

Detailed Planning Approvals
- Select private development partners
- Fix financial and legal agreements

Operations on Site
- Secure detailed planning approvals
- Site enabling and construction works

Development Review
- Formal review procedure

Estate Management
- Estate management system
- Establish community trust

Long-term Development
- Undertake successive phases
- Initial development team withdraw

Chapter 9

Project management

Mike Hollingsworth, Ben Denton and Chris Brown

With the client and consultant teams in place, the baseline conditions for a scheme established and the process of preparing the framework, masterplan, design guidance and detailed design completed, the project moves on to the delivery stage. This may run through a series of phases and may last for several years before all construction works are complete and a system for long-term management is established. This chapter focuses on the delivery stages of a project and concludes with guidance on estate management.

Left:
Looking across the neighbourhood park to the Tango housing at the Bo01 Expo, Malmo

Challenges for implementation

Experience gained during the 1990s has demonstrated that most mixed-use schemes are extremely challenging to deliver. As a general rule, two key preconditions are required: at the start of the development process the public sector or promoter needs to own, or at least have overall control of, the land; and, if the development is not financially viable, the public sector needs to bridge the financial gap.

It is generally the case that only through the involvement of the public sector can many of the less commercially viable social components of an urban village be delivered. Although there may be some concern about the compulsory acquisition of private property, this has to be weighed against the public benefit accrued through mixed-use urban regeneration.

Of the five early examples of successful urban village delivery – Hulme, Crown Street, Poundbury, Ancoats and West Silvertown – three have been on land that has passed through public sector ownership. Poundbury provides an unusual example of a private landowner (the Duchy of Cornwall) seeking a higher goal than mere short-

Below:
A comprehensive management regime for all of Great Notley's public spaces was put in place at the outset of construction

term financial return. The delivery of Ancoats Urban Village has been delayed for a significant period because of fragmented land ownership and the activities of property speculators. Much of the site will only be delivered through land assembly by the use of CPO powers by the Regional Development Agency.

Financial return is a critical issue. In the short term, which is the time frame used by the UK development industry, and by house-builders in particular, urban villages do not maximize financial returns. Over many years the industry has evolved into a low technology, low-skill, box-building, financially driven culture. In time, this is likely to change in response to the activities of organizations like the Prince's Foundation and the Urban Task Force, which are encouraging a longer-term, more collective view of this form of development. As consumers place a higher emphasis on the quality of the urban environment and the range of facilities mixed-use neighbourhoods can offer, the market should begin to change. It can be argued that only then will the house-building industry seriously start changing its standard development patterns and be prepared to invest the time and money necessary to create comprehensive urban developments.

Until then, only the public sector or 'third way' developers, such as development trusts and a few of the more enlightened and skilled registered social landlords or developers, will be in a position to deliver the wider public benefits which urban villages can provide. These benefits are often clearly more valuable to society than the costs of achieving them and certainly provide the greatest social benefit within an urban village development. This can only be achieved if such developers are able to work closely with the mainstream development industry, as only the latter sector has the financial and human capacity to deliver urban villages on the scale the country needs.

Funding strategies have to be established on a scheme-by-scheme basis and identified through rigorous appraisal methodologies such as the RICS comprehensive project appraisal.[1] Regional regeneration agencies must ensure that potential projects fit within the objectives of the regional economic strategy and that they are eligible to receive grant funding. The development appraisal process will need to establish that the assessments of value are reasonable; the regeneration agencies will generally use in-house or independent experts to undertake this. As part of this process, all property values will need to be certified by independent chartered surveyors in accordance with the RICS Red Book.

Choices for implementation

Although mixed-use projects can be delivered in a number of ways, two of the more common approaches are through:

– public ownership of the land to be developed, and public subsidy, or cross-subsidy, of the non-commercially viable elements; and
– public investment in improving the public realm and public services, combined with strong planning controls, to encourage private investment.

The choice of route for implementation depends on an analysis of development land values. Some edge-of-city-centre locations may have a relatively strong economic position even though values are depressed because of a poor-quality environment. In such cases, the environment can be significantly improved by a relatively small investment in the upgrading of streets and squares. In some cases this will naturally occur over time with funding released through traditional market forces when the economy is buoyant.

The likelihood of this happening can be assessed by an analysis of the development land values. These values can be calculated by subtracting from the value of a development, the cost of construction and the margin for risk, overhead and profit required by the market. This figure is particularly sensitive to residential sales values and development density where values are greater than cost. The higher the sales prices and the greater the density of the development, the greater the development land value will be.

The resulting valuation should then be compared with the cost of buying land. This will be determined by its existing use (perhaps

Right:
Right:
The delivery of Ancoats
Urban Village has been
made harder by a complex
pattern of land ownership

warehouses or car parking), or by its value for other types of permitted development. Usually the value for urban village development will be lower than these values, which is one clear reason why such development rarely happens without some level of support. Where the figures are close it may be judged that some public realm improvements may be sufficient to tip the balance and make urban village development values rise above the alternative options.

Where this development pressure exists, or can be generated, urban villages can be achieved through the use of a proactive planning strategy and associated financial obligations, although it should be recognized that this is an extremely unusual circumstance. In most cases, public ownership and subsidy will have to be adopted, as projects are often located in economically depressed areas and developers are often reluctant to take the long-term risks associated with investing through long, and more uncertain, economic cycles.

Partnering during implementation

Partnerships are an integral part of the urban village process and should continue on through to the construction process as individual phases of development are released for private sector development. There are several contractual ways to deliver both the residential and mixed-use components of each scheme; these include traditional contractor agreements, staged tendering, design and build contracts and project partnering. The essence of the process is to minimize financial uncertainty and construction

inefficiency whilst maintaining the design objectives of the masterplan and the quality in the detailed components.

Project partnering throughout the implementation stage is gaining greater acceptance. This technique proved invaluable during the development of Brindleyplace in Birmingham. It is described in detail in a useful and informative publication on the project.[2] Partnering does not just happen; it has to be actively sought, and considerable effort is required to extract its benefits. The process has to be built on trust, which in turn can only be established through mutual respect between the individual partners – and that comes with experience and a successful track record. Although it is impossible to avoid many of the difficulties associated with all construction projects, the aim is to anticipate potential problems at an early stage through preparation and advanced planning. All parties need to be involved at the outset and difficulties should be shared and solutions sought across the entire team structure, rather than through the traditional compartmentalizing of responsibilities. Ten key stages can be identified during the process:

1 Appointment of the concept team – the individual built components are established within an overriding masterplan.
2 Presentation to the contractor – cost plans are prepared and perceived problems and difficulties outlined.
3 Contractor presentation to the client – the approach to the construction is outlined, including elements where improvements can be made, solutions sought and risk minimized.
4 Value engineering – costs are brought down, in line with the initial budget.
5 Subcontractor partnering – subcontractors should have a significant input into the design to prevent irreversible decisions that cause problems later on in the development process.
6 Detailed design – a separate design team is appointed by the contractor to share ideas and seek creative alternatives.
7 Partnering workshop – these are held towards the end of the pre-contract period to take stock of the process and establish future

programmes of work.

8 Agreement of contract sum – this produces a
fixed-price, all-risks lump sum for the project
through an open book negotiation.

9 Construction – the concept design team
maintains a watching brief on the process to
ensure that the larger objectives of the
masterplan are achieved.

10 Review – this is essential to ensure continual
modification and flexibility in problem-solving.

Long-term ownership and management

Following the construction of an urban village, and
particularly in situations where this has been
achieved through large-scale urban regeneration, it
is easy to lose many of the achievements that have
been made and see the area quickly slip back into
decline. This is often the case where a high quality
management structure has not been established.
Failing to clean or police the streets, or to repair

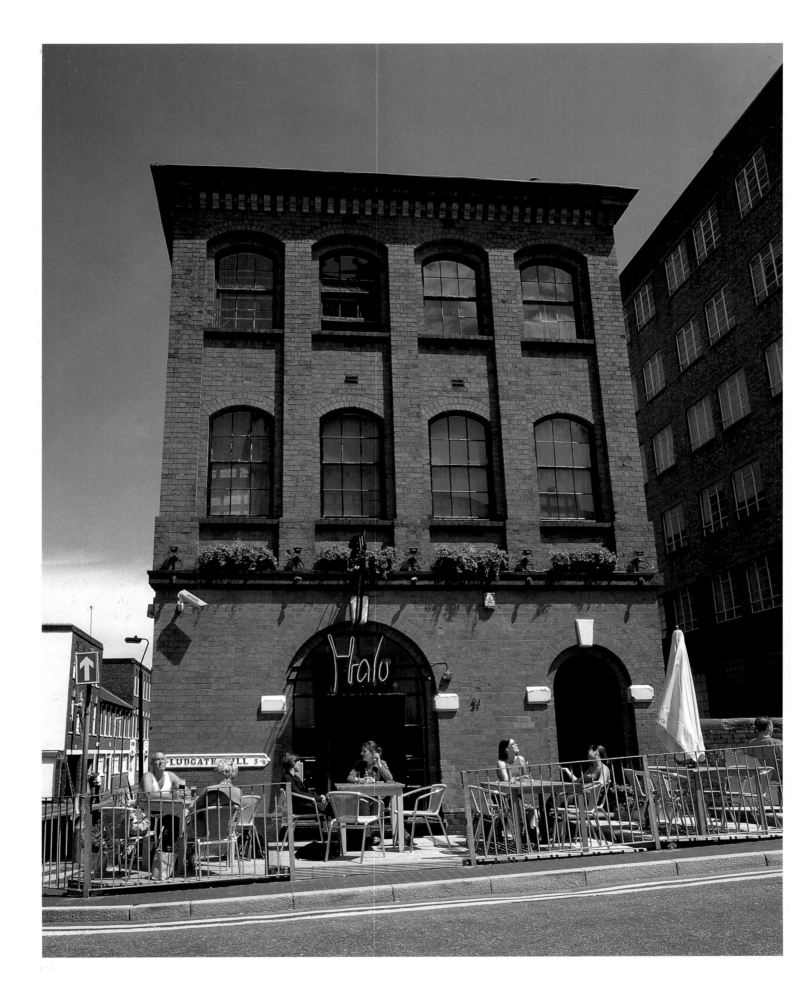

damage promptly, can have a devastating knock-on effect in a very short time.

In return for the considerable increase in property taxes, local authorities should be expected make a significant commitment to the management of an urban village. However, it is clear that this is often not sufficient to preserve the standards necessary for an urban village to prosper, and a higher level of care is often required. Typically, on large private sector developments, this has been secured by a traditional system of service charging, managed by an elected committee of occupiers. Where this works satisfactorily, it can completely displace the services provided by public agencies.

One alternative approach would be to establish a community trust that has a rather wider remit than would be given to service-charge-based management company. The objectives of a trust are generally to manage for the benefit of the entire neighbourhood; its operation can be part-financed by development endowment of cash or income-producing property, by ground rents, by a local tax reinvestment programme, by a business improvement charge or via a more traditional service charge. Such a trust should not be controlled by and for the occupiers, but should have a wider, community-based board. It would be the natural organization for the urban village promoter to hand over to when finally exiting from a project. It would seek to have surplus income beyond that needed for basic services, in order to provide the extra 'community glue' necessary in all successful neighbourhoods.

Detailed estate management procedures need to be tailor-made for each project and should avoid being overly prescriptive. Long-established estates have been able to preserve the values, if not the communities, in large areas of central London, whilst many neighbourhoods across the country work well because they have been able to evolve organically and adapt to changing needs, and this is an essential part of their charm and success.

Managing and governing

Although long-term management and governance of an urban village comes at the end of the development process, it should be considered at

the outset. The implications for management should be taken into account from the first stages of planning onwards. As part of this reverse feedback, early decisions on management must be taken in parallel to the design decisions. As each phase of an urban village is constructed and completed, provision should be made for:

- Disposal – the transfer of the completed construction, by sale or rental, to those wishing to carry out the activities, with appropriate covenants designed to promote good management.
- Management – provision to ensure that individuals or organizations are responsible for the costs of occupation, management and maintenance. Responsibility for this normally falls on occupiers, but for some uses such as open space, roads and schools, this cost must be met by the community.
- Government – the completed community will fall within the boundaries of one or more government administrations, local and/or central, and in some cases, special government agencies such as development corporations.

Left:
A proactive management strategy has focused on improving many of the public spaces in Birmingham's Jewellery Quarter

Right:
River Place in Portland, Oregon, has established a comprehensive management company to service all public and private facilities

Opposite:
Brindleyplace in Birmingham demonstrates that the long-term success of a project is dependent on the quality of management
© Simon Hazelgrove

Common management arrangements

Conventionally, following completion of development, the occupiers – be they private individuals or public organizations – share management costs. They remain responsible for the particular properties that they occupy under title. Responsibility for the maintenance of common parts, such as the public and social facilities, falls on one or more government or quasi-government agencies that collect taxes or charges to meet the costs. More often than not, a management organization should be established in which the responsibility for wider issues of management should be vested.

In an urban village, such bodies often work outside a conventional central and local government framework. The management arm of the urban village could actually take over some of the functions traditionally carried out by local or central government or their agencies, drawing on the management experience and resources of a diverse range of organizations. The choice of management structures would need to take account of the location of the urban village – be it an infill, brownfield or greenfield project – and the surrounding community. There will probably be greatest opportunity for innovation on a greenfield site, since existing administrative systems will not yet be geared to serving an existing urban settlement.

It may be preferable to transfer responsibility for management and funding of the majority of local services from local government and public agencies to the village community. Control and management should, as far as possible, be in the hands of those who live and work there. One vehicle for achieving this would be a community trust, which would also set up and pay for services not typically provided by local government. Such a transfer cannot be carried out across the board, as it will require careful consideration of each element of the 'common parts'. The consideration would relate, for example, to:

– services traditionally provided by central government or its associated organizations, such as certain local health services;
– services traditionally provided by local government, such as other social services, local roads, fire services, and parks and playing fields; and
– utility services that are generally provided by privatized companies, including water, sewerage, gas, electricity, telecommunications and cable television.

Towards a neighbourhood management structure

Most of our successful places work because people have used them over long periods, during which both the places and uses have adapted to strike a workable balance. No matter how well we plan, the way in which any new urban village works is bound to adapt over time, as actual usage puts the design assumptions to rigorous, real-life testing. It is important to incorporate a degree of flexibility that will allow individuals to put their mark on the neighbourhood over time; over-rigorous discipline stifles personal expression and behaviour and may have the opposite effect to that intended.

Estate management professions, driven by the potentially competing demands of institutional landlords and corporate tenants, have evolved sophisticated bespoke management models for niche and specialized property markets over the last three decades. Estate governance for high-value assets, including shopping malls and business parks, provides sophisticated and useful examples of the effective resolution of the complex mix of demands from all stakeholders, be they local authorities, investors, occupiers or visiting users.

Urban villages present a unique opportunity for the property profession to create an equally effective long-term management solution for this complex asset class. It is crucial that an effective, cohesive and sustainable management structure be formulated and applied from the outset of development and that the interests of stakeholders, the business population, residents and visitors be cared for in perpetuity.

The challenge for neighbourhood managers is to provide a specialized management service, which is founded on the well-established principles

of good estate management, but which is flexible and innovative, and complementary to the complex character and commercial mix of each urban village scheme.

Management structures

It is likely that each individual property within the scheme will have a dedicated and distinct management regime. However, to sustain a cohesive community, it is essential that a strong management body be established for the maintenance and administration of the entire neighbourhood. One solution would be to grant an overriding lease to the neighbourhood management company on all shared and public areas of the scheme that are not otherwise allocated to or the responsibility of the owners of individual buildings.

The management company shareholders, including promoters, individual building owners and occupiers, will be the key stakeholders in the community. The shareholding structure and voting rights would be designed to deliver the best and most equitable delivery of the objectives and aspirations of the community. The management company would be responsible for the upkeep of all public areas, and the processes for managing the neighbourhood could be incorporated in the corporate governance.

An apportioned estate charge would be levied on the owners of the freehold and long leasehold interests in the constituent buildings to fund the neighbourhood management. It is unlikely that the charge would be large in relation to the size of the buildings, given the high urban development density that is normally proposed.

Management centres

The community might benefit from a central management centre, funded from the service charge budgets of the estate and the individual buildings, which could provide a focus for coordinating the various services. It could also represent a tangible point of contact where the occupiers could communicate with the management team. The centre could also be the control hub and monitoring station for security services, including manned patrols and CCTV

Above:
**The maintenance of
individual buildings is
an important element
of any neighbourhood
management plan**

monitoring and any centralized control of access/
entry points.

Estate management teams

The management company should be encouraged
to recruit locally to appoint a dedicated site
manager, whose role will be key to the
coordination of the community management and
event management services delivery. The site
manager should embrace the objectives of the
management strategy and should supervise a team
of dedicated service personnel. These members of
the team would be recruited under local
employment initiatives and trained by the
management function to be fully conversant with
set procedures of quality. It is likely that the role of
the site manager will include:

–   estate management coordination;
–   supervision of the management centre
    reception and security;
–   a communication link between the various
    scheme occupiers, including opportunities for
    a neighbourhood intranet facility;
–   administration, management and supervision
    of public space and car parks;
–   event management and coordination of PR
    initiatives; and
–   liaison with the wider local community and
    other interest groups.

Key management issues

At the outset of the management operations and
throughout the life of the neighbourhood a number
of management issues are anticipated.

Security regime

The essence of the urban village is to provide a
vibrant and popular location which people choose
to visit regularly. The success of an urban
community will depend on a management policy
that delivers an effective and visible security
regime, which should be both manned and
electronically monitored. It is essential to be able
to deliver a secure and well-managed
neighbourhood from the launch of the scheme.

Transportation and vehicular access

A sustainable and progressive vehicle management
strategy that is consistent with local, regional and
national government policy should be developed at
an early stage. One of the core aims will be to
encourage the use of public transport in the area,
while maintaining good access for essential trips
made by private cars. Pragmatic initiatives from
the neighbourhood management team, including
car-pooling and cost-effective vehicle hire may
alleviate the problems of congestion.

Site-wide refuse and waste management strategy

In consultation with the relevant local authority
environmental and operational services
departments, an effective regime will be
established for managing refuse production from
the various types of occupiers. Wherever viable,
the opportunities for recycling and reuse should be
fully exploited.

The public realm

The integration of secure and clean public areas
will improve the flow of pedestrians through the
scheme, which will in turn benefit the commercial,
retail and leisure components of the scheme.
Opportunities should be sought to stage well-
conceived, well-managed public events that will
enhance the public perception of the area and
provide a beneficial resource to the location. A
carefully planned strategy to maintain safe, well-
lit, litter-free public spaces that include a
sustainable mix of hard and soft landscape
elements in a busy urban location increases the
commercial potential of adjacent areas. Good
management will encourage the use of public areas
of the scheme by visitors and ensure their security
and comfort. This should be achieved without
compromising the enjoyment, privacy and safety of
the commercial occupiers and residents.

Management of the phased development

The phasing programme of a scheme will have
significant implications for the implementation of
the estate management function. The
neighbourhood management regime must be
capable of implementation in stages, with each

Left:
**Concert Square in
Liverpool is a popular
public component of
the regeneration strategy
for the wider area**

stage being independently administered and sustainable, but complementary to the other stages and capable of being combined within the totally completed scheme.

The management of each individual property must be capable of integrating with the wider scheme. The community management regime must include measures to accommodate the continued development undertaken during the various phases of the scheme in order that the development process does not affect the quality of life of the occupiers of completed phases. Good liaison and communication between the parties, sensible accommodation of construction works and flexible interim contingency regimes will form the core elements of successfully managed phased development.

Carefully orchestrated consultation and publicity initiatives that adhere to set site-management goals will allow the identity of the community to evolve in tandem with the physical development of the entire scheme. The community management function should be structured in order to provide an accessible forum for future phases to engage within. In addition, initiatives that liase with adjacent communities and interest groups will lead to an increased integration of the evolving neighbourhood within the wider community.

The value of community groups

The most successful communities are often to be distinguished by their wealth of voluntary groups, including parochial church councils, amenity groups, and parent-teacher organizations, local social groups, sports clubs, and all manner of special interest groups. Although they operate at negligible public cost, they greatly enrich community life.

These existing patterns have broadly worked well. It is important, therefore, to seek to establish systems for the continuing management of the urban village that positively encourage the growth of a strong network of voluntary groups within a supportive management framework. A community development trust or neighbourhood management organization can also give a valuable stimulus to the creation of a intricate network of voluntary

organizations that will provide much of the social 'glue' that holds communities together.

Controlling the objectives of the masterplan

Urban villages and mixed-use developments should be built to a masterplan, supported by attendant codes that must be the subject of a binding development agreement between the local planning authority and the promoter – and landowner if the promoter does not own the land. As stated, it is important to have a management structure in place, ready to take over each section of the village as it is completed and occupied. This ensures that controls provided by the development agreement can fall away and be replaced by a permanent system of management that can immediately begin to look after that which has been completed. Historically, the large estates have successfully handled these issues through the leasehold system, which has given them extensive control over management and alterations in appearance and use. The attractive and consistent character of such neighbourhoods is often the result of such control.

There is some support for the introduction of new commonhold tenures and to allow lessees of residential property to purchase freeholds against the wishes of the existing freeholder. Yet, if freehold and leasehold interests merge, there is a risk that controls provided by covenants enforceable by the freeholder will effectively be lost. This would make the traditional systems of estate management based on the leasehold system less effective; if an urban village were to depend on them, its long-term environmental quality and balance of uses would be at risk. There is, in any event, ample evidence that house purchasers strongly prefer freehold property, which gives better investment value. This will, of course, not apply either to commercial property or housing for rent, which should be addressed differently. If an umbrella neighbourhood management structure is put in place in the manner described, there are fewer potential complications associated with leasehold, commonhold or freehold interests.

Establishing covenants for management

The legal agreement to be made with the local planning authority must at the outset define those parts of the development that will be taken over or dedicated to the managing authority. There will, however, be additional elements of an urban village that are best administered by the landowner or promoter, or some other body to whom responsibility is devolved. It is important that the neighbourhood community play a meaningful role in this process.

In order to separate the long-term legal and financial structure of management from the initial development process, it may be useful for the promoter to constitute a separate management company at the outset of the development. The obligation to contribute to the overall cost of neighbourhood management can then be established and enforced by the management company, whether a building is sold freehold or let.

In essence, it would be valuable for a management structure to be established right at the conceptual stage of an urban village development. Under this, the promoter (whether the landowner or not) enters into a binding agreement to develop the urban village on land in common ownership. This will probably require the landowner to conclude a separate agreement with the local planning authority, and to agree to be bound by the covenants and obligations it contains. The promoter will, at the time that planning approvals are issued, enter into a Section 106 agreement that sets out the promoter's intentions. This, together with the original agreement, will bind all three parties – promoter, landowner, planning authority, and in some cases other local government bodies – to the concept and intent.

These agreements will contain the basic covenants that will make effective and long-term management possible. The covenants will cover matters beyond the development period; they will be ongoing, and – to ensure enforceability – will be mainly restrictive in their operation. Examples of such covenants include agreements:

– not to change the character and concept of the urban village as described in the masterplan without the approval of the local planning authority;
– not to seek consent for the enlargement of the village;

– not to use, or treat otherwise than as open spaces, those areas so designated, including peripheral green open spaces; and
– in any works carried out in future, not to depart from either the masterplan or the design codes.

As stated, the urban village will require the provision of public services normally provided by local government. Specified local authority obligations to provide such services may conveniently be included in a Section 106 agreement, although some may well be excluded by agreement, and made initially the responsibility of the promoter.

Maintenance obligations

Local authority obligations to be covered by the Section 106 agreement or, in some cases, transferred to the promoter, might usefully include obligations to clean, maintain and renew when necessary:

– roads and footpaths;
– street lighting;
– open spaces, parks and squares;
– sewers and public drainage; and
– signage and street furniture.

Services provided by statutory bodies, including privatised companies, should also be covered by such agreements. These will provide for and specify the obligations and standards of provision and maintenance, and should try to avoid the necessity for successive service providers to repeatedly excavate one area. The coordination of these activities should be achieved by agreements which cover installations, structures and buildings associated with:

– water supply;
– electricity supply and distribution, including sub-stations;
– gas supply;
– sewerage and surface water drainage;
– postal and telecommunications services, including post and telephone boxes; and
   buses, taxis, trains and other public transport.

Such agreements would still have to include the statutory rights of undertakers to enter land and carry out works.

Development agreements

Once the form and basic infrastructure of the urban village is established, the promoter will still generally wish to provide building opportunities – residential, commercial or voluntary sector projects – for other developers and also, perhaps, individual owner-occupiers.

The arrangements for these developments will typically be embodied in development agreements between the promoter and individual developers. These oblige the parties to carry out individual projects to a defined timescale and to the approval of the promoter, the land being transferred at an agreed stage in the process. All development agreements must provide for such transfers to pass on the relevant obligations as set out in the Section 106 agreements and, where relevant, any requirements and responsibilities established by the original landowner. The development agreement will also provide for additional covenants relevant to that particular development. Typical covenants might include undertakings:

– not to extend or significantly alter the appearance of any building;
– not to use a building for certain prohibited purposes;
– not to sell or transfer properties without passing on the obligations and rights under the covenants;
– to reimburse the management company for the appropriate share of management expenses;
– regulating the way in which properties are let or sub-let;
– restricting the display of signage, boards or other advertising; and
– controlling the location and planting of substantial trees.

Individual developers are obliged to pass on the obligations and benefits of these covenants that refer to specific buildings and circumstances as they complete each project and wish to sell or let individual buildings. The promoter thus acquires both rights and obligations, notably the obligation to manage by carrying out particular activities and performing specific services. Such obligations might conveniently be carried out by the management company, which may initially be controlled by the promoter.

It would assist the development of community participation if every party with a legal interest in any part of the urban village were automatically a shareholder in the management company and thus had a voice in management. The community development trust could play an active role by agreeing to take on some of the duties of the management company along with activities associated with the promotion of the urban village.

Building management

In order to maintain a uniform and consistent appearance, an umbrella management company may choose to carry out certain functions that are usually the responsibility of individual owners or tenants. These obligations – in most cases, to manage, repair and where necessary renew specified parts of the fabric of buildings separately owned or occupied – fall into two or more types.

Those affecting all buildings may include:

– fences, hedges and gates;
– pathways visible to the public;
– television and radio aerials; and
– subject to local authority powers, the numbering and naming of houses and other buildings, and naming of streets.

Covenants affecting properties that are part of a block or terrace and in which common maintenance is required for architectural integrity might cover:

– roofs;
– external walls;
– front doors in all respects;
– windows;
– external redecoration; and
– external areas used communally to the benefit of specified occupiers.

Since the promoter will be obliged to undertake, through the management company, specified works, all transfers and legal agreements must also provide a compensating right to charge to the occupiers the cost of carrying out these works, along with administrative and other overheads. These costs will best be dealt with by collection of service charges and the accumulation of a management fund to provide for unforeseen contingencies.

Some buildings will be separate entities entirely surrounded by public realm, but will nonetheless need to be covered by these arrangements. They will include buildings with public or semi-public uses where there may be good reasons for leasehold rather than freehold tenure.

Community ownership

A community development trust could be granted an overall lease for key social facilities, including community halls and meeting rooms, sports pavilions and other leisure buildings. These can then be made available for use by voluntary groups, charities and sports clubs in a way that will maximize public benefit. Such an arrangement could also cover enterprise buildings such as shared workshops. Community buildings, including churches, medical centres and children's nurseries, are best owned or leased by their users, who will be under a legal obligation to comply with covenants affecting them and to contribute their share of management costs.

Maintaining mixed tenure

In order to maintain a balance of available tenures, provision must be made for affordable housing – affordable, that is, not just to its first occupiers, but also to subsequent occupiers in the future. There is also a need to provide economic support to certain commercial buildings, including shops, before they are fully viable to ensure that convenient facilities are established at an early stage.

The providers of such advance or non-commercial elements in the urban village are likely to include housing associations, companies established under business expansion schemes, and investors who are prepared to take a long-term view. This social provision will, by making the urban village more attractive, help to enhance the values of all properties in it. From the promoter's point of view, it will also mean that some sites have a negative value. To facilitate such provision, it may be possible to donate or allocate sites for a modest sum or even contribute to the initial building costs.

In these circumstances it will be possible to attach covenants to the transfers restricting the way in which the buildings may be let and used, and what rents may be charged, although this will clearly have financial implications. Established restrictions should be set for as long a period as commercial considerations allow, reflecting the extent of the cross-subsidy the promoter feels able to support.

In summary, these initial guidelines for the management of an urban village reflect three essential points:

– the importance attached to maintaining the quality and integrity of the masterplan, the detailed elements of the development and the planned mixture of uses and tenures;
– the commercial interests that must be protected if the urban village concept is to attract developers and funding institutions over the long term; and
– the need for a healthily developing community to have a stake and a voice in its day-to-day management.

Successful neighbourhood management needs both an established organizational structure and a clear framework of easily understood, realistic and enforceable obligations and rights. Each and every owner and tenant will not only be bound by this system of covenants but stands to benefit significantly from its existence and enforcement.

Afterword

David Lunts

It is 14 years since Trevor Osborne established the
Urban Villages Group. In 1992 the word 'Group'
was dropped in favour of 'Forum' to reflect the
breadth of interest the campaign generated. But
when the original, eponymous report was
published in 1992, it was greeted with rather more
scepticism than enthusiasm. The property business
was reeling from the deepest depression for many
years, following the boom of the late 1980s, the
previous decade had witnessed a huge expansion
of out-of-town shopping malls, leisure parks,
business campuses and housing estates. More than
three million people had moved to new suburban
housing developments in the previous 20 years.
The new, drive-in retail centres had fundamentally
altered patterns of shopping to the detriment of
traditional town centres. Many cities faced
catastrophic collapses of populations and economic
fortunes as traditional industries folded, and urban
riots during the 1980s and 90s seemed for many to
beckon the nemesis for inner cities. Urban flight
had long been a British phenomenon, but a laissez-
faire national planning policy during these years
seemed destined to encourage, rather than
discourage, the trend.

Many architects appeared to have little interest
in cities, and still less experience of creative
urbanism, and were increasingly obsessed with a
post-modernism that appeared to celebrate kitsch
and flamboyance almost entirely at the expense of
urban context. Planners, widely blamed for the
failures of post-war reconstruction and
redevelopment, often bore the brunt of massive

cutbacks in local government spending, and had
become a beleaguered and defeated profession.

The voices that had spoken out for a
celebratory urbanism were few. The Prince of
Wales had instigated the original urban villages
campaign, and Leon and Rob Krier, Christopher
Alexander and a few others had refused to
abandon the virtues of historic (or what Roberta
Gratz here describes as 'authentic') urbanism. The
moment was right for a new campaign. There was
a widespread enthusiasm for a more
environmentally responsible approach to land use,
transport and lifestyle, and resentment that so
many cities were apparently being left to rot.

Today, just ten years on, things look very
different. National planning guidance is strongly
supportive of mixed urban development, and is
rigorously resisting unnecessary greenfield
development. There's much talk of 'urban
renaissance'. The work of the Urban Task Force and
the consequent Urban White Paper has given
credence to much that the Urban Villages Forum
was created to achieve. There have been some
welcome – and important – concessions too. New
tax breaks offer incentives for cleaning up
contaminated land, VAT reductions are now
available for certain types of building
refurbishments, and Stamp Duty exemptions have
been approved for many poorer urban areas. New
regeneration agencies have also been set up, not
least the new Urban Regeneration Companies –
sponsored by government, but independent – to
act as promoters of local urban improvement.

Left:
**The clock tower has
been preserved as a
central landmark within
the regeneration of
the Jewellery Quarter,
Birmingham**

Above:
The redevelopment of Britannia Mills has brought new life to these redundant historic warehouses
Urban Splash

Opposite (above):
More than 2,000 homes have been constructed during the regeneration of Hulme in Manchester

Opposite (below):
Poundbury in Dorchester provides an alternative and successful model for extending towns on greenfield sites

There's also heaps of official planning and design guidance, which, together with the work of the Commission for Architecture and the Built Environment, have persuasively urged that urbanism should be rehabilitated. Greenfields should be the option of last resort. It seems that the future's urban; the future's brown.

But despite the exhortations, and the wealth of new advice and guidance, progress has been patchy, and often contradictory. So, what's the story, ten years on?

The urban lobby has certainly begun to gather its forces in the last decade, and there have been some impressive practical successes. After more than a century of urban flight, populations in many of the core cities have stabilized, helped by a welcome migration into city centres, and as single household professionals realize, the urban offer can be an excellent one. Ten years ago, few predicted how substantial, and apparently sustainable, this market would prove to be. The conversion of rotting warehouses and abandoned offices in Manchester, Leeds, Newcastle and Birmingham into upmarket loft-style apartments was only for daring entrepreneurs. Today, such opportunities, if they can still be found, are snatched up by the volume house-builders. The urban pioneers have begun to be replaced by the urban settlers.

But this welcome return to urban living for some of the prosperous, has been in stark contrast to the collapse of entire communities, often in the very same cities that are enjoying a revival in city centre fortunes. In east Manchester, large parts of Salford, Newcastle's West End, parts of Leeds, Sheffield and Birmingham, homes are all but impossible to sell or let. In many of the northern mill towns and former manufacturing settlements in the west Midlands, the same predicament prevails, as the wealth-creating foundations have disintegrated. Today, nearly 900,000 homes are officially ranked as suffering from 'housing market failure'. This at a time when nationally, there are record level house prices, surging ever higher, driven by rising incomes, increasing rates of household formation, low interest rates, and a chronic shortfall in building (amazingly now at the lowest peacetime level since 1924). In part, this is

a north-south issue, as Peter Hall has described in some detail, but only in part. Of more concern is the extraordinary proximity of rampant house price increases in city centres such as Manchester to the moribund housing markets just a mile or two away, in neighbourhoods where comprehensive clearance is now once again the order of the day.

While the northern and provincial cities have more or less stabilized their populations with some welcome signs of urban renaissance, London's population is growing at a fast and furious pace, and is projected to rise by 700,000 by 2016. The buoyancy of the national economy for the last few years, coupled with immigration to the capital, has accelerated the trend, leading to spiralling housing costs and real concerns about the affordability of housing for key service workers. London, as ever, offers stark contrasts in the wealth and poverty of its communities, although the city's enduring attraction as an economic and cultural powerhouse is witnessing the rapid renewal, and gentrification, of many neighbourhoods, especially towards the east, encouraged by improved transit and the regeneration of Docklands.

These pressures, both north and south, coupled with a more robust national planning framework, should offer considerable scope for urban village-style development activity. Comprehensive reconstruction of inner urban areas in many provincial cities, together with the growing conviction that major new greenfield and brownfield settlements may be required to ease the pressure on southern housing costs, point strongly towards such an approach.

It is heartening that a few large-scale schemes have already begun to appear which have explicitly used much of the urban village model. Strong and visionary leadership, coupled with rigorous masterplanning and a robust challenging of the standard rules of urban design and development, have left a small, but influential legacy through the 1990s and beyond. Encouragingly, the best of them appear to be very successful, often confounding the sceptics who once claimed they were naive or wrong-headed.

In Glasgow, the Crown Street regeneration project in the heart of the Gorbals has successfully

rehabilitated the traditional Glasgow grid, and the versatile density of the tenement, in an iconoclastic piece of urban renewal. The new neighbourhood has more than 600 new homes, together with a new shopping and residential high street and an urban park, and is proving an economic and community success.

In Hulme, Manchester, more than 2,000 new homes have been constructed around an infrastructure of linked streets and squares, in an explicit attempt to capture something of the character of the dense urban neighbourhood that was torn down to make way for disastrous municipal flats in the 1960s.

At Poundbury, the Duchy of Cornwall is developing an influential extension to the historic market town of Dorchester which, when complete, will group a number of walkable neighbourhoods together in a site totalling some 450 acres. Leon Krier's masterplan has enabled the street to become the focus for urban exchange and communication, and although only the first phase is fully complete, it is already proving a commercial success, despite breaking most of the

Above:

The regeneration of Crown Street, Glasgow, has turned around the character and economic potential of the area

Below:

Successful reuse of brownfield sites, such as Llandarcy in South Wales, will be essential to the delivery of an urban renaissance

pre-existing rules of greenfield site development.

These three projects are important because they set out, quite explicitly, to reintroduce traditional urbanism within their design as a precondition for creating memorable and lasting places for people to both live and work. In each case, rules have been broken and reinterpreted around the premise that what matters is what works for the place-making whole, rather than any individual piece or function within it.

There are many other schemes that either lay claim to being 'urban villages', or have borrowed some of the core concepts of the campaign. They tend to be of mixed quality. Some are little more than orthodox housing projects pretending to be more. Others are flawed because they are of insufficient scale or density to achieve their stated aims, or fail to provide adequate coherence to their internal and external connections.

There are, though, some promising schemes that may set new standards for large-scale urban village-type developments in the years ahead. Some have been assembled with the help of project teams from the Urban Villages Forum and, more recently, the Prince's Foundation. Large sites include the Llandarcy refinery, outside Swansea, and a western extension to Northampton, while estate renewal strategies in Nuneaton and Havant are following similar principles.

What, then, has the urban villages campaign achieved, and what can be learned that may help

improve our urbanism in the years to come?

The original urban village model, expressed in both the first Urban Villages report and the subsequent *Economics of Urban Villages*, had both the merits and drawbacks of exactitude. The preference for a precise size of site (30–50 hectares), a unified landownership, long-term finance and, most intriguingly, a nominal 1:1 ratio of residents to jobs, was at best naive and, at worst, unworkable. It also rather confused the virtues of a well-defined mixed neighbourhood with that of self-contained sustainability at the same spatial scale.

On the other hand, the model did point towards a precision in the principles that should inform the masterplanning of neighbourhood-scaled projects and, insofar as it neatly tied these principles of place-making into a clear procurement regime (the notion of the 'promoter'), it had its feet firmly on the ground. The influence of Howard and the new town movement was self-evident in the carefully argued case for achieving sustainable urbanism through patient investment in parallel to community endowment and governance.

It is noteworthy that all the substantial 'urban village' success stories in recent years, whether in this country, or through the New Urbanism in the United States, have depended on a unified site ownership and a strongly motivated 'promoter'.

The urban villages campaign has now been absorbed in a broader current of sympathetic urban discourse and practice. The Forum is now a central part of The Prince's Foundation, itself a home for teaching and debate around a wide theme of humane urbanism, craft, architecture and art. The emergence of other campaigns such as the Urban Design Alliance has also helped to influence policy makers and, at the margins at least, practitioners.

What then, are some of the implications and challenges for the coming years, and what can we perhaps draw from the contributions in this volume?

First, we badly need more sophistication and precision in the interventions we make in our towns and cities. It is difficult not to despair when one considers the skill, craft intuition and discipline that produced our historic townscapes, compared with more recent times. In the United States, the New Urbanism has created a lexicon, codes and operating systems which may offer inspiration for similar techniques in the United Kingdom. Andrés Duany makes a powerful case for urban coding and precision that draws directly on this country's own legacy, particularly that of Raymond Unwin and Patrick Geddes. It is ironic (and sad) that Unwin's seminal *Town Planning in Practice* has long been unpublished in this country. Even today, it is only available because Princeton University has recently produced a new edition. The clarity and usability of Duany's notion of the transect is perhaps a starting-point for working up a UK model for designing sustainable and interconnected urbanism.

Second, if we are to secure a step change in technique, then it needs to be matched with a new definition and methodology for the elusive notion of 'sustainability'. It is surely time to move beyond the measurements of traditional land-use planning and engineering, and find systems that are far more responsive to the overall needs of urban sustainability and the broader environmental agenda. A particular priority should be the quest to create urban environments that are as responsive and adaptable to change as many traditional cities.

Third, it seems clear that we need to devise new strategies for assembling land, whether by site acquisitions via state-funded agencies, or by land pooling and joint ventures. The opportunities available through substantial urban renewal programmes on the one hand, and major urban extensions on the other, demand an assertive approach to bringing about neighbourhood-scale development.

Fourth, the financing of urban regeneration remains a challenge. The viability of many urban masterplans often relies on commitments to front-fund elements that will only become fully viable over time. Schools, shops, health facilities, libraries and public transport will need to be factored in to funding mechanisms and project plans.

Fifth, there has to be a major investment in the skills of practitioners in all the key endeavours that impact on urbanism. This calls for a sustained and imaginative effort to learn from the best of

international practice and a long-overdue reappraisal of the UK's own urban heritage, from which a great deal can be learned.

Six, as Roberta Gratz and Ken Worpole make clear, cities and their communities usually defy easy categorization, and we need both precision and humility in dealing with the organized complexity that makes them work best. We need to celebrate diversity, and avoid tempting 'big bang' solutions that may rest on little more than egotistical and misplaced design visions. This is perhaps the single most compelling critique of twentieth-century urban planning and design, but it retains a continuing seductiveness. Ambition of vision doesn't have to mean inappropriate solutions or stereotypes, but it does demand a counterweight of technical rigour and humility.

Lastly, if the transcendent theme in this volume is about people, and the way they use, enjoy, or suffer the spaces and habitats they use, then we need to find better ways to engage them in the process of planning. The success of techniques like Enquiry by Design and Planning for Real need to become more firmly embedded into the practice of urban visioning and regeneration. Experience suggests that most communities have a clear and intuitive understanding of the kinds of environments they enjoy and admire. A commitment to embodying these aspirations into local, regional and national plans is an important component in the urban renaissance.

There are grounds for a cautious optimism. Few doubt that serious choices lie ahead for how, and where, we build decent human habitats. This remains an increasingly crowded country, where a uniquely rich urban heritage has been curiously at odds with a long-standing reluctance to develop a 'new urbanism' built upon this legacy. Yet recent policy strictures, fuelled by deep underlying trends that are analysed throughout this book, are already driving a renewal of urbanism which, despite the extent of its challenge, is finding converts and ambassadors, many of whom are making the city an investment of choice, not fate. Long may it continue.

Urban retrofit and infill

The Jewellery Quarter, Birmingham

Little Germany, Bradford

Temple Bar, Dublin

King-Spadina, Toronto

Urban renewal and brownfield

The Pearl District, Portland

Crown Street, Glasgow

Bo01 Housing Expo, Malmö

Llandarcy, South Wales

Urban extension and greenfield

Upton, Northampton

Poundbury, Dorset

Kirchsteigfeld, Potsdam

Newington, Sydney

A compendium of case studies

This compendium illustrates the structure, character and ongoing delivery of a dozen new and regenerated urban neighbourhoods. Throughout this book it is clear that the mixed-use characteristics of the urban village model can be realized and implemented in a number of ways. Early urban village literature set out the guiding principles of such neighbourhoods and presented these through illustrations of existing and theoretical places. The projects examined in this section follow the principles established at the outset of the urban village movement as a means to create a rich variety of medium- and high-density urban neighbourhoods. Many include a good mix of tenure, diverse social facilities and opportunities to live and work within the neighbourhood. They also encourage walking and cycling and many are served by a good public transport network. Fundamentally, these projects are about creating places that are popular, economically successful and attractive, and which embody a real sense of community.

To provide diversity, the case studies have been selected from a wide geographic and urban context that includes Great Britain, Europe, the United States and Australia. They have been chosen to illustrate three different urban conditions: centre, middle and edge. The first group address issues of urban infill or retrofit, where the existing urban fabric is in need of repair. Many of these districts are often close to the core of city centres but have outlived their original purpose and have generally gone through a period of decline. All these projects deal with areas that still retain a wealth of attractive, and often historically valuable, buildings that provide a significant cultural asset for redevelopment.

The second group focuses on situations where extensive, if not wholesale, renewal strategies have to be initiated on a large scale. These tend to involve recycling large tracts of brownfield land. The final selection of projects addresses issues of the urban edge where previously undeveloped greenfield land has had to accommodate an increasing demand for new housing. Such projects, often described as urban extensions, are capable of forging new connections with the existing urban fabric.

Each case study focuses on salient characteristics and key elements in their delivery. Some highlight the value of extensive and well-planned public consultation, others demonstrate the key role that focused and energetic delivery teams play in the process. Many have created a variegated yet harmonious architecture with clear character and identity, whilst the strength of others lies in their environmental and social sustainability. All the projects have been selected to provide an urban design aide-memoire for the complex process of making communities.

Authentic urbanism is a continual process of change that should be carefully and sensitively managed. All the selected projects have clear strengths and weaknesses, but the important lesson is to learn to interpret these theoretical and practical lessons. As Raymond Unwin suggested some hundred years ago, while we can study and admire, it does not follow that we should directly copy. It is important to understand that one of the key objectives is to learn to intelligently and proactively manage the dynamic process of urban change. Popular neighbourhoods are living human habitats and they need to be loved, nurtured and looked after to ensure that their full potential is released.

Category	Urban retrofit and infill
Project name	The Jewellery Quarter
Location	Birmingham, UK
Size	107 hectares/265 acres
Key milestones	1997 Framework Plan commissioned
	1998 Framework Plan adopted within UDP
	2002 Conservation Area Management Plan adopted

Case Study 1

The Jewellery Quarter, Birmingham

Birmingham's Jewellery Quarter, which was established in the late Georgian and early Victorian era to serve a growing jewellery industry, has become the foremost centre for production of jewellery in the United Kingdom. Praised by English Heritage as 'a place of unique character and a national treasure' the area is typified by a network of small industrial workshops and live/work premises that were originally built to serve the needs of the craftsmen working in the industry.

The Quarter extends over 100 hectares and although it is adjacent to the city centre, it was isolated from the city's commercial and retail activity by the construction of the Inner Ring Road in the 1960s. It went through a period of significant decline in the 1970s, with the loss of over 60,000 jobs and a rapid increase in the number of vacant or derelict properties. With growing interest from developers in the mid-1990s – buoyed by an improving economy and the success of nearby Brindleyplace – the City Council

sought to adopt a more proactive approach to regenerating the district. In partnership with Advantage West Midlands RDA, English Partnerships and the Urban Villages Forum (now the Prince's Foundation), the city commissioned the 'Jewellery Quarter Urban Village Framework Plan'. Prepared in 1997, the plan is seen as an important component in defining a new vision for the centre of Birmingham, which is now concentrating on the creation of a series of distinct quarters including the Gunsmiths Quarter and the Chinese Quarter.

Essentially, the Framework Plan sets out a strategy to retrofit and infill the existing urban quarter through a number of planned regeneration initiatives. From the outset the primary aim was to protect the existing architectural heritage of the area and reuse where possible the existing urban fabric. The strategy chose to adopt an approach more akin to keyhole surgery rather than transplanting, and radically altering, large areas of the district with new development.

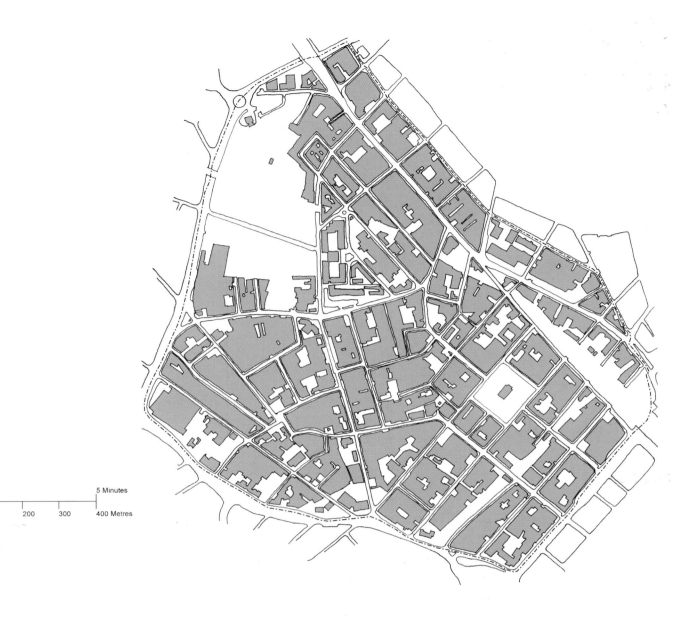

5 Minutes

100   200   300   400 Metres

At the outset an agreed vision for the project was established by the partnership to 'create a *complete* community, which is home to a thriving business and residential population; supported by other social and economic facilities and set within a high quality environment respectful of the area's unique heritage and existing industrial activity'.

As a means to deliver this vision the Framework Plan was formally adopted by the City in November 1998 and subsequently incorporated as Supplementary Planning Guidance within the Birmingham Unitary Development Plan. It has guided development and investment in the quarter since that date by playing to the area's strengths – its legacy of fine industrial buildings and its close proximity to the city centre. It adopts a flexible approach towards introducing new mixed-use development on a series of priority sites, which:

– consolidates the Quarter as an important centre for the jewellery industry and secures the historic context for future generations;
– achieves a significant commitment to new residential development in the heart of the city and provides a balanced mix of tenures;
– develops real opportunities for new forms of business activity;
– provides new social and communal facilities that now support a growing community;
– promotes the artistic, cultural and tourism potential of the Quarter;

○ Activity Node
◌ Gateway
→ Key Primary Link
-→ Key Secondary Link
▬ Key Active Frontage
○ Key Landmark Corners
▬ Significant Structures
▬ New/Reinforced Public Realm
▭ Opportunity Sites
▭ Open Space

Priority Opportunity Sites
1. Great Charles Street Car Park
2. Ludgate Hill South
3. Assay Office Car Park and adjacent Car Park
4. Former Science Museum
4a. Caspar Site
5. Canal Side Warehouse
6. Fleet Street
7. James Cond Building
8. Newhall Hill/Newhall Works
9. Tenby Site, Warstone Works
10. Albion Square/Carver Street
11. Legge Lane
12. Moulinex/Swan Factory Complex
13. Icknield Street
14. Warstone Lane
15. Spencer Street Block
16. Former Lucas Factory, Great Hampton Street

Other Opportunity Sites
17. 96 Newhall Street
18. 35-57 Summer Row
19. George Street
20. 10 Caroline Street
21. 43-47 Vittoria Street
22. Vacant Land and Buildings, St Paul's Square
23. Caroline Street
24. Car Park Site, Northwood Street
25. Vyse Street
26. Great Hampton Street
27. 23-25 Constitution Hill
28. Vacant Land, Water Street
29. Car Park/Vacant Land, Lionel Street

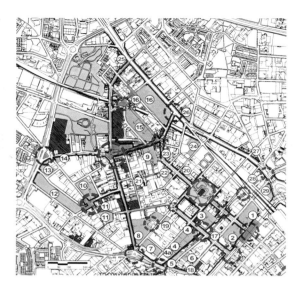

Above left:
The Jewellery Quarter Urban Village Framework Plan, prepared in 1997 EDAW Limited

Above right:
New buildings have been carefully integrated into the existing fabric of St Paul's Square

– enhances the quality of the environment and builds on the Quarter's unique urban architectural heritage; and
– achieves a delivery mechanism that allows a sustainable investment strategy to be secured that can release the full potential of the Quarter and enable it to reassert its role within the wider urban area.

These changes are now beginning to establish an enhanced identity and sense of pride for the neighbourhood and improve its standing within the city centre. As a priority, several substantial improvements to the public realm have been undertaken and a new mix of uses and cultural facilities has been integrated. Specific achievements include:

– a significant increase in the residential population of the area, with over 1,600 new housing units being either complete, under construction or with planning consent;
– an expanding business and office community that includes the headquarters for the Bass Brewery and the College of Law;
– many new leisure and retail units that represent a 50 per cent increase in jewellery retail outlets, in addition to a number of cafés, restaurants, a regular street market and a new Pen Museum;
– a modern apprenticeship scheme and a customized training scheme that has been

launched to enhance local employment opportunities;
– environmental improvements along Newhall Street and the coordination of street furniture within the Quarter, alongside a new CCTV package and neighbourhood watch schemes that have enhanced a sense of security within the area.
– improved pedestrian links that have established connections with adjacent districts, the closure of Newhall Street underpass, improvements to the canal towpath and a number of signed pavement trails within the district.

These achievements represent a significant change of fortune and have directly contributed to the growing economic and social confidence in the area. Gentrification is now becoming a particular concern, with spiralling property prices pressurizing existing jewellery manufacturers to relocate elsewhere. One development that has begun to address this problem is the Big Peg, which offers around 120 low-cost workplaces for a variety of arts and crafts activities. Named after a jeweller's workbench, which is known in the trade as a 'peg', the building makes a significant contribution to the cultural life of the area. Over the coming years it will become increasingly important for the City Council to maintain a good mix of tenure of the area to ensure that lower cost live/work facilities can continue to exist alongside more costly apartments and business premises.

Right:
An aerial view of
Birmingham's Jewellery
Quarter in 1993,
centred on St Paul's
Church and Square

Key framework statistics (set at 1998)
Capacity for new residential units:
2,000
Projected residential population:
4–5,000
New and refurbished workspace:
10,000 sq m
Reusable vacant space: 50,000 sq m
Learning and Development Centre
Business and office space
New leisure and retail units
Environmental improvements
Improved pedestrian links and
connections

Project partners
Birmingham City Council
Advantage West Midlands RDA
English Partnerships
The Prince's Foundation
British Waterways
Groundwork (Birmingham)
Jewellery Quarter Association
British Jewellery and Giftware Federation
English Heritage
University of Central England

Consultants
EDAW – town planning and urban design
Hillier Parker – property market
assessment
WSP Consulting Engineers – transport
and parking

References
Regeneration through Conservation:
Birmingham Conservation Strategy,
Birmingham: City Council, 1999.
The Birmingham Jewellery Quarter:
an introduction and guide,
English Heritage, 2000.
K Hughes, *The Jewellery Quarter*
(Brum Trail 6), Birmingham: Birmingham
Urban Studies Group, 1994.

Web sites
<http://www.the-quarter.com>

Category	Urban retrofit and infill
Project name	Little Germany
Location	Bradford, UK
Size	9 hectares/22 acres
Key milestones	1971 Designated a Conservation Area
	1985 Area renewal started by City Council
	1995 Renewed regeneration drive by EP and City Council
	1999 Urban Village established
	2002 Planning Framework adopted as SPG

Case Study 2

Little Germany, Bradford

The townscape and architectural form of Little Germany, a part of Bradford named after its late-nineteenth-century German residents, is considered to be unique, not only in the city of Bradford, but also within the UK. Established at the peak of the woollen and textile manufacturing industries, this urban quarter is typified by its sloping terrain and a compact network of imposing buildings that originally provided distinctive warehousing and office space for merchants to store and sell their goods.

Set adjacent to the northeastern side of the city, the district was built between 1855 and 1890 to accommodate the growing numbers of European merchants who settled and invested in the area. By the end of the nineteenth century Bradford had become a major economic force in the woollen and textile trades, and the resulting architectural quality and character of the district remains a testament to the wealth that was generated at that time. The compact townscape, designated as a conservation area in 1971, incorporates over 85

buildings, most of them Victorian, of which 55 have been listed. Several key landmark buildings have been identified as making a significant contribution to the character of the townscape, including Eastbrook Hall (which was previously a Methodist Chapel); the former Silens Works on Peckover Street; Capital House; Delaunay House, which has a frontage on Burnette Street; and Behrens Warehouse on East Parade.

By the late twentieth century many of the buildings had become vacant and were rapidly deteriorating through poor maintenance and vandalism. There was growing concern that the district would become irreparably damaged by neglect and inappropriate development as the city strove to maintain some form of economic role for the area. The clear challenge was to identify new uses and economic activities for the district that were compatible with the existing historic fabric and which could be used to create a new mixed-use community in the heart of Bradford city centre. Establishing Little Germany as an urban village

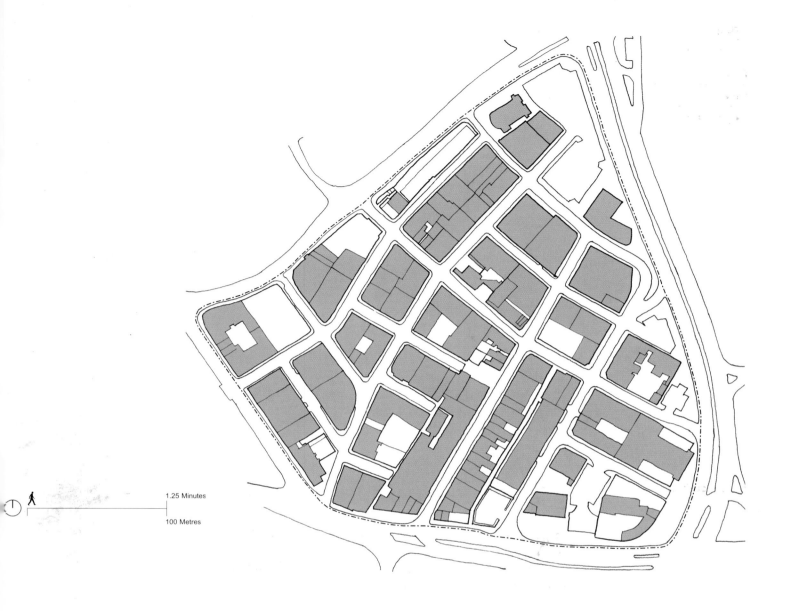

1.25 Minutes

100 Metres

offered a clear and identifiable strategy that could refocus economic, social and physical investment for this inner-city area and restore the district's identity and stature within the wider City of Bradford.

The Little Germany Urban Village Company (LGUVC) was established in the autumn of 1999 through a partnership between the City of Bradford Metropolitan District Council, Yorkshire Forward, The Prince's Foundation, Bradford Cathedral and local representation from a network of business and community groups. This partnership between the public and private sectors has been able to raise the status of the district and promote unified support for new initiatives that have grown from the existing base of local businesses and tenants. Five key themes have been defined to underpin the vision. These are:

–   the provision of a well-integrated mix of uses and activities;
–   the introduction of residential and commercial tenures that encourage social and economic cohesion, diversity and opportunity;
–   the creation of a pattern of development and residential density that encourages a mix of uses and amenities within easy walking distance;
–   the promotion of high-quality urban design and architecture within the planning and development of the area, recognizing its high value as a heritage asset for the city; and
–   a strong input from local stakeholders in the planning, design and management of the area.

To ensure the conservation and enhancement of the area's architectural and industrial heritage, a physical development framework for the district has been prepared by LGUVC. Initial guidance has been set by policy BN/R1 of Bradford's Unitary Development Plan, which defines the inner part of the city as a Strategic Regeneration Area. Supporting guidance is set within National Planning Policy Guidance (PPG) Notes 12, *Development Plans* (1999), and 15, *Planning and the Historic Environment* (1994). The Little Germany Planning Framework has now been adopted by Bradford City Council as Supplementary Planning Guidance. This safeguards the valuable built heritage of the area, promotes high quality urban design and forges direct links with the adjacent Cathedral Quarter and the Foster Square redevelopment area.

There is an expressed desire to attract new, high-quality uses to the area. These include residential, office, leisure, employment and training activities. In parallel, there is the need to reinforce the existing urban environment with new live/work opportunities to complement the current mix of elements and to increase the residential population that is becoming established. The tight urban form of the area means that there is a real shortage of suitable public space, consequently, the strategy emphasizes the opportunities to create pedestrian-biased spaces at Festival Square and in front of Delaunay House, and a new square at the old Quaker School playground.

In addition to attracting over 100,000 visitors per year, who are drawn in part by its architectural and industrial heritage, Little Germany is now home to over 110 companies and organizations providing over 3,000 jobs in a variety of service industries. Many of the buildings, including those in Well Street and Vicar Lane, have been converted into modern, high-specification offices that support insurance and financial service companies. New investment in the public realm will include better lighting, pavements and an integrated CCTV facility. The residential component to the district is growing, with the conversion of listed warehouses into new apartments and flats. North British Housing Association has transformed the listed warehouse on Currer Street into 49 self-contained flats. With £885,000 of gap funding from English Partnerships and Yorkshire Forward, the Silens Works, a former brass foundry, has been converted into a series of loft-style units to encourage a more diverse community for the area.

The regeneration of the historic quarter is seen as an important element in Bradford's bid for European Capital of Culture status in 2008 and it also forms a key component of Bradford's 2020 Vision. As a means to underpin the commercial and residential components of the regeneration strategy, investment in cultural, leisure and arts facilities has been actively pursued. These facilities include the Bradford Community Arts Centre, Bradford Design Exchange and the Priestley Centre for the Arts, which are popular local theatre, music and film venues. Additional cultural and leisure activities include the Gurdwara Sikh Temple, two independent radio stations, a fitness centre and a growing number of cafés, bars and restaurants that are supported by the residential population and also benefit from the close proximity of the quarter to Bradford's city centre.

Left:
Traditional building and paving materials provide a unified character for the entire district

Right:
Little Germany Urban Village looking east from the city centre

Above:
**A summer event held
at Festival Square in front
of Delaunay House**

Right:
**Vicar Lane and Priestley
House – improved lighting
has made the district far
more attractive to visit
in the evening**

Development statistics (at end 2001)
Projected residential community: 2,000
Projected full-time jobs within the
quarter: 4,000
Percentage of affordable homes: 30

Project partners and organizations
Little Germany Urban Village Company
City of Bradford Metropolitan District
Council
The Prince's Foundation
Yorkshire Forward
English Heritage
Cathedral Quarter partnership
Little Germany Community
Business Forum

Developers
J. J. Gallagher
North British Housing Association
Yorkshire Design Developments
Blue Room Properties
Aldersgate

Consultants
Scott Wilson Planning Consultants
Westmorland & Worcester Properties Ltd
Shared Intelligence
KPMG
Priest Woodward Associates

References
Bradford's Merchants Trail (self-guided
walk), Bradford: Bradford City Centre
Management.

Web site
<http://www.Bradford.gov.uk/little-
germany>

Category	Urban retrofit and infill
Project Name	Temple Bar
Location	Dublin, Ireland
Size	11 hectares/28 acres
Key Milestones	1991 Temple Bar Area Renewal and Development Act
	1991 Temple Bar Properties established
	1991 Framework Plan prepared by Group 91 Architects
	1993 Irish Film Centre and the Music Centre opened
	1996 Meeting House and Temple Bar Squares complete
	1996 Completion of Phase 1
	2001 Completion of Phase 2

Temple Bar, Dublin

The catalyst for Temple Bar's regeneration was inspired by two important, yet contrasting factors – the threat of redevelopment for a new bus terminal by the state transport company and the designation of Dublin as European City of Culture in 1991. Although the district has only occasionally been described as an Urban Village, Temple Bar has over the past decade re-emerged as a popular, dense, mixed-use neighbourhood. At the core of the strategy has been the elaboration of a mixed-use scheme that has placed equal importance on the simultaneous development of cultural, residential, retail and commercial activities. John Montgomery, writing in the January 1995 edition of *Urban Design Quarterly*, suggests that 'Temple Bar is the first example of an urban place being planned, managed and designed on principles derived from Jane Jacobs'.

Located next to the centre of Dublin and on the southern banks of the River Liffey, Temple Bar first acquired its name around the seventeenth century. With the development of the docks along the river in the 1800s, the area grew to become a bustling commercial centre that was soon home to an eclectic mix of activities, including bookbinders, tailors, drapers, cobblers, actors, stockbrokers and stationers. As new theatres, music halls, coffee houses and dozens of taverns opened, this flourishing area became recognized as an important entertainment quarter for Dublin. The 1950s marked the advent of mechanized mass production that reduced the demand for traditional skilled traders and established a growing preference for suburban rather than urban living. In response to this, the area began to stagnate and many of the buildings fell vacant and became derelict.

In the early 1980s, CIÉ, the State transport company identified Temple Bar as a prime location for a bus and coach terminal and began to acquire property in the area. During the extended planning process the district became known as the 'left-bank community' and gained a bohemian reputation for alternative fashion, art and cultural uses attracted

5 Minutes

| 100 | 200 | 300 | 400 Metres |

by low rents and alternative lifestyles. By the time CIÉ had finalized their proposals a grass-roots movement had emerged within Temple Bar that sought to conserve the existing qualities of the area. To champion their cause they established their own form of local government – the Temple Bar Development Council (TBDC).

In partnership with central and local Government, the Arts Council, the Tourist Board and the Employment and Training Agency, the TBDC put forward their own alternative vision to develop the area as a cultural, tourist and recreational quarter for Dublin. It was fortuitous timing, for in 1991 Dublin was designated European City of Culture and the renewal of Temple Bar was identified as one of the city's flagship projects. In the same year the Temple Bar Area Renewal and Development Act was adopted by Parliament and An Taoiseach (Central

Government) set up Temple Bar Properties (TBP) as a publicly-owned company with the remit to guide the revitalization of the area as a new cultural quarter. The company established an innovative urban renewal plan that set six key objectives to steer the regeneration process. These addressed:

- the urban renewal of the area;
- the consolidation and development of cultural activity;
- the regeneration of a resident population;
- the expansion of interesting retail outlets and service industries;
- the marketing of Temple Bar with the aim of attracting an increasing amount of business activity and people to the area; and
- the improvement of the external environment in cooperation with the appropriate authorities.

The process began with an architectural competition to prepare a framework that would stand the test of time and allow proposals for individual sites to be developed in a structured, yet flexible way. Group 91, a consortium of eight local architectural practices, won with their Framework Plan for Temple Bar. In the words of their submission, the plan established 'no single solution; rather a flexible series of integrated responses to release the dynamic potential of Temple Bar, while reinforcing its unique sense of place in our capital city'.

Importantly, the plan avoided large-scale building proposals and instead chose to enforce the existing character of the area and conserve the current urban fabric. The plan came with two key objectives: it chose to clearly emphasize the role of the public realm in the city by creating a series of urban spaces, and it stressed the need to increase the resident population of the area by including a significant proportion of new housing.

Throughout the regeneration process extensive archaeological investigations were undertaken and it became an established rule that all new development had to respect the scale and the medieval pattern of the Temple Bar area. The majority of the reconstruction work has been split over two phases and this is comprehensively documented in the Development Programme for Temple Bar published by TBP.

Phase One (1991–1996) saw the realization of many specific structural objectives, including the construction of many public and privately funded buildings. These included the creation of two new public squares – Temple Bar Square and Meeting House Square – and the Irish Film Centre. The latter was designed by O'Donnell and Tuomey and built within a disused Quaker Meeting House bounded by Eustace Street, Dame Street and Sycamore Street. Phase Two (1996–2001) focused on increasing the residential population of the area on the west of Parliament Street and bounded by the Liffey Quays, Fishamble Street and Lord Edward Street.

Much of the success of the programme must be attributed to the participation, on many levels, of individuals, partnerships and stakeholders. These have included local groups, cultural

Key statistics (as of 2001)
Number of new/refurbished
cultural facilities: 16
Total number of cultural
organizations now based in
Temple Bar: 65
Increase in residential
population 1991–2001: 2,800
Proportion of social housing:
30 per cent
Increase in number of new
long-term jobs from 1993 to
2001: 410
Total public funding 1991–99:
IR £ 40.6 million
Total temporary loans for
redevelopment:
R £60 million
Estimated private sector
investment: IR £100 million

**Project partners and
organizations**
Temple Bar Properties
The Department of An
Taoiseach
The Department of the
Environment and Local
Government
The Department of Arts,
Culture, the Gaeltacht
and the Islands
Dublin City Council
The Arts Council
European Regional
Development Fund

Group 91 Architects
Shay Cleary Architects
Grafton Architects
Paul Keogh Architects
McCullough Mulvin Architects
McGarry NíÉanaigh Architects
O'Donnell & Tuomey
Architects
Shane O'Toole Architect
Derek Tynan Architects

References
Jobst Graeve (ed.), *Temple Bar
Lives! – Winning Architectural
Framework Plan*, Dublin:
Temple Bar Properties, 1991.
Patricia Quinn (ed.), *Temple
Bar – The Power of an Idea*,
Dublin: Temple Bar Properties,
1996.
Eve-Anne Cullinan (ed.),
*Development Programme for
Temple Bar Phases I and II*,
Dublin: Temple Bar Properties,
1996.

Web site
<http://www.temple-bar.ie>

organizations, state, semi-state and statutory
bodies, experts in conservation and heritage,
business groups and European funding
organizations. In parallel, the private sector
has played a vital role in the regeneration process
by matching, and more often exceeding, the
IR £40.6 million financial investment that has
been made over this last decade by Temple Bar
Properties.

Of particular value has been the role of the
Framework Plan, which established from the start
a concrete set of objectives that had a flexible
and 'non-compelling' structure. Yet the return of
Temple Bar's status as one of the key entertainment
districts in the city is not without some inevitable
conflict. Delivering the mixed-use aspirations in a
dense urban neighbourhood highlights specific

incompatibilities between certain uses. 'Living
over the shop' is now an accepted planning idea,
but conflict between an increasing residential
community on the one hand, and late-night bars
and clubs that attract large numbers of revellers
on the other, does require more proactive and
selective zoning.

The achievements of Temple Bar certainly
highlight the clear benefit of establishing
TBP as a single-purpose agency with appropriate
managerial and executive responsibilities to
deliver the objectives of the plan. Much of the
development has been achieved through a
combination of the 'bottom-up' initiatives
established at the outset by local people alongside
'top-down' facilitation from TBP that has
proactively nurtured the regeneration process.

Category	Urban retrofit and infill
Project name	King-Spadina
Location	Toronto, Canada
Size:	93 hectares/230 acres
Milestones	1996 Zoning By-law amended for the Kings
	1997 Community Improvement Plans adopted
	2001 Completion of Key Residential Projects
	2002 First Official Plan for City of Toronto adopted

Case Study 4

King-Spadina, Toronto

King-Spadina and King-Parliament, often referred to as 'The Kings', are located immediately to the west and east of Toronto's downtown core and just north of Toronto Bay. Named after King Street, which runs from west to east through the heart of both districts, the areas grew during the nineteenth century as traditional manufacturing districts. They became home to a wealth of old industrial complexes and warehouse buildings, many of which have significant architectural and historical merit.

During the 1970s, like many other inner city manufacturing districts, the areas started to decline as businesses began to migrate out of the city to cheaper, expressway-serviced, suburban sites. Planning regulations and measures put in place at the time aimed to preserve the viability of the city's Central Industrial District for manufacturing and warehouse activity. Such a defensive policy framework attempted to protect the areas from the incursion of non-industrial activities that would compound the situation by

raising land values and rents thereby, forcing further industrial migration. By the early 1990s it was conceded that such single-use districts could no longer compete as viable locations for manufacturing. There was a growing interest in reducing existing land use restrictions and opening up the area to a variety of other activities and uses.

The Kings are an easy walk from Toronto's financial district. King-Spadina, bounded by Bathurst Street on the west, Queen Street West to the north, Simcoe and John Streets to the east and Front Street West to the south, is located on the western flank of the financial district. In the financial boom years of the 1980s it was specifically identified as the next logical place to grow Toronto's financial and commercial centre, but a severe recession in the early 1990s put a halt to further speculation. By 1995 the need for a more proactive planning strategy to stimulate economic activity was acknowledged by both political leaders and planning staff. Between 1987 and 1995 the Kings districts lost approximately 50

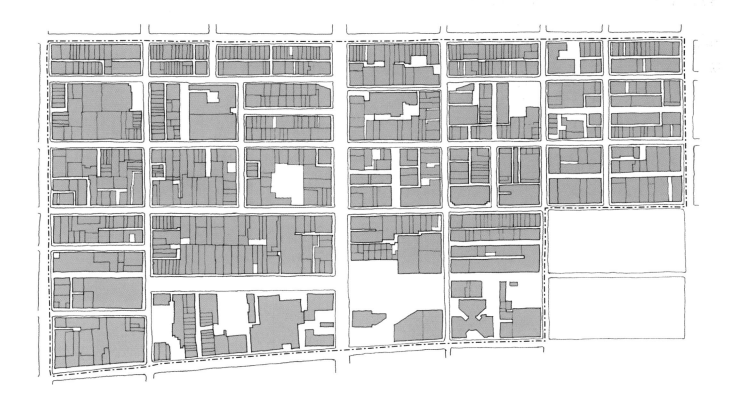

2.5 Minutes

100   200 Metres

per cent of their manufacturing businesses, representing a loss of 5,000 full-time jobs in King-Spadina. It became clear that the area needed urgent remedial action, and three broad objectives were established to drive a new approach. These were:

– the creation of a positive environment for regeneration and economic growth;
– the retention of the special physical and heritage character of the built environment; and
– assurance of a high-quality working and living environment.

In 1996 Toronto City Council approved new Part II Official Plans and Zoning By-law amendments to encourage reinvestment and regeneration in the Kings. The traditional approach of segregating land uses and regulating the size of development with density and parking regulations was replaced with a more flexible planning approach that included:

– as-of-right development permission with general height limits;
– maximum flexibility in land use policies to permit new buildings and conversions of existing buildings to almost any commercial, light industrial or residential use;
– the removal of density numbers from Part II Official Plans and Zoning By-laws;
– new built form regulations focusing on building height, massing and light, view and privacy standards; and
– the relaxation of a number of general by-law standards regulating parking and loading, with exemptions being given to existing and heritage buildings.

Since 1996 both the King-Spadina and King-Parliament districts have grown to become highly desirable residential communities and competitive locations for new economic activity, including dot-com startups that have begun to reuse much of the older building stock. King-Spadina includes Toronto's Fashion District, which has had mixed fortunes in recent years but still provides part of the economic focus to the area. Further growth has been concentrated on computer services, radio, television and film, utilities, entertainment, and accountants and management consultants.

One of the key objectives for new development within the Kings is to ensure that it reinforces the look and feel of the area. Explicit building form controls create a built form-based zoning envelope within which a wide range of land uses is permitted. This is designed to ensure that new development:

– is compatible with existing buildings, and especially heritage buildings;
– has regard for its own light, view and privacy requirements, as well as those of adjacent buildings;
– relates well to the character, scale and dimensions of adjacent public streets and open spaces; and
– achieves good sunlight and wind conditions at street level.

Built form guidelines have been developed for areas of special identity and key streets. In King-Spadina these are Clarence Square, Wellington Street, Draper Street and St Andrews Playground. Early in the process it was recognized that improvements to the public realm would also be needed to make these industrial districts more attractive to new businesses and create a high-quality living environment. A set of Community Improvement Plans was adopted in 1997 to enhance the heritage character, upgrade the quality of public spaces and improve public safety; as King-Spadina was formerly an industrial district, minimal attention had been paid to pedestrian amenity in the past.

A series of improvements to the pedestrian realm is gradually being implemented and should primarily be funded through planning approvals for new development. Within King-Spadina proposed improvements to Victoria Memorial Square, located between Wellington and Niagara Street, will provide a valuable open space for the neighbourhood.

Between April 1996 and September 2001, 84 residential development projects had proceeded

through the planning approvals process in the Kings; approximately two-thirds of these units are being built in King-Spadina. Once built, these developments, representing a total of over $396.2 million Canadian dollars of investment, will have added 6,595 new homes within walking distance of Toronto's financial core. Over 21 per cent of this investment is going to the revitalization of older buildings and two-thirds of investment is within King-Spadina. Investment has occurred across a mix of uses, with 27 per cent directed to commercial, institutional, and industrial activity, 49 per cent directed to residential in mixed-use buildings and 24 per cent focused on residential construction.

Changing the zoning laws was a bold move for the City Council to take and there were initial concerns that most, if not all, new development would be purely residential. Yet the experience in the Kings has shown that urban regeneration can be successful and meet a number of 'quality of life' objectives, including the creation of high-quality urban living environments that combine both housing and economic opportunities.

The approach has proved that through careful and sensitive guidance it can successfully be used to regenerate a mixed-use, city-centre neighbourhood. A similar technique is now being adopted within the drafting of the first Official Plan for the newly amalgamated City of Toronto.

Above:
Many of the existing buildings are now used for mixed commercial and residential activities

Below:
The successful refurbishment of historic warehouses has occurred alongside the construction of new residential buildings

Key statistics
Number of residential units
under construction: 244
Number of live/work units: 56
Increase in residents since
1996: 1,136
Percentage of population
walking to work: 44
Percentage of residents not
owning a car: 38

Coordinating organization
City of Toronto, Urban
Planning and Development
Services, City Planning
Division

**Key King-Spadina
Development Projects**
168 Simcoe Street
126 Simcoe Street
136-150 Simcoe Street
326 King Street West
250 Wellington Street West
– Tridel's Icon
254 Wellington Street West
– the Soho Development
150 Spadina Avenue
– Morgan
400 Richmond Street West
– District lofts
20 Niagara Street
– apartment and townhouse
development

References
Tracking the Kings, Toronto:
Urban Development Services
City Planning Division,
February 1998.
Regeneration in the Kings,
Toronto: Urban Development
Services City Planning
Division, November 2002.

Web site
<http://www.city.toronto.on.
ca/torontoplan>

Right:
**Looking south from
Willcocks Street with
the introduction of
Light Rail transit**

Category	Urban renewal and brownfield
Project name	The Pearl District
Location	Portland, Oregon, USA
Size	106 hectares/262 acres
Key Milestones	1988 Central City Plan provides strategic foundation
	1992 River District Vision Plan
	1994 River District Development Plan
	1998 Adoption of River District Urban Renewal Plan
	1998 River District Design Guidelines
	2001 Adoption of Pearl District Development Plan

Case Study 5

The Pearl District, Portland

The City of Portland has a long and established track record in the strategic planning of its future growth. This proactive approach to shaping change in the city centre began in the early 1970s and was led by an appraisal of key development opportunities, major road investments, improved public transit and parking, new parks and associated commercial and cultural opportunities – all of which would influence the future form of the city. Most of this work was drawn together in the 1988 Central City Plan, which has provided the main foundation for all subsequent spatial development. This overlying strategic concept plan for the city has been detailed by finer-grained urban design plans for individual districts and backed up by a series of robust action proposals with broad time horizons assigned to both public and private implementing agencies. Such an approach illustrates the clear long-term benefits that can accrue from preparing comprehensive city plans. It has established a 'top-down' set of design theories and principles and a 'bottom-up' means to

regulate the individual projects and actives, ensuring that each scheme directly contributes to the overriding vision for the city.

Portland's Pearl District is one such neighbourhood unit of the Comprehensive City Plan. Once an area of marshland to the north of the city centre and adjacent to the Willamette River, the area became the transport hub of the city. It was home to a vast network of railway goods yards and warehouses built to support rail transport in the late nineteenth and early twentieth centuries. Created by extensive landfill and planned initially as part of Couch's addition to the city, the area became a prosperous industrial and warehouse district with associated manufacturing and support services until the mid-1950s. As transport patterns moved from rail to road and then air, primary users began to relocate, leaving the district vacant and marginalized from the rest of the city. Fringe uses and activities started to occupy the district, attracted by its proximity to the city centre, casual environment and low rents. The area developed a

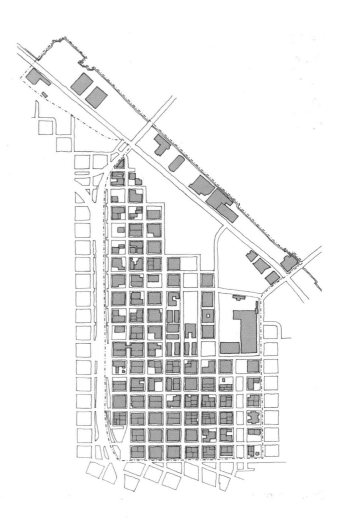

bohemian character, acting as an incubator for small start-up businesses and developing a flourishing artistic community who enjoyed the benefits of spacious warehouses that could be used in a flexible manner for both living and working. This lead the district becoming known as 'the Pearl' – a reference to the neighbourhood of rough old buildings each concealing 'pearls' in the form of artists' studios and art galleries.

Following the strategic work within the Central City Plan, the Pearl District became the focus of planning efforts to convert the under-used warehouses and derelict rail and goods yards into a new mixed-use neighbourhood. The process culminated in the adoption of the River District Urban Renewal Plan in 1998, which now provides the focus for tax increment financing for improvements within the district over the next 20 years. One of the key strategic objectives for the area has been to establish the district as a form of urban village or high-density urban neighbourhood to help relieve the increasing pressure on Portland's

Urban Growth Boundary and significantly contribute to City and State goals for housing and growth management.

The Pearl District is set within Portland's River District and the Pearl District Development Plan. Formally adopted in 2001, this now guides all future development. The process has established both a vision and extensive set of actions and priorities for the area and addresses five key issues for the district. These focus on how:

- the city can maintain the unique character of the Pearl District;
- the city can encourage a diverse mix of uses that include housing, employment and shopping;
- the district can become a model for compact urban development;
- the artistic community that makes such a significant contribution to the identity of the district can be supported; and
- existing businesses and industries that make the Pearl unique can be supported.

The plan identifies the goal of creating neighbourhood amenities as the creation of 'a successful high-density neighbourhood that will be a vibrant urban neighbourhood with a range of quality amenities that support people who live and work in the neighbourhood, as well as those people who come to enjoy its services and amenities'. Included within a series of objectives to meet this goal, the plan seeks to attract nursery facilities to support residents and employees and create additional community space for local residents. Both are identified as high priority actions that are assigned to the Portland Development Commission and the City's Parks and Recreation Department for implementation.

Fundamental to the success of the regeneration initiative has been the establishment of the Pearl District Business Association and the Pearl District Neighbourhood Association (PDNA). Working through a set of three focused committees, the PDNA addresses planning, transport and design review, and liveability and is formally governed by a set of by-laws establishing that it:

–   provides a facility for education, research and an exchange of information for citizens within the general area of the Pearl District so they may relate to their total environment;
–   broadens channels of communication between the residents and businesses within the Pearl District and City officials in matters affecting neighbourhood liveability; and
–   assists in furthering activities and developments that will raise the level of the residential, commercial and industrial activity consistent with the interests of the Portland citizenry and sound economic practices.

Above:
The Pearl District has incorporated new loft and appartment buildings within the existing fabric of warehouses

Below:
The development plan integrates private space with good quality public open space

The process of change, familiar so many urban districts, has always been a hallmark of the Pearl. The challenge has been to be able to respond to the new forces of change in a proactive and constructive manner, so as to ensure that the essential components of its unique character are protected and enhanced alongside future opportunities for development. 'The essence of the Pearl as a community is that this is a neighbourhood where people choose to come because of its unique mix of activities and its grit and contrasts,' suggests the Development Plan, which goes on to say that it should be 'an urban place where daily life can be seen as much on the streets as in the buildings'.

The Development Plan is built around seven key urban components: the built environment; neighbourhood amenities; housing; arts and culture; economic opportunities; edges and gateways; and transportation and parking. It sets out an overriding goal for each component and provides a set of objectives that are prioritized within a comprehensive action plan identifying key organizations that are responsible for its delivery.

Significant time and money has been invested in the regeneration of the Pearl District. Although much of this has been focused on the built environment, the social structure and needs of the neighbourhood have not been ignored and are now proactively supported by the work of the PDNA. In the words of the development plan, 'The success of the neighbourhood is not only the number of units built and people who live there, but the way in which people experience a healthy, engaging and intriguing community.'

Left, top:
Looking towards the Willamette River with the Brewery Blocks redevelopment in the foreground

Above:
Play space has been incorporated within a number of parks, including Jamison Square

Development statistics (2001)
20–30 year projections
Residential population 12,500 (currently 1,300)
Local jobs 21,000 (currently 9,000)
Housing units: 8,080
Commercial space: 4,505,000 sq ft
Retail Space: 1,225,000 sq ft

Project stakeholders
Portland Development Commission
Portland Bureau of Planning
Portland Bureau of Traffic Management
Portland Bureau of Parks and Recreation
Portland Institute for Contemporary Arts
Pearl District Neighbourhood Association
Housing Authority of Portland
Northwest District Association
US Post Office

Architects, developers and consultants
Ankrom Moisan Associated Architects
Carroll Investments
David Evans & Associates
Dehen Company
GBD Architects
Gerding/Edlen Development Company
Hanna Anderson
Hobson Ferrarini & Associates
Hoyt Street Properties
HGW Inc.
Robert Leeb Architects
Roberts Merryman, Barnes Architects Inc.
SERA Architects
Stastny Brun Architects Inc.
Thompson Vaivoda & Associates
Wieden & Kennedy
WPH Architecture

References
City of Portland Central City Plan, Portland Development Commission (PDC), 1988.
Pearl District Development Plan, PDC, 2001.
Pearl District Development Plan, Appendix, PDC, 2001.

Web sites
<http://www.neighborhoodlink.com/portland/pdna>
<http://www.thepearl.citysearch.com/1.html?>
<http://www.portlanddev.org/pdf/pubs/dev/dev_river_map.pdf>
<http://www.portlanddev.org/pdf/pubs/dev/pearl_district_devel_plan.pdf>
<http://www.portlanddev.org/pdf/pubs/dev/pearl_district_devel_plan_appendix.pdf>

Category	Urban renewal and brownfield
Project name	Crown Street
Location	Glasgow, UK
Size	16 hectares/40 acres
Key Milestones	1960s Hutchesontown in the Gorbals redeveloped
	1990 Crown Street Regeneration project established
	1990 CZWG commissioned to prepare a masterplan
	1995 First private and rented homes complete
	1996 Shopping centre and convenience store opened
	1998 New Gorbals Park completed
	2000 Crown Street Management Trust established
	2003 Projected completion of the initial proposals

Case Study 6

Crown Street, Glasgow

Crown Street richly illustrates the cyclical fortunes that many of Britain's inner city districts have experienced over the last century. Originally a single street village that grew up around the River Clyde's most westerly crossing point, the district and community has always played a prominent and distinctive role in the life of Glasgow. Known from early in its life as the Gorbals, the area grew rapidly at the beginning of the twentieth century and by the 1930s it was supporting a population of over 90,000 packed into its tight network of streets and tenement blocks. At this time the area was the epitome of a diverse and mixed community, with over 1,000 shops and 130 pubs – a home for a succession of Highland, Irish and Jewish immigrants.

Inevitably such overcrowding, compounded by poor sanitation and building decay, led to massive social problems and a proliferation of gang violence, graphically detailed by Alexander McArthur in his book, *No Mean City* (1935). The Gorbals soon become synonymous with the most severe levels of poverty and became recognized as one of the worst housing areas in Europe.

With the advent of Comprehensive Development Area strategies in the 1950s Glasgow identified 29 areas across the city for wholesale redevelopment. Hutchesontown, which included part of the Gorbals, was to be the first, and a new masterplan for the area was formally approved in 1957. Having commissioned the architectural practices of Sir Robert Matthew and Sir Basil Spence, the City embarked on a massive social experiment for the area: only 10,000 of the existing 26,000 residents were to be resettled in a mix of mid-rise and high-rise blocks that reflected the Corbusian dream of a city of towers.

Before redevelopment the Gorbals had at least 444 shops and 48 public houses. Subsequently the area had just 57 shops and 9 pubs. Labelled as 'filing cabinets for people' and latterly referred to as the 'dampies', the Hutchesontown E blocks lasted only 14 years before they were completely vacated due to excessive condensation and dampness. In 1987, following significant

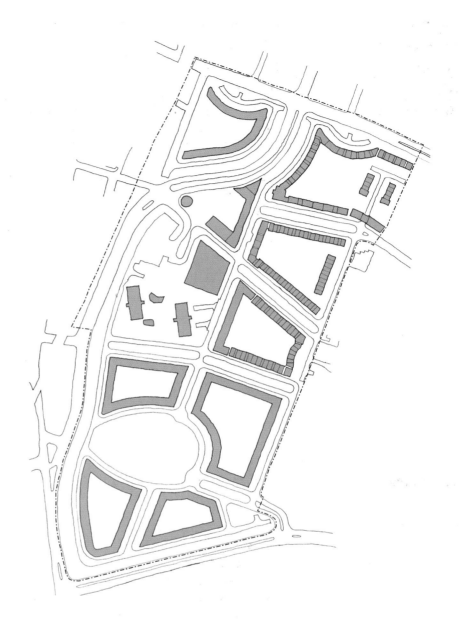

vandalism and considerable local campaigning, the towers were finally demolished and 13 hectares in the heart of the Gorbals became vacant.

Given the failure of the post-war Comprehensive Development Area strategies, Glasgow's lead public agencies sought a more sensitive and intuitive approach to housing-led regeneration for the area. In 1990 the Crown Street Regeneration Project (CSRP) was established. In partnership with Scottish Enterprise Glasgow, Communities Scotland, Glasgow City Council and members of the local community, the CSRP set out to improve the social, economic and environmental quality of the Gorbals through a process of careful urban renewal. At the outset four

key objectives were established. These were to:

–   make the Gorbals a place in which people want to live;
–   develop a new and positive image for the Gorbals as a popular, well-balanced urban community;
–   assist in the regeneration of the local Gorbals economy; and
–   physically, socially and economically integrate the new development with the existing community.

These objectives provided the basis for a national urban design competition for the area. This was won by CZWG Architects with a proposal that

Above (clockwise from top):
The dilapidated and derelict character of the Gorbals around 1965

The high demand for family housing is met with ground- and first-floor family maisonettes within each tenement block

A section of the competition-winning masterplan prepared by CZWG in 1990

The reintroduction of tenements provides both a street frontage and gardens to the rear

Opposite:
Crown Street forms the backbone to the masterplan, whilst adjacent streets connect to the surrounding urban fabic

sought a return to many of the innate qualities of Glasgow's original urban fabric. Piers Gough suggested a 'stitching of the area back together again' to create a more liveable city built around the local grid, the block, the street and the tenement. Importantly, the role of the winning masterplan was to act as a starting point for discussions with all the local stakeholders rather than providing a fixed blueprint for the area.

The strategy proposed an urban village concept that would again respect the street as the fundamental urban space of Glasgow and re-establish a varied mix of new development to help revive the Gorbals community. Crown Street had always been the central north-south axis through the Gorbals and the masterplan restored this as the main structural component of the scheme. A loose grid of secondary streets, articulated with an occasional circus or crescent, connected through to the surrounding street pattern to ensure that adjacent communities were fully integrated.

Within the framework a block structure allowed each dwelling to face both the street and private courtyards, offering a clear hierarchy of open space. Private courtyards within each block

allow children to play safely, and most of the ground floor occupants enjoy the benefits of private gardens. The new street pattern reverses the traditional hierarchy of street widths, with residential streets established as wide, leafy boulevards that are quiet, pedestrian-friendly and able to accommodate on-street parking.

The tenement has been re-established as the City's preferred form of housing in a number of recent regeneration initiatives, although concerns have been raised as to their suitability for family housing. Crown Street has adapted the model to provide three- and four-bedroom family homes on the first two floors, with direct access to both the street and courtyard. The third and fourth floors are then used for two- and three-bedroom flats that can be accessed by a separate common entrance.

One of the real strengths of the CZWG masterplan has that it can be broken down into manageable development parcels. These have been released incrementally in line with market demand and the regeneration programme. Urban design briefs, written for developer/architect competitions, have been prepared to guide the development of each parcel, with land values being

Key statistics (at 2000)
Total of privately owned
homes: 682
Total of socially rented
homes: 168
Total area of retail floor
space: 2,400 sq m
Total of office accommodation:
5,000 sq m
Total business space in railway
arches: 2,000 sq m
Total of student apartments: 204
Number of hotel rooms: 114
Number of shops: 12

**Project Partners and
organizations**
Communities Scotland
(formerly Scottish Homes)
Crown Street Management
Trust
Hutchesontown Community
Council
Laurieston Community Council
New Gorbals Housing
Association
Scottish Enterprise Glasgow
(formerly Glasgow
Development Agency)
Stewart Milne Homes
Residents and Tenants
Association
Tay Homes Residents and
Tenants Association
Crown Street Tenants and
Residents Association

Consultants
Turner & Townsend –
project managers
CZWG – masterplanners
URS Corporation – civil
engineers
Douglas Baillie – transport
DEP landscape initiatives –
landscape architect
Maclay Murray & Spens –
solicitors

References
Mike Galloway, 'Crown Street
Regeneration, Glasgow',
Urban Design Quarterly, no. 63,
July 1997.
Tom Macartney, 'No Mean City
– No Mean Achievement',
Urban Design Quarterly, no. 72,
October 1999.

Web sites
<http://www.crownstreet.org>
<http://www.gorbalslive.org.uk>

fixed for each stage and every proposal being
evaluated on design quality, standards of building
and the comparative need for grant funding. To
ensure that the regeneration strategy delivers a
balanced community, 25 per cent of the new
homes are for social housing; these are rented
through the New Gorbals Housing Association.

Although the regeneration of Crown Street has
been led by residential development, the initial
objectives called for the creation of a new
community that integrated a mix of uses that could
be incorporated throughout the entire scheme. The
preliminary strategy promoted the concept of the
urban village. This has been met by the provision
of a number of ancillary uses and activities that
now serve the local and wider communities and
includes re-establishing the traditional shopping
street, a neighbourhood supermarket and over 10

shops, a new park, a new budget hotel and a
business centre. In addition, a refurbished listed
mill building now supports startup businesses and
includes flexible small office accommodation.
Over 200 student residences for the Glasgow
Nautical College have been built and several new
workshop spaces have been incorporated within
existing railway arches.

Crown Street can be credited with a number
of remarkable achievements over the last decade.
The local community has regained its faith in the
area and investors have demonstrated real
confidence in the Gorbals as a place to both live
and work. The impact of this success is now being
felt in adjacent areas, with new regeneration
initiatives now stretching out to Queen Elizabeth
Square, Oatlands and Laurieston.

Category	Urban renewal and brownfield
Project Name	Bo01 Housing Expo
Location	Malmö, Sweden
Size	30 hectares/74 acres
Key Milestones	1995 Sweden decides to hold European Housing Expo
	1998 Malmö's comprehensive plan identifies Bo01 site
	1999 Masterplanning begins
	1999 Designs for public spaces begins
	2001 Bo01 Exhibition is held

Case Study 7

Bo01 Housing Expo, Malmö

Bo01: The City of Tomorrow was the title of Sweden's first International Housing Exhibition, held in Malmö between 17 May and 16 September 2001. Initiated by the Swedish government and supported by the housing ministers of the European Union, the exhibition, translated as *Living 01*, sought to explore the way we live today and ways we may choose to live sustainably in the future. Specifically, it chose to present its version of 'an ecologically sustainable information society in an era of well-being'. While quantifiable requirements for sustainability are important, the Expo also attempted to address the emotional and social needs in development suggesting that 'beauty and humanism are the true foundation of a sustainable society'. Economically, the benefit of Bo01 was to last far beyond that of a short-term event, for it was one of a series of strategic initiatives, including the construction of the Øresund Bridge and the opening of the Malmö University, that were designed to transform the region's economy.

Set within these ambitious ideals there are both relevance and clear parallels to the philosophy of urban villages. The project attempts to define a sustainable and ecologically viable strategy to convert a vacant brownfield site into a new mixed-use urban neighbourhood. Located at Västra Hamnen, part of Malmö's western docks, the Bo01 site was previously used for heavy industry and landfill. From this industrial wasteland adjacent to the centre of Malmö a new, tightly-knit urban district has emerged that offers new opportunities for living, working and study. The masterplan for the new neighbourhood includes homes, workplaces, shops, restaurants, cafés, day-care centres, schools and a library. In the words of the Expo, these combine to provide 'imaginative visions of future living, where high demands on aesthetics, ecology and high technology' are united.

The Expo follows a long tradition of European housing exhibitions that includes those held in Paris in 1925 and Stockholm in 1930. Specifically,

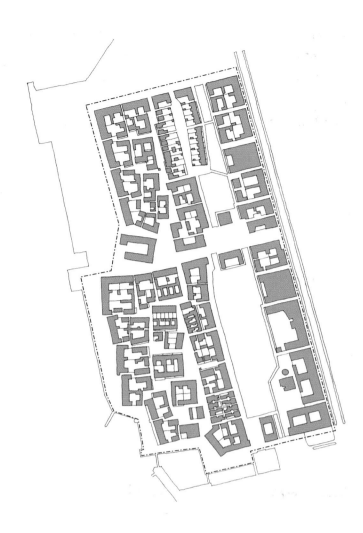

2.5 Minutes

100   200 Metres

Bo01 follows principles established by Berlin's 1979 IBA (International Building Exhibition) with the urban design proposals adopting qualities that are typical of a northern European city – low, tight, intimate, dense and efficient in the use of land. The exhibition was split into two distinct halves: a permanent housing area called the Boplatsen (the living area), and VISION – a series of five temporary exhibitions focused on the home that explored subjects that could not be fully realized in the permanent development.

The built component of Bo01 makes up the first stage of Västra Hamnen´s conversion into a completely new district and is within walking distance of both the city centre of Malmö and the beach at Ribersborg. The aim has been to create an attractive area that combines education, research, recreational activities, housing, and cultural opportunities. In essence, the Expo has produced the precursor to a truly mixed-use and dense urban neighbourhood. A strong environmental framework for the materplan was established at

the outset, to ensure that green spaces and water are visible from all dwelling units. A network of parks seeks to enhance local biodiversity and includes the Strandparken (Beach park) to the west of the development, the Kanalparken (Canal park) through the heart of the neighbourhood and the Kajpromenaden (Quay Side promenade), which borders the sea and can be used by both pedestrians and cyclists.

An important part of the strategy is to ensure that there is a wide mix of apartments and houses that support a broad community, including the elderly and students. In the centre of the development two- to four-storey houses have been built; that rises to four- and five-storeys for the multi-family dwellings that provide a windbreak along the promenade facing the Öresund, the large expanse of water between Copenhagen and Malmö. In line with previous international exhibitions, Bo01 provided the opportunity to showcase new forms of building designed by a number of prominent international architects

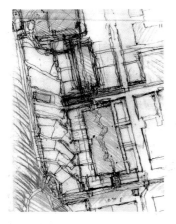

Above (clockwise from top):
An initial open space concept plan established the Canal Park at the heart of the project

The Bo01 expo was held on the Västra Hamnen, a former industrial and dock site overlooking the Öresund

Cafés, restaurants and other mixed uses enliven the waterfront promenade

Opposite:
An eclectic mix of architecture was tempered with strong references to traditional Scandinavian detailing

including Ralph Erskin, masterplanner of the Greenwich Millennium Village, and Moore Ruble Yudell, who have worked on Kirchsteigfeld in Potsdam, Germany. The highest architectural award was given to Kjellander and Sjöberg's flexible and energy-efficient housing, which offers an alternative approach to traditional, mixed-tenure housing. Because each unit has a significant amount of additional living space, it can be rented out if not needed or can provide the opportunity to be used as loft-living studios for live/work units.

A key goal for the Expo was to create a sustainable and ecologically robust urban community through the exploration of creative, and at times innovative, techniques for development and long-term management, including resource-efficient construction techniques, renewable energy, water management, waste treatment, information technology and alternative forms of transport.

The development relies on 100 per cent renewable energy that is provided entirely from locally-produced electricity. A large proportion of the heating needs are met from seawater and groundwater, complemented by wind power and

solar energy. Bo01 makes extensive use of photovoltaic technology and claims to be Sweden's largest urban solar project. Energy demand and supply is balanced through its connection with Malmö's renewable energy system, which ensures that any surplus production from Bo01 is exported to the wider network. Rubbish and waste is recycled at the point of production and collection whilst all organic material is used to produce biogas that generates additional energy. Most waste water is treated on site, with much of the reclaimed water being used for environmental and horticultural uses.

The area is planned to keep car dependency to a minimum, with parts of the development designated as car-free zones. Provision of a comprehensive cycle network that links with adjacent areas is the most important element in the area's transport strategy, with cyclists being given priority over vehicles. Public transport has been integrated within the development from the beginning to establish regular patterns of use with vehicles that should primarily be powered by environmentally-friendly fuels. In addition, there is a car pool that has a number of electric and gas-powered vehicles, further limiting the need for private car ownership.

At the outset of construction the integration of high-specification networks for information technology was incorporated into the design to help build what the project defines as an information society. Broadband and wireless networks serve all the dwellings and offices, along with facilities for voice activation and digital control and communication for individual premises. The impact of this new technology goes beyond the relatively simple control and management of the buildings and is also used to provide smart distribution and delivery systems for electronic shopping.

The ambitious programme of elements and activities put significant financial strain on the project as it neared the opening of the Expo. Although the economic viability of the scheme has been in question, the exhibition has provided a unique opportunity to test and publicly present a number of significant environmental and technological innovations for the design of new urban neighbourhoods.

Development statistics (2001)

Ratio of housing to offices, shops and services: 1.0:0.5
Total number of new homes: 800
Area zoned for commercial uses: 30–50,000 sq m
Area for the VISION exhibition: 180,000 sq m
Development/open space ratio: 0.5
Net development ratio: 0.7 raised to 1.0
Target reduced energy consumption for housing; 40 per cent

Project stakeholders

Svensk Bostadsmässa – Controlling Company
Svenska BoProjekt AB – Exhibition Organizer
The Swedish Government
The City of Malmö
Sydkraft
Telia
HSB
SBAB
The European Commission

Architects/Consultants include

Adrian Geuze, Netherlands
Bertil Öhrström, Sweden
Dalgaard and Madsen, Denmark
Gert Wingård, Sweden
Kai Wartiainen, Sweden
Karmebäck and Krüger, Germany.
Mario Campi, Switzerland
Martha Schwartz, USA
MooreRuble Yudell, USA
Ralph Erskine, Sweden
Stig Andersson, Copenhagen

References

Bo01 City of Tomorrow (European Housing Expo brochure), Malmö, Sweden, 2001.
Bo01-Staden: Byggnaderna, Planen, Processen, Hållbarheten, Svensk Byggtjänst
'Bo01: the city of tomorrow in Malmö', *Topos*, vol 30, March 2000.

Category	Urban renewal and brownfield
Project name	Llandarcy
Location	Neath, Wales, UK
Size	Approximately 565 hectares/1,400 acres
Key milestones	1997 Closure of BP Oil Refinery
	2000 Start of initial framework planning
	2001 Completion of site clearance
	2002 Preliminary phase received outline planning consent
	2003 Commencement of works on site
	2022 Anticipated completion of the project

Case Study 8

Llandarcy, South Wales

The conversion of Llandarcy's disused oil refinery site at Neath in South Wales into a new sustainable community has been identified as one of the most challenging and ambitious redevelopment projects ever undertaken in the UK. Named after William Knox D'Arcy and given the traditional welsh prefix 'Llan' meaning church or parish, the site became the UK's first crude oil refinery and storage facility in the 1920s. By the late 1970s a sharp decline in demand for oil-based goods and the impact from the global competition led BP to finally close the works in November 1997 and begin the process of identifying a new use for the site.

The project represents the first urban village development to be undertaken in Wales and is potentially the largest of its type anywhere in Britain. It directly follows guidance established by the Urban Task Force that encourages the creation of high quality, mixed-use neighbourhoods in areas that are particularly in need of regeneration. In addition it reflects the Government's commitment to reusing brownfield land in preference to a continued release of greenfield sites and also follows strategic planning objectives for South Wales. The distinctive topography of the South Wales valleys has significantly limited the availability of development land over the years and in parts of Deeside, Cardiff and Newport there is a real shortage of appropriate greenfield land. This has led to efforts by local authorities to maximize brownfield opportunities; in the case of Llandarcy, this has been embodied in Neath Port Talbot Council's Unitary Development Plan, Deposit Draft 2002.

Before the regeneration project could start, approximately 565 hectares of land has had to be decommissioned and cleared. Without BP's conscientious approach to the remediation of the site and its future use, the viability of the project might well have been in question. At the outset significant social and environmental issues have had to be addressed, including the impact of the project on the adjacent Llandarcy village, which was developed in the 1920s for BP employees. In addition, the site adjoins a number of major

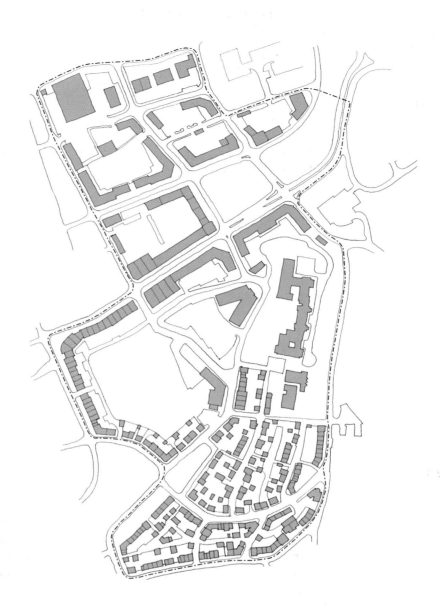

2.5 Minutes

100   200 Metres

Above:
**Figure-ground illustrates phase
one of the master plan**

environmentally sensitive areas including the Crymlyn Bog, which, under the European Directive, is a candidate for Special Area Conservation. The Crymlyn Burrows, an area of tidal marsh and sand dunes, have been designated as both a RAMSAR wetland of international importance and a Site of Special Scientific Interest. Provisional technical and feasibility appraisal has included a detailed assessment of the remediation works, traffic impact statements, full landscape and ecological assessments, historical analysis and a broad-based commercial market appraisal.

The project is lead by a partnership that includes the Welsh Development Agency, BP, Neath Port Talbot Council and The Prince's Foundation.

Initially the intention has been to draw in local stakeholders and members of the community, through the UDP consultation process. Maintaining extensive participation and establishing local ownership of the project is regarded as critical to the success of the scheme over the longer term. Early dialogue with the surrounding community has helped set a number of clear aspirations that include the provision for better homes, employment opportunities, local shopping and leisure facilities. The overriding aim is to respond to these desires by creating an integrated community that will be able to provide homes and a range of employment activities, a school, and shops, along with other local amenities and social facilities.

Top:
Initial architectural elevations reflect the use of local construction materials and vernacular detailing

Middle:
Significant industrial infrastructure has had to be removed from the site as part of the remediation process

Below:
An initial perspective for the first neighbourhood centre establishes a hierarchy for building form and public space

Initial scoping work has indicated that around 120–160 hectares of land could be used for new development as part of efforts to reclaim the site and regenerate the wider area. A Strategic Development Framework has been prepared to guide the comprehensive redevelopment of the site and integrate new facilities with the existing residential, manufacturing, leisure and environmental resources that the site currently offers. At the heart of the proposals will be a new village centre that should be well served by public transport to reduce the need for private car travel. In addition, several secondary centres have been proposed, which will focus localized activity around retail and community facilities. An arrangement of streets and squares will contain a dense urban form rising to three storeys and capable of accommodating over 3,000 residential units and 65,000 sq m of additional uses in addition to new primary schools. In line with key principles of sustainability, an integrated public transport network will include regular bus and cycle routes that will connect with the adjacent districts of Swansea and Neath.

With reference to established New Urbanist techniques, a preliminary town code has been prepared for Llandarcy to guide the design development in the coming years. Following the structure of the urban transect, the code establishes building and street design principles from the centre to the edge of the entire development. Within this framework, street patterns and the architectural form and detail of buildings can be established early in the design process. This should ensure that a coherent and sequential structure for Llandarcy is established at the outset, in advance of future stages of detailed design and development.

The development, which is spread over six phases, should attract up to £500 million of private investment and have the potential to create more than 3,000 permanent jobs over a 20-year period. The project is to have a major economic impact on the region and the site has already benefited from being selected as one of ten in the UK to be assessed for European Objective 1 Funding. Existing development on the site includes the BP D'arcy Business Park, which is already home to more than 80 small and medium-sized companies, providing employment for over 1,000 people. Further development will integrate with the existing Business Park, and will include the construction of a new headquarters for the Environment Agency and an initial 5-hectare phase of mixed-use development.

**Key provisional statistics
(as of 2001)**

Total area of brownfield land developed: 538 hectares

Total area of greenfield land developed: 15 hectares

Total area of net developable plots: 117 hectares

Area required for infrastructure: 16.5 hectares

Total area for parkland: 67 hectares

Area designated for ecological protection: 66 hectares

Total number of residential units: 3,000+

Total area for employment and industry: 49,000 sq m

Total area for retail activities: 65,000 sq m

Area reserved for school and community buildings: 6,000 sq m

Total number of jobs created direct employment opportunities: 3,200

Anticipated temporary construction person years: 4,300

Project partners
BP
The Welsh Development Agency
The Prince's Foundation
Neath Port Talbot County Borough Council

Consultants
Wyn Thomas Gordon Lewis
Alan Baxter & Associates
Percy Thomas Partnership
DTZ/Pieda
Mott MacDonald
Ove Arup & Partners
TACP
URS Dames & Moore

Web sites
<http://www.bpdarcy.com>

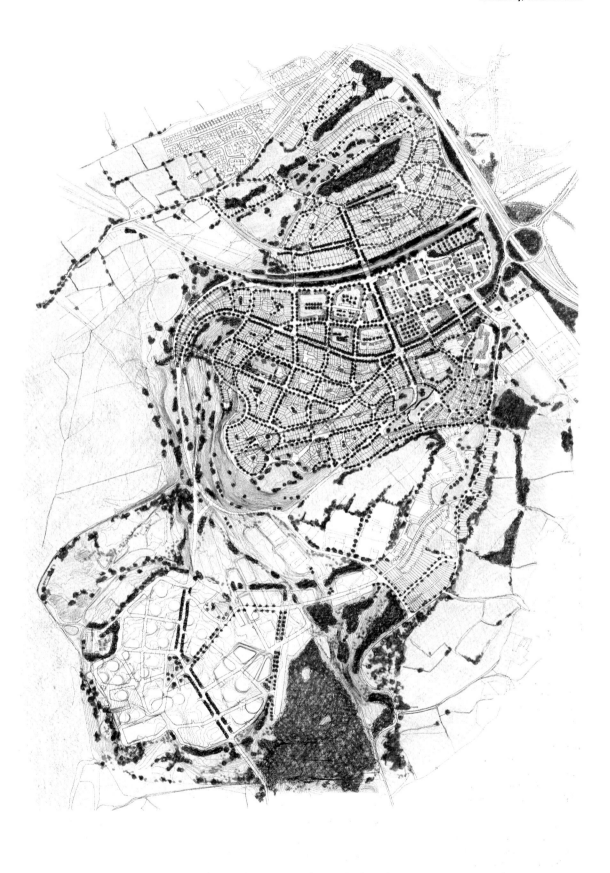

Right:
The initial illustrative framework spreads the development of Llandarcy over six phases

Category	Urban extension and greenfield
Project name	Upton
Location	Northampton, UK
Size	44 hectares/110 acres
Key milestones	1997 Outline planning application submitted
	1999 Preliminary EbD workshop
	2000 Outline planning consent granted
	2001 Full EbD workshop held
	2002 Urban Framework Plan prepared
	2003 Anticipated start of infrastructure works on site
	2015 Projected completion

Case Study 9

Upton, Northampton

The Structure Plan for the County of Northamptonshire, in line with Regional Planning Guidance for the east Midlands (RPG8), calls for at least 15,000 additional dwellings by 2016. This provides a clear illustration of the pressure for new homes that is being felt throughout the county. Although many of these homes can be built on existing brownfield sites, some greenfield land in Northamptonshire will have to be developed to meet this target.

The 44-hectare site of Upton, southwest of Northampton, is one such greenfield location. Of particular interest in this project is the collaborative and inclusive planning and consultation process that has been undertaken in advance of more detailed development proposals. Originally under agricultural production, the site was acquired by Northampton Development Corporation and passed to the Commission for New Towns in 1985. Allocated for residential development in the Local Plan for Northampton, the site is now within the ownership of English

Partnerships, a central government agency established to regenerate and develop vacant, derelict and contaminated land, as well as land that has been reserved for urban extensions.

In 1999 a partnership was formed between English Partnerships, The Prince's Foundation, The Council for the Protection of Rural England and The Department of Transport, Local Government and the Regions to launch a major national initiative promoting sustainable urban extensions. This represented a shift in thinking away from existing models of suburban expansion, typified by the monocultural and disconnected housing estates that had been built over the previous 30 years. This new approach seeks to create more sustainable and liveable extensions of existing urban areas in line with many of the early principles established by the urban village movement. Through the careful integration of uses and with intelligent planning and design, it is believed, the opportunities for social and economic interaction can be maximized and a stronger sense

of community can be achieved.

An essential part of this process is to ensure that members of the local community and stakeholders who have a common interest in the area are able to actively participate in the planning of these new neighbourhoods. To facilitate this approach a collaborative planning technique called Enquiry by Design (EbD) was pioneered in the UK by English Partnerships and The Prince's Foundation. Late in 1999 the first EbD exercise was held for the site at Upton to demonstrate that an intensive design workshop involving key stakeholders could successfully contribute to the masterplanning of a large area and help to define an agreed and locally acceptable solution for development.

Outline planning consent, establishing the principle of development, was granted in 2000 and from this basis a further EbD workshop was undertaken in late 2001 to prepare a more detailed set of proposals. The workshop was run through an intensive series of meetings spread over four days, which brought together key stakeholders and members of local communities to thoroughly examine specific constraints, opportunities and aspirations for the project. Landowners, the local authority, developers, existing residents, statutory agencies and interest groups all worked together to achieve a consensus for the pattern of future development and take forward the proposals jointly for this new community.

Through this process an Urban Framework Plan was prepared that reflects the principles required to build a sustainable urban extension.

Above:
Throughout the Enquiry by Design workshop, regular presentations were held to discuss the elements of the emerging masterplan

Particular attention is focused on:

– building height and density;
– networks for transport and movement;
– landscape and public realm infrastructure;
– sustainable urban drainage systems; and
– the potential phasing of the development.

The adopted plan includes a mix of uses that increase opportunities for living and working in close proximity to each other and significantly reduces the reliance on the private car. It builds on the requirements set out in the outline planning consent given in 2000, which allowed for the development of up to 1,020 new homes, a school, community facilities and shops. As part of the original legal agreement, the project had to make adequate provision for public transport, respect the character of the adjacent country park and adopt appropriate flood prevention measures.

The proposals establish a new local centre with medium-density commercial development along the northern boundary with the existing arterial road. Space has been given for flexible commercial and live/work units along a new main street. These frontages are designed to change

Right (above):
The existing greenfield site, reserved for a town extension, lies on the edge of Northampton's south west district

Right (below):
Existing roads and paths are to be connected to, and integrated within, the movement framework

from residential to retail and commercial uses if required as Upton grows and the demand from local services increases.

The plan allows for a range of housing types and densities that encourages a diverse population and a range of tenures. Densities at 35 units per hectare are achieved by two- to four-storey buildings, with the tallest concentrated along the main street and arterial roads. Affordable housing units are incorporated throughout the scheme and are planned to be indistinguishable from private market housing. A combination of shops, cafés, restaurants, commercial facilities and community services are located around the main street to maximize the commercial benefits of the proposed circulation network. A new school and playing fields provide a focus within the central square to enhance the social activity at the centre of the neighbourhood and maximize the catchment for those able to walk to school.

Particular attention has been given to the public realm. Different kinds of spaces, including formal squares, informal greens, green footpaths and urban boulevards, are combined to create many opportunities for outdoor recreation and leisure that directly connect with the adjacent country park. Opportunities for cycling and horse riding will link in with surrounding pathways to provide an integrated green network that is set apart from vehicles. Transport and circulation patterns will be biased towards the pedestrian, and a dedicated bus link to the centre of Northampton will be provided within the new development. Early concerns about the potential for the site to flood are addressed by a sustainable urban drainage system, located within the network of green corridors, that is connected to a series of retention and detention ponds located above local flood lines.

Following technical appraisal of the Framework Plan and review by the participants of the EbD workshop, the proposals need to be submitted for formal approval. To maintain control over the quality of future development a set of design codes and development briefs will be prepared before the first parcels are offered to the market for development, detailed planning approval and implementation.

Above:
The preliminary masterplan was prepared in response to the key issues and opportunities raised during the Enquiry by Design process

Outline planning statistics (as of 2001)

Number of homes having outline planning consent: 1,020
Proportion for affordable homes: 22 per cent (224 in total)
Residential units to be built per annum: 100–150
Land allocated for local centre: 1.5 hectares
Land allocated for retail uses: 700 sq m
Land reserved for a new school: 1.15 hectares
Land reserved for playing pitches: 1.8 hectares
Land reserved for children's play facilities: 1,700 square metres

Project partners

English Partnerships
Northampton Borough Council
The Prince's Foundation

Local stakeholders

Northamptonshire County Council
County, District and Parish Council
The Environment Agency
Health Authority and Local Health Trust
Local Chamber of Commerce
Local Residents Groups
Wildlife Trust

Consultants

EDAW – town planning and urban design
Alan Baxter and Associates – transport and engineering
Lambert Smith Hampton – property market assessment
Paul Murrain – urban design consultancy

Category	Urban extension and greenfield
Project name	Poundbury
Location	Dorset, UK
Size	160 hectares/400 acres
Key milestones	1987 Duchy land selected for town expansion
	1988 Preparation of initial masterplan
	1989 Poundbury Planning Weekend
	1993 Start of Phase One on site
	1995 Poundbury primary school opened
	2001 Start of Phase Two
	2020 Projected completion

Case Study 10

Poundbury, Dorset

In the late 1980s Dorchester was facing growing pressure to expand in response to a chronic shortage of affordable housing and increasing pressure from businesses that wanted to move to the area. Following agreement with the Duchy of Cornwall, which owned of much of the surrounding land, the District Council proposed a westward expansion across adjacent agricultural land towards the boundary with the newly-built bypass.

Part of the agreement with the Duchy to release land for the development ensured that the Duke of Cornwall, HRH The Prince of Wales, was directly involved in to project from the outset. This came at an opportune time for the Prince as he was establishing a personal view of architecture in his book and exhibition, *A Vision of Britain*. The book re-examined many of the prevailing principles of urban planning, and this project in Dorchester was seen as a unique chance to create an alternative model for urban development. It was a real opportunity to collaborate with the local council to create a well-crafted and exemplary urban extension to the ancient market town of Dorchester.

Poundbury takes its name form an adjacent iron-age hill fort and one of the original farms upon which the new development is being built. Dorchester has grown from its historic core to some 300 hectares but has remained very much a single-centre town. At the outset there was significant public concern about the 160-hectare size of the development and the impact this would have on the existing character of the town. The initial strategy proposed that Dorchester should grow to have a number of centres, or quarters, and the new development should be seen as an organic extension to the existing urban fabric. It was important that these new districts should reflect a clear association with the vernacular of Dorset that goes beyond simple architectural detail to respected local characteristics of scale, hierarchy, harmony and enclosure. Specifically, it was the expressed desire of the Prince that when complete

1.25 Minutes

100 Metres

Above:
Figure-ground illustrates phase
one of the master plan

and viewed from Maiden Castle, a local landmark, Poundbury would be seen as an integral part of Dorchester and appear as if it had existed for many years.

With this strategy in mind, Leon Krier prepared the original masterplan for Poundbury in 1988. Four distinctive urban quarters of appropriate scale were proposed, each with around 500–800 households. Essentially, each district was to embody the key urban village principles of mixed use, mixed tenure, and localized provision of commercial premises and shops that placed everyday needs within easy walking distance. The irregular and non-standard street pattern was established to visually articulate each quarter

around key buildings and create a variety of attractive and individual public spaces. The urban form was specifically designed to limit the impact and speed of vehicles and place parking and servicing facilities within rear courtyards. Road junctions were set with tight radii that limited sightlines, thereby forcing drivers to slow right down to negotiate narrow turnings.

To ensure that the general public and key local stakeholders were able to participate in the masterplanning process, a Community Planning Weekend was held in June 1989 to present initial design objectives. Although much opinion was positive, real concerns were voiced about the size of the proposal, the perceived incompatibility of

Above:
Careful attention to architectural craft and detail is achieved throughout the development

mixing housing and industry and the expectation that the majority of housing would be beyond the means of first-time buyers and local residents. There was a specific desire to be kept informed of the evolving proposals and ensure that there continued to be opportunities for public debate. With this in mind, a temporary planning centre was opened in a vacant shop in the centre of Dorchester, and this provided an opportunity for direct consultation on the project.

From the outset the project has been seen as a long-term exercise spanning some 20–25 years of incremental development. Following public concern and a more detailed appraisal of the property market, the initial proposals planned for first phase on the Middle Farm site were scaled down from 600 houses to just 250. The first quarter was designed to connect directly with the existing neighbourhood of Victoria Park and was to be focused around a central public square. A network of urban blocks set around this central space was planned, with continuous frontages giving access to planted mews, courtyards,

workshops, additional office buildings and the occasional public house. Work started on site in 1993 and much of this initial phase of development is now complete. All the commercial premises are now occupied and a number of public facilities have been opened, including a new doctor's surgery and a central public hall, the Brownsword Hall, which is home to a monthly farmer's market.

Architectural development remains tightly controlled at both the design and management stages. The initial Poundbury Building Code was prepared by Alan Baxter and Associates with input from Duany Plater-Zyberk and used to establish the physical parameters for building. Current Design Guidance retains its control on development with the sanction of freehold rights being withheld on properties for non-compliance. House owners also face restrictive covenants on property deeds that regulate conditions for maintenance and architectural alteration.

Although most development has been residential, including both three- and four-bedroom

Above:
The street pattern prioritizes pedestrians above vehicles and introduces a variety of attractive public spaces

Right:
Leon Krier's analysis of Dorchester and Poundbury, showing the boundaries of existing and new urban quarters

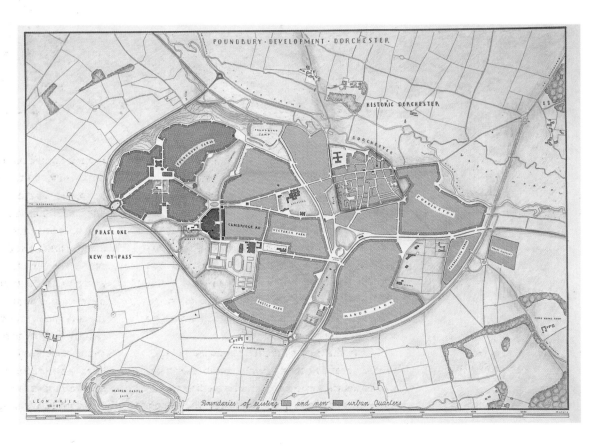

Development statistics (mid 2002)
Area of Phase One development: 14 hectares
Affordable houses in Phase One: 55
Private houses Phase One: 141
Shops in Phase One: 370 sq m
Café in Phase One: 70 sq m
Offices in Phase One: 880 sq m
Number of full-time jobs: 220
Area of Phase Two development: 73 hectares
Total area of parkland to date: 40 hectares
Projected number of residents on completion: 5,000

Project partners and organizations
The Duchy of Cornwall
West Dorset District Council

Developers
C. G. Fry & Sons
Morrish Builders
The Guinness Trust
Renaissance Developments

Consultants
Leon Krier – masterplanner
Alan Baxter and Associates – engineers
Hunt Thompson Associates – community development consultants

References
New Practice in Urban Design, Academy Group Ltd, 1993.
Leon Krier, Architecture and Urban Design 1967–1992, Academy Editions, 1992.

Above:
A key objective for Poundbury has been to reflect a Dorset vernacular that connects with the surrounding town and landscape

terraced and detached houses of mixed tenure, Poundbury is also home to a wide variety of light industrial and commercial businesses. The West Dorset Council Enterprise Centre encourages new business to move to the region and provides a number of small serviced offices. A business centre and three factories have opened, and more than 220 people are now fully employed in a variety of activities that include advertising, media, food processing, light engineering, a veterinary centre and a chocolate factory.

From the outset the project has had a high profile, receiving considerable attention and numerous visitors each year. The architectural profession has been quick to criticize the so-called pseudo-vernacular detail of many buildings and has questioned the ideology and perceived historical pastiche of the traditional building form, and this question of architectural detail will probably continue to attract a disproportionate level of attention for some time to come. The success of the scheme to date lies in the structure and form of the urban design, the prioritizing of pedestrian movement over that of vehicles and the ability to deliver mixed use and tenure in relative high density. Significantly, the Government chose to cite Poundbury in its Urban White Paper as a practical example of good design and an innovative way to build sustainable and environmentally responsible communities.

Category	Urban extension and greenfield
Project name	Kirchsteigfeld
Location	Potsdam, Germany
Size	60 hectares/148 acres
Key milestones	1991 Land acquired for redevelopment
	1991 Preparation for planning
	1992 Community participation workshop
	1993 Development approval granted
	1993 Works start on site
	1998 Completion of tram connection with Potsdam
	1998 Majority of development complete

Case Study 11

Kirchsteigfeld, Potsdam

Over the course of a decade the new community of Kirchsteigfeld has been built from what in 1991 was a stretch of vacant greenfield land just over 3 kilometres southeast from the centre of Potsdam. Located between the village of Drewitz and the Berlin-Hanover Autobahn, this new urban district has already become home to over 6,000 people and has marked a significant change in the approach to neighbourhood planning for the City of Potsdam.

Until the 1980s the city's urban development department planned to simply expand the large-scale high-rise apartment blocks that were familiar to the Potsdam-Kirchsteigfeld region. Adopted by the former GDR since the 1960s, residential tower blocks had been the favoured and standard way to plan and expand housing areas. Following reunification, the city began to recognize that many of these original high-rise dormitory towns were the cause of enormous social problems and an alternative model for housing was sought. Kirchsteigfeld was to be planned as one of the first

new mixed-use, high-density districts in the former GDR that would reflect the integrated principles of 'life-home-work'. A particular requirement was that it would be well connected and pedestrian-friendly; it was hoped that in time Kirchsteigfeld would become known as the 'city of short distances'.

With foresight, and reflecting many of the initial urban village precedents established in the early 1990s, the city planners established three strategic objectives for the new neighbourhood. The new district would have to:

- serve as a bridge between the eighteenth-century Old Town of Potsdam and the high-rise apartment blocks of Kirchsteigfeld;
- be based on a comprehensive concept of urban sustainability, taking account of social, economic and ecological aspects; and
- promote the use of public transport and reduce car use and car ownership.

The shift from high-rise development to low-rise

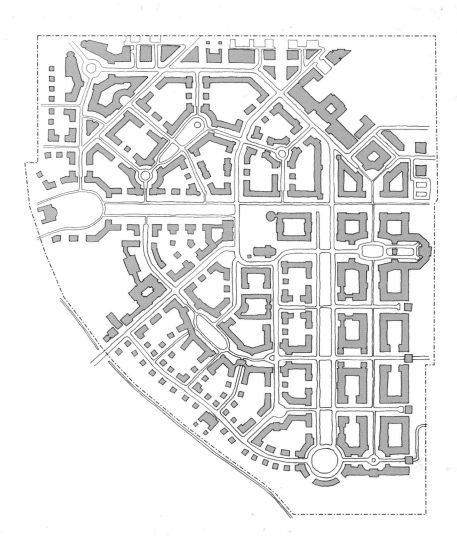

5 Minutes

100   200   300   400 Metres

mixed use required a number of changes to the adopted land use plan for the Brandenburg region. These were made in 1991 and rather than simply creating a new residential development, there was a clear desire from the outset to create a new community. A precondition for the project established the need for schools and nursery schools, shops and restaurants; together with buildings for leisure and sports activities, which would all need to be integrated within the new development. Mixing state-subsidized and privately-owned apartments would ensure the development of a heterogeneous population who would in time come to know Kirchsteigfeld as their 'Kiez' or neighbourhood.

In 1991 the Berlin property investment company Groth + Graalfs GmbH acquired approximately 60 hectares of the undeveloped land and established a comprehensive team for

the project including the Potsdam City Planning Department, the developer, regional planners, landscape architects, colour consultants, urban designers and a coterie of over 80 German and international architects.

Successful negotiations between the Federal State of Brandenburg, the City of Potsdam and the developer established an Urban Development Contract, a legally binding agreement of cooperation. This broke new ground in Germany, as it put the principle of a public-private partnership into a legally binding form that saved time and money, prevented uncertainty and regulated the rights and duties of the two equal partners. The public side is responsible for all aspects of building law and making the necessary public funds available. The developer assumes responsibility for private investment and for

Right:
Garden courtyards close to all apartments provide informal opportunities for play

adhering to the construction deadlines.

For the private developer, the obligation was to construct 2,800 residential units, reserve enough land for the requisite social facilities and provide the entire supporting infrastructure, including roads and drainage. The local government was responsible for subsidizing 2,000 units as low rent apartments, providing 450 public-assisted houses, and funding all the schools and kindergartens. In addition the local authority had to guarantee that convenient public transport connections would be made at an early stage to serve the new development.

Before a masterplan for the project was commissioned, a three-month process of preliminary, interim and final discussions was held in a series of workshops with six international groups of architects. An alternative to the more traditional design competition, this method had the advantage of providing the opportunity for intense discussion with all stakeholders with an interest in the project from the outset. Each competing team was able to view each other's work at each of the various stages and contribute positive and negative criticism as the individual schemes evolved. At the end of this process Rob Krier and Christoph Kohl's initial concept was selected to take forward the urban development plan.

Kirchsteigfeld's development is comprehensively described in Krier and Kohl's book, *The Making of a Town*. This provides the rare opportunity to see a well-documented and sequential development of the final urban plan. This was finally composed of four urban quarters and established a network of streets, squares, public spaces and green corridors to articulate the urban fabric. It takes the form of a tight grid that develops west from the boundary with the eastern forest and highway, with each residential quarter being given a local centre and distinct identity. Importantly, the block formation of the urban plan provides the opportunity to create a varied spatial pattern for the public spaces. This gives the entire development a familiar and individual character typical of a Berlin neighbourhood. The entire development shares a common centre at the Marktplatz and the Kirchplatz, and from here a central boulevard leads towards the commercial area, which provides

Above:
Four- and five-storey apartment blocks line the Horseshoe Square

Below:
Public landscapes, including the pond and the 'Hirtengraben', are central componets of the masterplan

a link with the centre of Kirchsteigfeld.

The provision of good public transport infrastructure was established as an essential component of the masterplan from the outset of the project. Just four months after most of the residential and social buildings were complete the new tramline was opened. The mixed use strategy of the development reduces the need to commute to work or to travel for shopping and leisure activities. The high residential density justifies good provision of public transport, which in turn significantly reduces the need for cars. Vehicle numbers have been further reduced by the use of traffic calming techniques and by limiting residential parking to one space per dwelling.

The strength of the project lies in the execution of a clearly articulated set of initial objectives. Securing the masterplan through a collaborative competition ensured that many architects who subsequently worked on the project shared a collective vision from the outset. In just eight years Kirchsteigfeld has grown to become a fully functional neighbourhood and even though a number of the commercial and retail elements of the mixed use strategy have yet to be delivered, the district is already served by good social facilities and efficient public transport.

Above:
An aerial view of
Kirchsteigfeld in 1997,
illustrating the phased
development of the project

Key statistics (at 1997)
Total number of residents: up to 7,000
Total number of workplaces: 5,000
Total number of residential housing
units: 2,800
Total number of social housing
units: 2,450
Residential use: 24.9 hectares
Commercial use and services:
9.8 hectares
Mixed use buildings: 9.5 hectares
Roads and public transport:
10.3 hectares
Open spaces: 4.5 hectares
Floor space for offices and retail:
110,000 sq m

Project partners and organizations
The State of Brandenburg
The City of Potsdam
Ministry for Urban Development
Ministry for Urban Development, Urban
Life and Traffic of the State of
Brandenburg
Berlin Free Planning Group

Design team
Rob Krier · Christoph Kohl,
masterplanners
Müller · Knippschild · Wehberg
Gartenarchitekten Lützow 7
Benzmüller + Wörner
Brandt/Böttcher
Augusto Romano Burelli e Paola
Gennaro
Dewey & Muller
Elw · Eyl Weitz Würmle
Faskel & Becker

Feddersen, V. Herder & Partner
Ferdinand + Gerth
Foellbach Architekten
Hermann & Valentiny
Wilhelm Holzbauer
Jürgens + Mohren
Kammann und Hummel
Kohn Pedersen Fox
KSV · Krüger Schuberth Vandreike
Lunetto + Fischer
Moore Ruble Yudell
Johanne Nalbach + Gernot Nalbach
Nielebock & Partner
Skidmore, Owings & Merrill
Steinebach & Weber

References
Rob Krier and Christoph Kohl,
The Making of a Town: Potsdam,
Kirchsteigfeld, Andreas Papadakis, 1997.

Category	Urban extension and greenfield
Project name	Newington
Location	Sydney, Australia
Size	90 hectares/222 acres
Key milestones	1993 Sydney selected to host the Olympic Games
	1996 Olympic masterplan approved for Homebush Bay
	1997 Construction of Newington begins
	1998 Precincts 2, 4 and 5 complete
	2000 Olympic Games held during September
	2006 Projected completion of Newington

Case Study 12

Newington, Sydney

The estates of Newington and Homebush lie close to the shores of the Parramatta River and just 15 kilometres to the west of central Sydney. Originally used in the 1800s for farming and salt production, the area was purchased by the government in 1882 for use as an armaments depot and munitions store. A significant portion of the site was designated a buffer zone between the depot and adjacent residential areas, which protected much of the original forests and wetlands on the northern part of the site.

In the early 1980s, following the closure of the armaments depot, the area was selected for renewal and the privately developed business park, the Australia Centre, was established at the site. This was followed by the opening of the State Sports Centre in 1984 and the Bicentennial Park in 1988. Attention was refocused on the Homebush Bay area in the early 1990s, when it became the central location for Sydney's successful bid to host the 2000 Olympic Games.

The city's successful 1993 bid set a commitment to make the 2000 Olympics the Green Olympics and established two predominant aims: the development of world-class sporting venues on a very constrained site and the protection of the natural environment. Greenpeace Australia was instrumental in developing a set of 'Environmental Guidelines for the Summer Olympic Games' that established a strong commitment to ecologically sustainable development (ESD). This specifically focused on:

– protecting biological diversity;
– energy conservation;
– water conservation;
– waste avoidance and minimization; and
– protecting significant natural and cultural environments.

The masterplan for the Olympics, approved in 1996, established four key components for the 760-hectare site: an urban core containing most of Sydney's Olympic venues; the Newington urban district to house over 15,000 Olympic and

Paralympic athletes; a major metropolitan ecological park, known as the Millennium Parklands; and a waterfront development, which would provide a ferry wharf and public access to the shores of Homebush Bay itself.

It was conceived at the outset that 90 hectares of land designated for Newington should be designed to meet part of the longer-term housing needs for Sydney and the surrounding district. In essence, the development of Newington was driven by its end use as a new medium-density, mixed-use suburb that would be well served by public transport, including bus, train and ferry connections. The post-games suburb will eventually house around 5,000 people in over 2,000 dwellings and include some 60,000 sq m of associated commercial space.

Early proposals for the Olympic Village were received from a number of development partnerships, including Greenpeace consultants who had previously contributed to Sydney's original Olympic bid. Although unsuccessful,

their urban village proposals established a number of influential ecological principles that established a more sustainable approach to the subsequent development.

The competitive tender process was won in 1996 by the Mirvac Lend Lease Village Consortium. Newington has been masterplanned by HPA Architects, the design division of Mirvac, in conjunction with a number of Australian residential architects. It is built around five integrated precincts – three residential areas, a retail centre and a business park – that are designed to maximize the amount of open space and limit the dominance of private cars. This strategy, although failing to integrate a comprehensive mix of uses throughout the scheme, does combine living, working and leisure opportunities within the overall development strategy.

The third precinct, designed for 550 dwellings and focused on a central community park, has been the first to be completed and was used to

Right:
The Olympic Boulevard leads across the Millennium Parklands and on to Newington

Top:
Medium-density detached and apartment buildings were initially used to house Olympic athletes

Middle:
Each neighbourhood precinct is centred on a public open space and children's play area

Bottom:
Each property is fitted with solar roof panels to generate a large proportion of its energy requirements

establish clear design and construction guidelines for the entire scheme. The retail core set at the termination of the western axis of the Olympic Boulevard covers over 3,600 sq m and includes shopping, leisure and childcare facilities. A new community centre is to be built, along with a new primary school that has been designed by Lindsay and Kerry Clare. A 9.5-hectare business park, masterplanned by Cox Richardson Architects, now acts as a transition zone between Newington and the neighbouring area of Silverwater.

As the site was relatively untouched by earlier development, and in line with the environmental principles established by the ESD Olympic bid, the new development has been designed to demonstrate an ecologically responsibility design philosophy. The development is fully connected to the 400-hectare Millennium Parklands, providing extensive opportunities for walking and cycling. As a means to reinforce the biodiversity of the district, over 90 per cent of the planting uses native species that contribute to the structure of habitats for the area. All storm water is recycled through the wetlands, which in turn provide water to irrigate the parklands.

At the time of the Olympics, Newington was the largest solar-powered village in the world, with the power to generate over one million kilowatt-hours of power annually. Twelve photovoltaic (PV) cells are installed on the roof of every house and are accompanied by a gas-boosted solar hot water system. The PV cells have the capacity to generate the equivalent energy needs of all 2,000 houses in the suburb. In addition to significantly reducing carbon dioxide emissions, this system may well earn residents rebates from the power company, as all surplus electric power is exported to the local electricity grid. Passive solar design principles have also been used to increase energy efficiency and thermal comfort within the homes. Most are oriented towards the north, cross-ventilated for indoor temperature control and insulated with recycled materials on ceilings and walls.

During construction, developers had to establish effective building-waste recycling systems that have reduced hard waste – including timber, concrete and broken bricks – by as much as 90 per cent. Soft waste, including insulation material, has

been reduced by around 60 per cent, with much being recycled within the site. Timber offcuts that would normally have gone into landfill have been converted to mulch, which is spread on the landscape areas to reduce water loss, and special concrete and brick recycling plants have provided base material for road underlays and landscape fill. An eco-rating for materials that calculated initial costs, durability, ease of construction, availability, performance benefits and environmental impact was used for much of the building construction, and many of the materials and products were selected on the basis of their impact on the environment.

Although Newington may not have established any really innovative environmentally-friendly technologies, it has conscientiously tried to meet many of the environmental objectives that were established as part of the original Olympic bid. In recognition of this, Newington was awarded the Prime Minister John Howard's Living Cities Award for Urban Environmental Leadership.

Key statistics (as of 2000)
Projected total number of
residents: 5,000
Total number of homes: 1,100
Total number of apartments:
1,000
Total area of commercial uses:
54,000 sq m
Total area of retail uses:
3,600 sq m
Places in childcare centre: 40

**Project partners and
organizations**
Government of New South
Wales, Australia
NSW Olympic Coordination
Authority
Mirvac Lend Lease Village
Consortium
Lend Lease Development
Mirvac Group

Architects/consultants
Virginia Kerridge
Grose Bradley
Richard Huxley
Gordon & Valich
Order Architects
Howard Tanner & Associates
Tonkin Zulaikha
HPA Architects
Bruce Eeles and Associates
Bruce Vote Associates
Peddle Thorp and Walker
Lend lease design group
Hassell Group
Cox Richardson Architects
EDAW

References
*Newington, a new suburb
for a new century*, Mirvac
Lend Lease Village
Consortium, 2000.

Web site
<http://www.newingtonvillage.
com.au>
<http://www.oca.nsw.gov.au>

Right:
**Principles of energy
efficiency have been
integrated within the
design of all apartment
buildings**

References

An urban village primer

1 D. Sucher, *City Comforts*, City Comforts Press, 1995, p. 7.
2 R. LeGates and F. Stout, *The City Reader* (2nd edn), London: Routledge, 2000.
3 Ibid., p. 468; Camilo City, *The Art of Building Cities*, 1889.
4 Ibid., p. 94; Lewis Mumford, 'What is a City?', *Architectural Record*, 1937.
5 Jane Jacobs, *The Death and Life of Great American Cities*, London: Penguin Books, 1972 (first published 1961).
6 Lewis Mumford, *The City in History*, London: Penguin Books, 1991 (first published 1961).
7 T. Aldous (ed.), *Urban Villages*, Urban Villages Group, 1992.
8 Gillian Darley, *Villages of Vision*, London: Architectural Press, 1975.
9 Ebenezer Howard, *To-morrow: A Peaceful Path to Real Reform*, London: Swan Sonnenschein, 1898; *Garden Cities of Tomorrow*; London; Swan Sonnenschein, 1902.
10 International Congress of Modern Architecture (CIAM), *Charter of Athens*, 1943. Dennis Rodwell, 'Identity and Community', *RSA Journal*, vol. 140, August/September 1992, pp. 631–3.
11 Jacobs, op. cit.
12 J. H. Kunstler, *The Geography of Nowhere*, New York: Touchstone, 1994, p. 15.
13 I. Colquhoun, *Urban Regeneration*, London: Batsford, 1995.
14 Department of the Environment, Transport and the Regions, *Our Towns and Cities: The Future*, Norwich: HMSO, 2000.
15 Urban Task Force, *Towards an Urban Renaissance*, London: E. & F. N. Spon, 1999.
16 A. Duany, E. Plater-Zyberg and J. Speck, *Suburban Nation*, New York: North Point Press, 2000.
17 M. Hebbert, *New Urbanism, Old Urbanism*, CNU VII Panel Presentation, Milwaukee, Wisconsin, 4 June 1999.
18 P. Katz, *The New Urbanism*, New York: McGraw-Hill, 1994, p. ix.
19 Ibid., pp. xvi.
20 *Charter of the New Urbanism* <http://cnu.org/cnu_reports/Charter.pdf> (accessed 5 December 2002).
21 D. Rudlin and N. Falk, *Building the 21st Century Home: The Sustainable Urban Neighbourhood*, Oxford: Architectural Press, 1999.
22 Office of the Deputy Prime Minister, *Planning Policy Guidance Note 1: General Policy and Principles* (PPG1): 22 August 2001.
23 H. J. Gans, *The Urban Villagers*, New York: The Free Press, 1962.
24 HRH The Prince of Wales, *A Vision of Britain*, London: Doubleday, 1989.
25 T. Aldous (ed.), op. cit.
26 Dennis Rodwell, 'Identity and Community', *RSA Journal*, vol. 140, August/September 1992, pp. 631–3.
27 C. Knevitt, 'Village Life?' *Building Design*, 6 November 1992, p. 15.
28 M. Biddulph, B. Franklin and M. Tait, *The Urban Village: A Real or Imagined Contribution to Sustainable Development?* Cardiff: City and Regional Planning, Cardiff University, 2002.

Authentic urbanism and the Jane Jacobs legacy

J. Jacobs, *The Death and Life of Great American Cities*, New York: Random House, 1961.
J. Jacobs, *The Economy of Cities*, New York: Random House, 1969.
J. Jacobs, *A Question of Separatism: Quebec and the Struggle over Sovereignty*, New York: Random House, 1980.
J. Jacobs, *Cities and the Wealth of Nations: Principles for Economic Life*, New York: Random House, 1984.
J. Jacobs, *Systems of Survival: A Dialogue on the Moral Foundations of Commerce and Politics*, New York: Random House, 1992.
J. Jacobs, *The Nature of Economies*, New York: Modern Library, 2000.
For book reviews and other journal articles on Jane Jacobs' work refer to: <http://www.people.virginia.edu/~plan303/biblio.html> (accessed 5 December 2002).
R. B. Gratz, *The Living City: Thinking Small in a Big Way* (4th edn), New York: John Wiley & Son, 1998 (first published 1989).

R. B. Gratz with N. Mintz, *Cities Back from the Edge: New Life for Downtown*, New York: John Wiley & Son, 1998.

1 Smart growth on two continents

1 Urban Task Force, *Towards an Urban Renaissance*, London: E. & F. N. Spon, 1999.
2 A. Power and K. Mumford, *The Slow Death of Great Cities? Urban Abandonment or Urban Renaissance*, York: Joseph Rowntree Foundation, 1999; R. Rogers and A. Power, *Cities for a Small Country*, London: Faber and Faber, 2000.
3 Urban Task Force, op. cit., pp. 32–4.
4 Ibid., p. 42.
5 M. Breheny and R. Rookwood, 'Planning the Sustainable City Region', in A. Blowers (ed.), *Planning for a Sustainable Environment*, London: Earthscan, 1993, pp. 150–189.
6 P. Hall and C. Ward, *Sociable Cities: The Legacy of Ebenezer Howard*, Chichester: Wiley, 1998.
7 Department of the Environment, Transport and the Regions, *Planning for Sustainable Development: Towards Better Practice*, London: DETR, 1998.
8 http://www.planning.odpm.gov.uk/sustdev/ (accessed 10 June 2003).
9 A. Duany, E. Plater-Zyberk and J. Speck, *Suburban Nation: The Rise of Sprawl and the Decline of the American Dream*, New York: North Point Press, 2000; P. Calthorpe and W. Fulton, *The Regional City: Planning for the End of Sprawl*, Washington: Island Press, 2001.
10 P. Salkin, 'States to the Fore', *Planning*, 2000, 66/1, 8.
11 Ibid., p. 8.
12 A. Lorentz and K. Shaw, 'Are you Ready to Bet on Smart Growth? *Planning*, 2000, 66/1, 5.
13 In *Planning*, 2000, 66/2, p. 4.
14 Duany, Plater-Zyberk and Speck, op. cit., pp. 47, 139.
15 Calthorpe and Fulton, op. cit., p. 202.
16 Ibid., p. 5.
17 Ibid., p. 6.
18 Ibid., p. 8.
19 Duany, Plater-Zyberk and Speck, op. cit., pp. 223, 230.
20 Ibid., p. 230.
21 M. Bernick and R. Cervero, *Transit Villages in the 21st Century*, New York: McGraw Hill, 1997; P. Calthorpe, *The Next American Metropolis: Ecology, Community, and the American Dream*, Princeton: Princeton Architectural Press, 1993; R. Cervero, *The Transit Metropolis: A Global Inquiry*, Washington, DC: Island Press, 1998.
22 *Planning*, 2001, 67/1, p. 5.
23 Duany, Plater-Zyberk and Speck, op. cit., p. 143.
24 Ibid., pp. 143–4.
25 Lorentz and Shaw, op. cit., p. 7.
26 Ibid., p. 9.
27 *Planning*, 2000, 66/6, p. 33.
28 Breheny and Rookwood, op. cit; Hall and Ward, op. cit.

2 Planning for sustainable communities

1 P. Hall, *Cities of Tomorrow*, Oxford: Basil Blackwell Ltd, 1988, p.61.
2 The House of Commons Sub-Committee for Transport, Local Government and the Regions Nineteenth Report *The New Towns: Their Problems and Future*, 29 July 2002, reported on the problems of particular new towns, and recommended that the new towns should be studied in detail so that lessons – about what works and what doesn't – can be learned.
3 P. Hall, op. cit., p. 347.
4 Brundtland Commission Report, *Our Common Future: From One Earth to One World*, Oxford: University Press, 1987.
5 Ibid., p. 255.
6 H. Giradet, *The Gaia Atlas of Cities*, London: Gaia Books Ltd, 1992, p. 179.

7   *The European Spatial Development Perspective*, European Commission, January 1999.

8   <http://www.iclei.org/europe/ac-eng.htm> (accessed 22 July 2002).

9   Department of the Environment, Transport and the Regions (DETR), *A Better Quality of Life, A Strategy for Sustainable Development for the UK,* The Stationery Office, 1999.

10 DETR, *Planning for the Communities of the Future*, HMSO, 1998.

11 Urban Task Force, *Towards an Urban Renaissance*, London: E. & F. N. Spon, 1999.

12 DETR, *Our Towns and Cities: The Future,* The Stationery Office, 2000.

13 Peter Calthorpe, *The Next American Metropolis*, Princeton: Architectural Press, 1993.

14 P. Hall and C. Ward, op. cit., p. 8.

15 Urban Villages Group, *Urban Villages: A Concept for Creating Mixed-use Urban Developments on a Sustainable Scale*, London, 1992. See, for example, paras 7.5, 7.11, 7.14–7.16, and p. 76.

16 Urban Villages Forum, *Economics of Urban Villages*, London, 1995. See, for example, paras 1.18, 1.27, p. 17, ch. 4 and para. 7.5.

17 *New Urbanism: Comprehensive Report and Best Practices Guide*, Ithaca, New York: New Urban Publications Ltd, 2001.

18 For example: DETR, *Planning for Sustainable Development: Towards Better Practice*, London, The Stationery Office, 1998; English Partnerships and the Housing Corporation, *The Urban Design Compendium*, 2000; Commission for the Built Environment (CABE) with DETR, *By Design, Urban Design in the Planning System: Towards Better Practice*, Tonbridge. Thomas Telford, 2000; CABE and Office of the Deputy Prime Minister (ODPM), *Paving the Way: How We can Achieve Clean, Safe and Attractive Streets*, London, 2002; Urban Design Group, *Urban Design Guidance*, London, 2002.

19 J. A. Dutton, *New American Urbanism: Re-forming the Suburban Metropolis*, Milan: Skira, 2000.

3 Emerging digital neighbourhoods

1   For further discussions of fragmentation and recombination see William J. Mitchell, *City of Bits*, Cambridge, MA: MIT Press, 1995; *E-topia*, Cambridge, MA: MIT Press, 1999, and William J. Mitchell, 'The Parable of the Pizza Parlor', *Scientific American*, vol. 272, no. 5 (May 1995), p. 92.

2   On the rise of digital telecommunications networks, and their broad social, economic, and political consequences, see Manuel Castells, *The Internet Galaxy*, Oxford: Oxford University Press, 2001.

3   William J. Mitchell, 'The Economy of Presence', in *E-topia*, Cambridge, MA: MIT Press, 1999, pp. 128–45.

4   For an introduction to the digital divide, and specifically its urban design and planning implications, see Donald A. Schon, Bish Sanyal, and William J. Mitchell (eds), *High Technology and Low-Income Communities*, Cambridge, MA: MIT Press, 1998. For a more recent discussion of the digital divide see Pippa Norris, *Digital Divide*, Cambridge: Cambridge University Press, 2001.

5   For introductions to wireless infrastructure and its uses see Rob Flickenger, *Building Wireless Community Networks*, Sebastopol, CA: O'Reilly, 2002, and Barry Brown, Nicola Green and Richard Harper (eds), *Wireless World: Social and Interactional Aspects of the Mobile Age*, London: Springer, 2001.

6   In his influential *Bowling Alone* (New York: Simon and Schuster, 2000), Robert Putnam, for example, suggests that America's social capital is declining, and further suggests that the rise of the Internet will further dissociate neighbours from one another.

7   See, in particular, Keith Hampton, *Living the Wired Life in the Wired Suburb: Netville, Glocalization and Civil Society*, Ph.D. dissertation, Department of Sociology, University of Toronto, 2001, and Keith Hampton and Barry Wellman, 'Neighboring in Netville: How the Internet Supports Community, Social Support and Social Capital in a Wired Suburb', *City and Community*, forthcoming.

8   For one approach to this, see Randal Pinkett, *Creating Community Connections: Sociocultural Constructionism and an Asset-Based Approach to Community Technology and Community Building*, Ph.D. dissertation, Media Laboratory, MIT, 2002.

9   For an early, cheerleading introduction to the idea of online virtual communities, see Howard Rheingold, *The Virtual Community: Homesteading on the Electronic Frontier*, Reading, MA: Addison-Wesley, 1993.

10 The literature on community networks, and their variant forms, is now significant. For introductions see Douglas Schuler, *New Community Networks*, Reading, MA: Addison-Wesley, 1996, and Stephen Doheny-Farina, *The Wired Neighbourhood*, New Haven: Yale University Press, 1996. There are some useful, more recent case studies in Toru Ishida and Katherine Isbister (eds) *Digital

Cities: Technologies, Experiences, and Future Perspectives*, Berlin: Springer, 2000, and Kostas Stathis (ed.), *Local Nets: Proceedings of the International Workshop on Community-Based Interactive Systems*, Siena, 1999, London: Electrical and Electronic Engineering Department, Imperial College, 1999.

11 For further details see William J. Mitchell, 'Reworking the Workplace', in *E-topia*, Cambridge, MA, MIT Press, 1999, pp. 98–111.

12 For further details see William J. Mitchell, "Homes and Neighborhoods," in *E-topia*, Cambridge, MA, MIT Press, 1999, pp. 70–83.

13 IEEE.802.11 is the Institute of Electrical and Electronics Engineers standard for wireless computer networks that allows for ad hoc configuration and network-free communication between computers.

14 Douglas Schuler, *New Community Networks*, Reading, MA, Addison-Wesley, 1996.

15 <http://www.parcbit.es> (accessed 12 March 2003).

16 <http://www.mawsonlakes.com.au> (accessed 12 March 2003).

17 <http://www.playavista.com> (accessed 12 March 2003).

18 Jane Jacobs, *The Death and Life of Great American Cities*, New York, Vintage, 1961.

19 See, for example, Andreas Duany, Elizabeth Plater-Zyberg and Jeff Speck, *Suburban Nation*, New York: North Point Press, 2000, and Peter Calthorpe and William Fulton, *The Regional City*, Washington: The Island Press, 2001.

4 Neighbourhood design in practice

1   Congress for the New Urbanism, *Charter of the New Urbanism*, New York: McGraw-Hill, 2000.

2   R. Unwin, *Town Planning in Practice. An Introduction to the Art of Designing Cities and Suburbs*, New York: Princeton Architectural Press, 1994 (first published 1909); see Andrés Duany's Preface, p. v.

3   C. Alexander, *A Pattern Language*, New York: Oxford University Press, 1977.

4   R. Unwin, *Town Planning in Practice*, 1994, p. 13, as quoted in J. Dutton, *New American Urbanism, Re-forming the Suburban Metropolis*, Milan: Skira, 2000, p. 21.

5   For a summary of Clarence Perry's Neighbourhood Unit see <http://www.chbooks.com/online/eastwest/166.html> (accessed 14 June 2002).

6   Duany Plater-Zyberk & Co., *The Lexicon of the New Urbanism* (version 3.2), ch.1–2, describes TND in further technical detail.

7   See Congress for the New Urbanism, op. cit., pp. 79–81.

8   US Department of Housing and Urban Development (HUD), June 1996. A digital version can be found at <http://www.orl.arch.ethz.ch/disp/displus/140/docs/neighbor.pdf> (accessed 7 December 2002).

9   For government-endorsed design on mixed-use nieghbourhoods, refer to: Department of the Environment, Transport and the Regions (DETR), *Places, Streets and Movement*, London: DETR, 1998; English Partnerships and the Housing Corporation, *The Urban Design Compendium*, London: English Partnerships, 2000; Commission for the Built Environment (CABE) with DETR, *By Design, Urban Design in the Planning System: Towards Better Practice*, Tonbridge: Thomas Telford, 2000; Department for Transport, Local Government and the Regions (DTLR) and CABE, *By Design: Better Places to Live*, Tonbridge: Thomas Telford, 2001.

10 A more detailed description of Geddes' Valley Section is available in V. Welter, *Biopolis: Patrick Geddes and the City of Life*, Cambridge, MA: MIT Press, 2002.

11 I. McHarg, *Design with Nature*, New York: Doubleday/Natural History Press, 1969.

Bibliography

A. Duany, *The Lexicon of the New Urbanism,* Miami: Duany Plater-Zyberk & Company, 1999.

A. Duany and E. Plater-Zyberk, *Towns and Town-Making Principles*, New York: Rizzoli International Publications Ltd. 1991, second edition 1992.

A. Duany, E. Plater-Zyberk and J. Speck, *Suburban Nation, The Rise of Sprawl and the Decline of the American Dream*, New York: North Point Press, 2000.

New Urban News, *New Urbanism: Comprehensive Report and Best Practices Guide*, Ithaca, New Urban Publications Inc., 2001.

5 Connectivity and movement

1   Department of the Environment, Transport and the Regions (DETR), *Design Bulletin 32 – Residential Roads and Footpaths,* 1977 (revised edition 1992).

2   The Department of Transport *Design Manual for Roads and Bridges* is a series of volumes published in the 1990s by HMSO, London.

3   A. Jacobs, *Great Streets*, Cambridge, MA: MIT Press, 1993, p. 3.

4   J. Jacobs, *The Death and Life of Great American Cities*, London: Penguin Books, 1972 (first published 1961), p. 39.
5   Clause 22 of the *Charter Of The New Urbanism*. Available online: <http://cnu.org/cnu_reports/Charter.pdf> (accessed 5 December 2002).
6   Ebenezer Howard, *To-morrow: A Peaceful Path to Real Reform*, London: Swan Sonnenschein, 1898.
7   For a detailed description of Copenhagen's 'finger plan' see P. Hall and C. Ward, *Sociable Cities: The Legacy of Ebenezer Howard*, Chichester: Wiley. 1998, pp. 91–5.
8   Refer to streets and circulation systems in P. Calthorpe, *The Next American Metropolis – Ecology, Community, and the American Dream*, New York: Princeton Architectural Press, 1993, p. 64.
9   SUSTRANS, *Safe Routes to Schools Information Sheet FS01*, 2001, is available on SUSTRANS' 'Safe Routes to School' website: <http://www.saferoutestoschools.org.uk/pdf/fs01.pdf> (accessed 25 March 2003).
10 Midland Mainline travel updates, for example, are available on WAP-enabled mobile phones: <http://www.mmlwap.com> (accessed 8 December 2002).
11 Office of the Deputy Prime Minister (ODPM), *Planning Policy Guidance Note (PPG) 13: Transport*, London: ODPM, 11 October 2002.
12 DETR, *Design Bulletin 32: Residential Roads and Footpaths*, 1977 rev. 1992
13 DETR, *Places, Streets and Movement – a Companion Guide to Design Bulletin 32, Residential Roads and Footpaths*, London: DETR, 1998.
14 Commission for Architecture and the Built Environment (CABE) and ODPM, *Paving the Way*, 2002.

6 The social dynamic

1   Beatrix Campbell, *Goliath – Britain's Dangerous Places*, London: Methuen, 1993.
2   François Maspero, *Roissy Express. A Journey Through the Paris Suburbs*, London: Verso. c. 1994.
3   Todd W. Bressi, 'Planning the American Dream', in Peter Katz, *The New Urbanism: Toward an Architecture of Community*, New York: McGraw Hill, 1994, p. xxvii.
4   Ben Jupp, *Living Together: Community Life on Mixed Tenure Estates*, London: Demos, 1999, p. 4.
5   Department of the Environment, Transport and the Regions (DETR), *Focus on Personal Travel*, London: The Stationery Office, 1998.
6   Anne Spackman, 'Rethinking suburban landscape' (interview with John Callcutt), *Financial Times*, 26/27 January 2002.
7   Bill Lucas and Liz Russell, 'Grounds for alarm', *Landscape Design*, May 1997, p. 46.
8   Manuel Castells, *The Rise of the Network Society*, Oxford: Blackwell, 2000, p. 500.
9   Household composition 1991 Census, cited in David Rudlin, *Tomorrow: A Peaceful Path to Urban Reform*, London: Friends of the Earth, 1998.
10 Cited in Urban Task Force, *Towards an Urban Renaissance*, London: DETR/ E. & F. N. Spon, 1999, p. 94.
11 See Helen Woolley et al, 'The Listening Game', in C. Jefferson, J. Rowe and C. Brebbia (eds) *The Sustainable Street: The Environmental Human and Economic Aspects of Street Design and Management*, Southampton: WIT Press, p. 118.
12 See Ken Worpole and Liz Greenhalgh, *The Richness of Cities: Urban Policy in a New Landscape*, Stroud/London: Comedia/Demos, 1999, p. 29. See also, Michael Young and Gerard Lemos, *The Communities We Have Lost and Can Regain*, London: Lemos & Crane, 1997.
13 Jane Jacobs, *The Death and Life of Great American Cities*, London: Penguin Books, 1964 (first published 1961). p. 44.

7 Project identification

1   M. Biddulph, B. Franklin and M. Tait, *The Urban Village: A Real or Imagined Contribution to Sustainable Development?* Cardiff: City and Regional Planning, Cardiff University, 2002.
2   HM Government Select committee, *The New Towns: Their Problems and Future*. Available online <http://www.parliament.the-stationery-office.co.uk/ pa/cm200102/cmselect/cmtlgr/603/603.pdf> (accessed 25 March 2003).
3   Department of the Environment, Transport and the Regions (DETR), *Places, Streets and Movement – a Companion Guide to Design Bulletin 32: Residential Roads and Footpaths*, London: DETR, 1998.
4   Further information on the Space Syntax Laboratory is available at: <http://www.spacesyntax.com> (accessed 25 March 2003).
5   For a more detailed analysis of Gloucester's Western Waterfront scheme see <http://www.glos-city.gov.uk/libraries/templates/page.asp?URN=418>

(accessed 25 March 2003).
6   Little Germany Urban Village Co. and City of Bradford, *Little Germany Urban Village, Supplementary Planning Guidance*, Bradford: City of Bradford, 2002.

8 Project procurement

1   The Urban Design Group, *Urban Design Guidance – Urban Design Frameworks, Development Briefs and Master Plans*, London: Thomas Telford Publishing, 2002.
2   See M. Breheny, T. Gent and D. Lock, *Alternative Development Patterns: New Settlements*, London: HMSO, 1993.
3   Royal Town Planning Institute, *Development Briefs: Practice Advice Note, Appendix 2*, London: RTPI, 1990.
4   DETR and CABE, *By Design: Urban Design in the Planning System, Towards Better Practice*. London: Thomas Telford Publishing, 2000.
5   Policy guidance for this is given in Department of the Environment (DoE) *Circular 1/97, Planning Compensation Act 1991: Planning Obligations*, London: Office of the Deputy Prime Minister (ODPM), 1997.
6   Nick Wates, *Action Planning*, London: The Prince of Wales's Institute of Architecture,1996; English Partnerships, *Brick by Brick. How to Develop a Community Building*, 1998; The Architecture Foundation, *Creative Spaces, a Tool Kit for Participatory Urban Design*, London: The Architecture Foundation, 2000; Nick Wates, *The Community Planning Handbook*, London: Earthscan Publications Ltd, 2000; DLTR and CABE, *By Design, Urban Design in the Planning System: Towards Better Practice*, Tonbridge: Thomas Telford, 2000.
7   Nick Wates, op. cit., 2000.
8   <http://www.creativespaces.org.uk> (accessed 26 March 2003).
9   RICS Research and DoE, *Quality of Urban Design, a Study of the Involvement of Private Property Decision-makers in Urban Design*, 1996.
10 CABE and DETR, *The Value of Urban Design*, London: Thomas Telford Publishing, 2001.
11 HM Treasury Guidance on appraisal and evaluation in central government (the 'Green Book'), can be found at <http://www.isb.gov.uk/faqs/faq_pdfs/greenbook.pdf> (accessed 26 March 2003). ODPM Guidance to Regional Development Agencies on approval of Successor Schemes to the Single Regeneration Budget (SRB) in 2001–2002 can be found at <http://www.urban.odpm.gov.uk/programmes/srb/guidance/> (accessed 26 March 2003). New Deal for Communities (NDC) guidance from the ODPM's Neighbourhood Renewal Unit can be found at <http://www.neighbourhood.gov.uk/ndcprognotes.asp?pageid=91> (accessed 26 March 03).
12 The IRR of a project is the discount rate at which the net present value of cash flows will be equal to zero. The IRR discounts future cash flows at a higher rate than that applied to current cash flows. Undertaking an analysis of the IRR of a project helps to indicate the scale and timing of cash flows and real returns.

9 Project management

1   RICS Policy Unity and The Environment Agency, *Comprehensive Project Appraisal*, 2001.
2   Ian Latham and Mark Swenarton (eds), *Brindleyplace, a Model for Urban Regeneration*, London: Rightangle Publishing, 1999.

Index